"Kelly Monroe Kullberg provides an engaging personal account of a nationwide effort to counter the shortcomings of secularized universities in pursuing one of their original goals: a quest for truth that is open to all the possible dimensions of reality."

GEORGE MARSDEN, Francis A. McAnaney Professor of History, University of Notre Dame, and author of *The Soul of the American University*

"The Veritas Forum is having a remarkable impact on college campuses, presenting the intellectual case for Christianity. But around Kelly Monroe Kullberg, 'intellectual' never means pedantic! In her account of the organization's founding, she welcomes readers into her life and ministry in prose that is refreshingly lively and spirited. Every page glows with her spunky personality."

NANCY R. PEARCEY, Francis A. Schaeffer Scholar, World Journalism Institute, and author of *Total Truth*

"The Veritas Forums have done a marvelous job of holding forth on many campuses the profound vision that gave rise to most of our great universities: that all Truth ultimately holds together in Jesus Christ. In this highly readable and wonderfully inspiring book, Kelly Monroe Kullberg tells us how the Forums came into being, and how they spread throughout North America and beyond. But she also weaves into the story— and often with a wrenching candor—a chronicle of her own personal journey of faith as she has promoted the Veritas cause."

RICHARD J. MOUW, President and Professor of Christian Philosophy, Fuller Theological Seminary

"Simply put, this is an extraordinary book. It evokes recurring memories of Anne Morrow Lindbergh's splendid *Gift from the Sea* in that it poignantly probes both the beauty and the pain of living, in this case of one very brave soul yearning to please God and live life to the fullest. It made me laugh and brought me to tears. It is a 'must read!'"

J. STANLEY MATTSON, Founder and President, C. S. Lewis Foundation

"Kelly Monroe Kullberg has written a warm and grace-filled book that blends the inspiring story of The Veritas Forum with a tender and deeply moving account of her own struggle to trust in the truth of Jesus Christ. In lively, graceful prose, Kullberg takes us along on her coast-to-coast adventures among college students who share a common hunger for truth—a hunger their secular universities failed to satisfy. Read *Finding God Beyond Harvard* to glimpse God at work in the secular academy and to see how the story of Christ's redemptive love continues to captivate young people in every generation."

COLLEEN CARROLL CAMPBELL, author of *The New Faithful: Why Young Adults Are Embracing Christian Orthodoxy*, fellow at the Ethics and Public Policy Center

"Kelly Monroe Kullberg has written a sparkling book, a passionate and deeply personal inside story of a burgeoning movement bringing Christian hope to an increasingly fragmented and alienating secular academy. Irreverent, inspirational, engaging, full of amusing stories, a page-turner . . . I couldn't put it down."

ARD LOUIS, Royal Society University Research Fellow in Theoretical Chemistry, Cambridge University

"The poetry of Kelly's journey to—and with—Veritas invites me to believe all over again! This is passionate storytelling, pointing to an adventure beyond the mountains and streams of universities and marketplaces. But it would be a sad mistake to reduce her story to simplistic conservative or liberal perceptions of higher education. Rather, Kelly calls every reader to consider honestly the wonder of learning and living together, in the light of truth. There's hope in these pages!"

JO KADLECEK, journalist, author of *The Sound of My Voice: A Novel* and instructor of creative writing

"In her first book Kelly Monroe Kullberg stepped aside, allowing others to tell their own stories of finding God at Harvard. In *Finding God Beyond Harvard* she tells, in her own richly imaginative voice, her own story of the journey of The Veritas Forum, of her own pursuit of truth and the experience of again and again being found by It."

MICHAEL CARD, songwriter, recording artist, and author of *Scribbling in the Sand* and *A Fragile Stone*

"In *Finding God at Harvard*, Kelly Monroe drew on some of the brightest Christian minds associated with America's first college to build a multidisciplinary case for the reasonableness of Christian faith. *Finding God Beyond Harvard* is the story of the movement that brought—and is still bringing—that conversation to universities around the world. Perhaps more significantly, *Finding God Beyond Harvard* is her personal story of a quiet journey through doubt and disappointment—and the lonely struggle to cling in private to the very truths she fought so hard to proclaim in public."

ERIC CONVEY, former religion reporter, *Boston Herald*

"What do you do if you find yourself lost after you had already been found? In *Finding God Beyond Harvard*, Kelly Monroe Kullberg tells the story of God's remarkable work in taking The Veritas Forum to dozens of universities. However, the rise of Veritas inversely parallels the breaking and numbing of her own heart. Woven throughout this public tale is Kelly's renewed personal quest for veritas. Her depiction of the Christian story enfolds adventure, suffering, laughter, nature and the scholarship of keen minds in many disciplines. With words vivid and full of grace she reports back to us what she sees: a world broken yet still enchanted by a loving God who is redeeming all things."

GLENN LUCKE, author of *Common Grounds: Conversations About Things That Matter Most*

FINDING GOD
BEYOND HARVARD

THE QUEST FOR VERITAS

KELLY MONROE KULLBERG

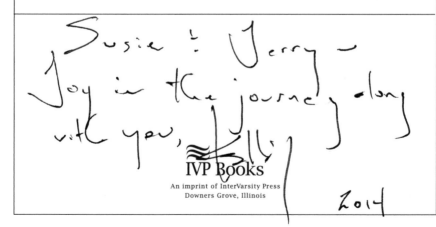

Susie + Jerry —
Joy in the journey along
with you,
Kelly

2014

IVP Books

An imprint of InterVarsity Press
Downers Grove, Illinois

InterVarsity Press
P.O. Box 1400, Downers Grove, IL 60515-1426
World Wide Web: www.ivpress.com
E-mail: mail@ivpress.com

InterVarsity Press® is the book-publishing division of InterVarsity Christian Fellowship/USA®, a student movement active on campus at hundreds of universities, colleges and schools of nursing in the United States of America, and a member movement of the International Fellowship of Evangelical Students. For information about local and regional activities, write Public Relations Dept., InterVarsity Christian Fellowship/USA, 6400 Schroeder Rd., P.O. Box 7895, Madison, WI 53707-7895, or visit the IVCF website at <www.intervarsity.org>.

All Scripture quotations, unless otherwise indicated, are taken from the Holy Bible, New International Version®. NIV®. *Copyright ©1973, 1978, 1984 by International Bible Society. Used by permission of Zondervan Publishing House. All rights reserved.*

"Martyrs and Thieves" by Jennifer Knapp © Gotee Music/West Hudson Music. All rights reserved. Used by permission.

"St. Paul's Song" by Pierce Pettiis. Used by permission.

"The Word" by Michael Card. Copyright © 1988 Birdwing Music/Mole End Music. All rights reserved. Used by permission.

Lyrics from the Passion play and musical Tetelestai, *written by Joel and Russ Nagy, 1972, Upper Arlington Lutheran Church, Columbus, Ohio, are reprinted with permission.*

Quotations on pages 118-19 of this book are taken from pages 17-19 of Ruthless Trust *by Brennan Manning. Copyright ©2000 by Brennan Manning. Reprinted by permission of HarperCollins Publishers.*

Trail map illustrated by Jody Sjogren. Used by permission.

Every effort has been made to provide proper credit for material cited in this book. Omissions and errors should be brought to the attention of the publisher for correction in future editions.

Cover design: Andrew Craft
Interior design: Cindy Kiple

Images: Claudia Geopperi / Getty Images

ISBN-10: 0-8308-3387-0

ISBN-13: 978-0-8308-3387-0

Printed in the United States of America ∞

Library of Congress Cataloging-in-Publication Data

Kullberg, Kelly Monroe, 1960-
Finding God beyond Harvard: the quest for veritas / Kelly Monroe
Kullberg.
p. cm.
Includes bibliographical references and index.
ISBN-13: 978-0-8308-3387-0 (cloth: alk. paper)
ISBN-10: 0-8308-3387-0 (cloth: alk. paper)
1. College students—Religious life. 2. College
teachers—Religious life.
3. Scholars—Religious life. 4. Universities and
colleges—Religion. I. Title. BV639.C6K85 2006 248.8'34—dc22

2006003977

P	19	18	17	16	15	14	13	12	11	10	9	8	7	6	5	4	3
Y	21	20	19	18	17	16	15	14	13	12	11	10	09	08				

To all Veritas volunteers. You are the unsung heroes.
A special thanks to Kurt Keilhacker, Jeff Barneson
and Brenda Birmann, the Bradleys, Shaws, Edgars,
Zartmans and VanCleaves, who are true in heart,
and live for an audience of One.

To my mother and father, Kay Monroe VanMeter,
and Lawrence John Monroe, and brothers
Daniel and Michael, each of whom I cherish.

To my husband, David, beloved of God,
who drew forth every story.

And to our children's children.

Contents

Foreword

In 1992 an event took place that put me on a track from which there was no turning back. It was the Veritas Forum at Harvard.

My involvement with the Forum was born out of a discussion I had in an elevator with a businessman who wanted to help bring the Christian faith before some of the finest minds of our time, to have it tested and challenged. A dedicated young woman doing pioneering Christian work on campuses asked me to be the Forum's inaugural speaker. That woman was Kelly Monroe. Kelly was, and is, one of the most effective communicators on the campus scene.

The first Veritas Forum was scheduled to take place at the busiest time on the Harvard calendar—the weekend of the Harvard-Yale football game—so no one could be sure what kind of turnout we might have. The venue was Harvard Law School. It was one of the most thrilling moments of my life. As I stepped to the lectern, I saw that the place was packed to overflowing. Every seat was taken, with students and faculty sitting on the stairs, on banisters, on the floor next to the podium where I stood. The impact of the Veritas Forum at Harvard was life changing for me and for many others involved.

As Kelly Monroe writes, "The keynote talks and students' questions and insights were like a prophetic sparkplug, and thousands of copies of the first few events went around the world by audiotape. Word about Veritas began to spread beyond Cambridge."

The Harvard experience opened to us university campuses not only in North America but also around the world. It was a defining moment for The Veritas Forum and in Kelly's unique story as well. She went on to edit *Finding God at Harvard,* which has been translated into other languages and read by United Nations ambassadors and heads of state.

Veritas Forums have since emerged in more than sixty leading universities, engaging the questions and ideas of a quarter-million students who will help shape our culture's future.

This does not surprise me, for in all my years of travel, Kelly is clearly one of the most knowledgeable and influential workers on campuses that I have met. She is both fun-loving and well-studied, with a keen understanding of the ideas that shape the academy as well as the points of entry into a meaningful dialogue of things eternal.

As you will discover in these pages, Kelly is also a gifted writer with rich insight into what it means to be human: to long for love, to experience beauty and loss, and to hope beyond sometimes seeming hope in the God who made and loves us. With poignancy and poetic phrases, Kelly describes a story that only God, who is *Veritas*, could weave together. I am delighted to be asked to introduce her book to you and hope that you might know the One who is the Truth.

Ravi Zacharias,
Author and speaker

Preface

A Note to the Reader

Friends have asked me, Will your new book be the story of the Veritas movement? Or is it the actual content of Veritas Forums? Or is it your personal memoir of sorts?

The answer is "all of the above, but prioritized in that order." Primarily this is the story of a spirited and semi-nomadic group of friends and their quest for true life—veritas. Up against some odds, they are willing to challenge, and wanting to change, the world. By sharing their lives and insights, they are creating a way for students to explore our deepest questions—The Veritas Forum. This is a particular and sometimes quirky story (as life is), filled with remarkable people, conversations and local color. Adventures take us from Cambridge to the rainforest of Peru, from Princeton to Dartmouth to Yale. We'll find ourselves on ski slopes and foreign mission fields, at Stanford, Ohio State, Cal Berkeley and many schools in between. We'll spend time in a lonely cabin north of Boston, and then back in universities in Los Angeles, Chicago, England, Asia, New York City and back to Harvard.

So, this is both the story of The Veritas Forum as a movement and the experience of veritas in our hearts and minds, in our relationships and adventures. The larger story is about God himself using our passionate bunglings and longings in the human epic of creation, the Fall and redemption. Our lessons of renewal may apply to many spheres of life: our communities, hospitals, schools, churches, workplaces and homes. In fact we see graduates follow callings into the work of justice, mercy, healing, art, scientific discovery and culture-making.

We are looking for Life as full as we can find it. We are rebelling against flat-souled agendas and authorities. We are, if you will, "post-postmodern," wondering about ancient and timeless truth as a golden key to the present and future, and experiencing a richness of life that is the yield of such truth. We are for that which is timeless, elegant, undying, abiding and beautifully real. Perhaps we're more like recreationists, eternalists or hopeful realists who find a confluence of beauty and truth on the far side of complexity. And so we are inspired to build in the ruins of our world.

This story isn't abstract and idealized, but gritty and particular. The book is not always linear because a chronology of events is not what the story demands; rather, I've written something more like a novel that asks the reader to put together the pieces of the puzzle.

I include some content of Veritas conversations, but only as fore-tastes. (The voluminous content is best absorbed from our website and in future Veritas Forum books.) This book just begins the adventure of "seeing all things" in light of the truth who has found us.

As it turns out, yes, some of my own story is included, culminating in the epilogue, mainly because preliminary readers urged me to do so, and as you'll discover halfway through, the hard questions of Veritas became my own questions, from the inside out. Also, my wonderful editor, Al Hsu, wanted the story told through the memory of a person whose life and family were shaped by the modern academy and who began The Veritas Forum—I am your travel guide on an intellectual road trip. So, with my husband's help and gentle prodding, I've tried to tell each story as clearly as I can remember it. Hundreds of Veritas talks were recorded, but not all dialogue in the book is verbatim (since I didn't carry a tape recorder as a norm); however, dialogue is at least representative of the conversations we often had in and beyond Cambridge. I was not present at all Veritas Forums and so I regret that so many stories will be untold and local heroes unsung in these few pages.

May all this help you see beneath and above the surface of our attempt to add spiritual, intellectual and cultural vitality to universities, to future leaders and to a world awaiting its redemption. May the particulars of this story yield something universal.

Finally, please join the journey in person (facilitated by the website) as new friends along with us.

Gratefully,
Kelly Monroe Kullberg
www.veritas.org

Prologue
A Sense of Wonder

One reason Henry Thoreau left Cambridge for Walden Pond was to return to his senses. Likewise, friends and I would leave Cambridge and, depending on the season, we'd be on bikes or skis or in my red canoe. We'd explore trails connecting the fields, streams and mountains of New England. Walden and other ponds and beaches became our swimming holes on hot summer days. Before long, our sense of wonder introduced us to kindred spirits in the landscapes, labs and cafés of other universities.

I suppose it's possible that my friends and I were a little crazy, seeing connections, design, even meaning now and then beneath most rocks. But I'd take our craziness over the world's dullness any day. What we saw was healing to our minds, hearts and lives.

Formations of Canadian geese. Lilting vocal harmony. Silence of snowfall. Migration of Monarch butterflies. The flavor of summer in a ripened peach. Reality has a way of wooing us.

As a hobby-photographer, I'm fascinated with light and optics and ways of seeing what is otherwise invisible. "Why do we see design everywhere?" asks Carnegie astronomer Allan Sandage. "Why are so many processes and ecosystems so deeply connected?" The more we look, the more we see. The more powerful the telescope or microscope, the more complexity we find.

Our lives are the result of a chain of more than a thousand scientifically verifiable but very unlikely events, each one essential in exact order of its occurrence—statistically less than one chance in trillions if by dumb luck. Reason cancels "random." Such is the wild improbability of the universe itself with its forces, gases and elements converging into an exquisite chemistry necessary to create and sustain complex life on even one planet (fortunately, ours).

How does a glass-knife fish process information faster than a computer? Who could create the colors, fragrances and clever packaging of an orange or lemon? Who could dream up the exquisite patterns of crystals, each one different? Who could imagine and animate the shape and power of a horse?

Translucent jellyfish. The trusting gaze of an infant. Rain forests. Beach fires and coral reefs. Wave upon sea, sand upon shore.

Even more stunning is the ability of "mind" by which we imagine each of these, by which we conjure out of nowhere, in the room in which we sit, images and sounds of horse and child and ocean. We human beings are the most complex miracle in the known universe, with minds inexplicably larger than brains. We are animated from within as if someone has breathed into us the breath of life.

The romance of dancing under the stars. Cows that help Ben & Jerry make Cherry Garcia. The buoyancy of a wooden boat. Swiss chocolate between ski runs. A letter from our dearest friend. These are neither drab continuum, nor fantasy, nor Matrix—such beauty in our actual world has color and texture and weight.

I love beauty. So much that it aches. I want in. Inside of things.

Put conversely, and bluntly, the secular world bores me to tears. Its sky is low and thick with clouds, blocking the sun. There is no Author and no great story of conquest against forces of darkness, advancing a kingdom of light, love and glory. All is relativized. Ideas are minimal. Eyes closed to revelation, the cynic sees no glory, no intrinsic value to human beings; thus man is laid low. Truth is dead, and so people grapple for power. Goodness is analyzed and dismissed by the skeptic's small heart and mind. Romance, imagination and enchantment fade, needing the transcendent to break in.

I know this contrast well. But my mind cannot accept a secular view. I don't have that much faith in the irrational. I can only have faith in what is real, even if it's not always visible. The brilliant mathematician Blaise Pascal wrote, "Reason's last step is the recognition that there are an infinite number of things which are beyond it." And so I am looking more carefully at things than I once did. I'm paying attention, which is fun if you like treasure hunts.

I am fascinated by that which is both invisible and real. History. Love. The laws of physics. The wind that fills my friend Kirstin's giant kite on the coast of Scotland, making us laugh and run as we try to guide it skyward—our joy as invisible and real as the wind. Such realities are enchanting, drawing us back to the One from whom all beauty flows.

Yet with wonder comes sorrow, and beauty can be hard to bear alone. We soon find that nature itself sheds no tears. We must expect suffering and think in advance about its meaning, because every one of us will be pierced by thorns and have to deal deeply in our lives with the problem of pain. This journey goes through the hardest questions and realities of a fallen world.

Any truth worth holding, or being held by, would welcome our questions and doubts with open arms. Truth wouldn't be exhausted but revealed by our search.

If we find, as many now are finding, Someone behind "nature," behind the beauty—the "yes" behind the universe—then we are in the realm of truth. Someone who, as author Francis Schaeffer said, "is there and is not silent." We are wise to ask for evidence, for authority. "Has an Author spoken? Has the Author ever entered the play and told us our story?"

Many are discovering both the realism and the romance of a story that clearly recognizes a good creation, a very bad fall, and the reality of redemption. To understand it at Harvard and MIT, Princeton and Berkeley and a hundred schools in between, we need only follow the sound of their singing and laughing and studying, their astute sense of wonder and work and worship. Theirs are becoming the most dynamic, large and even "hip" (according to *The Boston Globe*) student organizations on many once-"godless" campuses.

Might veritas hold a secret, both ancient and progressive? Perhaps Someone is trying to show us something, and he's given us both a treasure and a map to find it. That would mean that life is full of mystery to be revealed and discovered—to be laid hold of. That something was lost but could be regained—an intimacy for which we've been searching and a Tree of Life to which we belong.

Many on the front edge of research are finding that veritas is real and alive. Welcome to our campuses and research labs, to our conversations, sorrows and adventures.

On the far side of complexity we begin to see not an argument, but a light so lovely that those who want to see will be drawn to its presence. And in that light, all things will one day become clear. Welcome to the journey. Welcome to veritas.

1

Through the Darkness

*"I wish the ring had never come to me. I wish none of this had
happened," said Frodo.*

*"So do all who live to see such times," replied Gandalf, "but that's
not for them to decide. All we have to do is decide what to do
with the time given us. There are other forces in this world besides
the will of evil."*

J. R. R. TOLKIEN, *THE FELLOWSHIP OF THE RING*

*Our lives are not a random series of events; they tell a Story that
has meaning. We aren't in a movie we've arrived at twenty minutes
late; we are in a Sacred Romance.*

JOHN ELDREDGE, *THE SACRED ROMANCE*

Unable to sleep against the boxes marked "Biohazard," I sat in the
plane's jump seat, looked through the cockpit window at the stars and
moon and wondered, *What in the world am I doing on this cargo jet in the
middle of a cold winter night?* I was hitching a ride on a friend's plane—
the AirNet express.

AirNet was a network of pretty darn quick planes, the fastest carrier
of goods to a hundred cities. I had walked into the office earlier this
evening in a virtual and literal fog. "Hey, Kelly," Jim in Boston opera-
tions had said. "Where are you headed this week?" I'd had to stop and

think. "Denver for a few days, then out to Portland," I said. "Is a jump seat open?" He pointed out the window and down the tarmac. If they hadn't finished loading, I'd lend a hand and then toss my backpack and body on board. Within minutes we were headed off to wherever it was I was going.

I wrote a journal entry and lay back against the boxes of canceled checks, Red Cross blood and mystery boxes with the orange stickers. I was the cargo with the yellow earplugs and blue sleeping bag. And frankly, I missed Rob and my family, friends and books by the fire.

Falling asleep tonight was rough on the crates and cold metal. This was unusual for me, having once been a paid sleeper. As children, my brothers and I were among the "good sleeper" test group in my father's sleep lab at the University of Chicago and later at Ohio State where he did clinical psychology. These odd, groggy people called graduate students would put electrodes all over my head and body and later awaken me to ask about my dreams when my EKG, EEG and REM graphs did something they liked. I was still good at sleeping in general—though not tonight.

JOURNAL ENTRY

I talk to myself and when I include God the monologue becomes dialogue, and on a good day I simply listen. "Again," I ask God to help me remember, "what am I doing here?"

As a part-time college chaplain at Harvard, I believed, despite the university's long bout with amnesia, that the purpose of the modern university was the pursuit of truth—*veritas*. But I also heard the postmodern questions of the times: Whose truth? What good is truth? Who cares? Isn't truth relative? But then I wondered, do we just accept a loss of bearings, of true north? On every campus I saw signs of despair and emptiness. In every university the questions were similar: What story is real? What is the life that is truly life? To whom do I belong? And where? If God is love, why do we suffer? Is anyone here, for me?

I also needed to know what was true and why. I couldn't "believe" what my mind reasonably doubted. Who could, I wondered. Without a sound basis for knowledge, how could anyone act in the world with proper confidence? Within our community, from the grassroots up, the Veritas Forum at Harvard emerged as a way of exploring such questions about true life, as friends, together.

I was reminded—exploring true life by advising Veritas Forums in other universities—that's why I was on a cold plane that night. And many nights.

I sat up and eavesdropped—the pilots were talking about work, about family. They seemed so calm, shooting through the turbulent darkness in this metal tube. How did they know where we were going? I studied the indigo instrument panel. A compass read "southwest," based on the fixed reference of true north, I supposed. A radio controller broke in.

"Charlie one-niner, you've got the Chicago tower. What's your destination, over."

"Denver," said the pilot. "Over."

I borrowed their calm and tried again to rest. Eyes closed, I floated off into a memory—my first memory, age four, on my father's lap gazing up into the vaulted arches of Rockefeller Chapel at the University of Chicago during a Handel's *Messiah* Christmas concert.

"The kingdoms of this world have become the kingdom of our Lord."

I fell asleep in my father's lap, and as I attempted to fall asleep on the cargo plane, I could hear the majestic orchestral melodies of the *Messiah* hidden in my memory.

That memory morphed into another. I was once again in the dark, now twelve years old in my purple bedroom in Ohio with a lava lamp and beanbag chair, very alone and unable to speak to anyone about my parents' divorce. And then as a fifteen-year-old, I was hiding in a church balcony, hoping to see but not be seen since I'd announced to high school friends that I wouldn't go to a play about the Passion of Jesus. After all, my academic family was more sophisticated than that.

The play opened with three prophets foretelling the Messiah's coming, in humility, the Prince of Peace. "The eyes of the blind man behold now the sun. The ears of the deaf are undone. The lame run like children, the cries of the dumb say he's come, finally he's come."[1]

In my memory the lights fade and come up again to reveal sixty students from my school strewn across the stage as if sleeping or dead. A man enters and begins to gently resurrect them one by one, singing, "Awake, awake, the day is dawning clear and the sun returns to the sky. Behold salvation now is drawing near, and the king for whom you cry."

They come to life. They join the chorus. Some follow him as friends. Some have the guts to press the question of the Roman governor Pontius Pilate when he looks into the face of Jesus and asks, *Veritas, quae res veritas?*—truth, what is truth? Some crucify him and hear for themselves the life-changing cry, "Father, forgive them, they don't know what they are doing." Hundreds become eyewitnesses not only to his death but also to his resurrection that changes human hearts and history.

I returned to that balcony four straight nights. I didn't see religion but, instead, a wildly alive Person, the Life-Giver. I discovered God in flesh and blood, full of grace and truth, with the heart of a relentless lover. I saw the One who saw me, who knew me, even while I was hiding.

I encountered not only a resurrected Savior but also a vibrant community of people in whom I saw the light of life. I was invited to belong even while wrestling with belief. The leaders welcomed every question and doubt. They loved me more for them, not less. Mud fights, barn raisings, Bible studies, cross-country bike trips. I questioned, observed, played, sang and eventually trusted. Then I found myself walking through our empty house, giving little speeches to myself and to my family in my mind: "I'm not a Christian because it's popular or comfortable (it was neither), but because it's true. It's where the weight of evidence leads. And it changes lives, like mine." Before long I joined the Passion play called *Tetelestai,* and then began to lead groups of younger kids—rafting, camping, talking and doing life together. A decade later, I was a chaplain at Harvard.

I occasionally wondered if the gospel was myth, but I came to see the gospel as myth fulfilled in reality—in a real time, place and Person. Science and art reveal the reality of the biblical story. Astrophysics reveals a beginning and the necessity of an immaterial first cause. Biochemistry and DNA reveal a "language" of encoded instruction, a *logos* becoming flesh and blood. Archaeology and history reveal the Bible as accurate eyewitness accounts of real events, people and places. What—or rather, Who—I experience behind all the beauty seems too good to be false. Sometimes it's a haunting. Sometimes a glory. The story has what C. S. Lewis called "the ring of truth."

In my journey I often found myself travel-weary and mysteriously carried into a story I didn't fully understand, a story I am still learning to see, a story in the eyes and minds of remarkable friends who wondered about Jesus at and beyond Harvard—together.

Not imagining the crisis of sorrow nor the deeper joys that lay ahead, I was asking, what is my story? More importantly, I was asking, what is our quest for veritas? Now, at twenty thousand feet in the glimmer of dawn beneath a crescent moon, I began to remember how it was I came to be on this plane.

2

Bewildered in the City
The Journey Begins

*[We live in a culture that has] for centuries now cultivated the
idea that the skeptical person is always smarter than one who
believes. You can be almost as stupid as a cabbage, as long as you
doubt. . . . Today it is the skeptics who are the social conformists.*

DALLAS WILLARD,
THE VERITAS FORUM AT OHIO STATE UNIVERSITY

I was a photographer who wanted to produce documentaries that
would inspire hope, so in the late 1980s I left The Ohio State University
to attend Harvard Divinity School (HDS) as a visiting student in religion and media.[1] As an impressionable grad student from Columbus,
Ohio, I arose early—my first morning in Cambridge—and set out to
explore this American icon.

JOURNAL ENTRY

June 1987

*What a day to first experience Harvard. Cheerful
students milling about in academic robes huddling for
pictures with friends and parents. Party tents, balloons, and
caterers were welcoming visitors on verdant manicured lawns*

rolling up to massive schools of law and business and government. The Yard itself, the heart of Harvard's undergraduate college, as well as the larger university, was drawing everyone to itself. I soon realized I was witnessing Commencement Day, not every day.

Walking around the Yard, the most hallowed ground of American academia, I counted over a dozen gates, wrought iron and brick and stonework from centuries past. Over many of these gates were clues about Harvard's original vision. Some, a cross. One a Proverb. Others an inscription such as Christo et Ecclessiae (for Christ and the church), or simply, Veritas (truth). Thanks to former Latin teachers the stones themselves were speaking to me.

This new chapter in my life feels both scary and exciting. Scary because I've heard that HDS can be inhospitable to orthodox Christian faith. But I'm also excited—I love a challenge. If HDS has something important to say to me, to expose biblical faith as false hope, then I want to find out ASAP.

I went to HDS expecting to be challenged by both secular and Christian professors, students, and a broad curriculum. But by the end of an orientation lunch, I gathered that one was not to speak of Jesus or the Bible without a tone of erudite cynicism. I quickly learned that subtle mockery trumped reason. I thought of Genesis 3 (the serpent's subtle and sarcastic questions to the woman about God's word and character) and wondered what kind of ministers and teachers this school turned out.

Though there were exceptions, the attitude at the luncheon proved to be the norm. The overall ethos of HDS at the time was like this: We wear black and are tolerant of anything but belief in truth. We are sophisticated post-Christian intellectuals who understand, rather than stand under, any authority or truth claim. We are subject to no one. All things are subject to our interpretations and preferences.

Though some people were pleasant, HDS was in general a confusing mix. When I arrived Henri Nouwen, a deeply thoughtful Christian minister, had just decided to leave his professorship at HDS to work with mentally retarded adults. He later referred to the school as a spiritual desert.

Less than a month after I arrived at HDS, a secular Jewish student— I'll call him Michael—offered me Ecstasy, which was then the academic culture's recreational drug of choice. I passed on the drug and instead we went to lunch in the Square.

I knew I'd entered a cultural bubble when our Boston-born waiter heard my flat Midwestern accent and asked me, "Wea ya from?"

"Pardon me?" I replied.

"Wea ya from?" he said a little louder.

"I'm from Ohio," I answered, rather flatly I suppose.

"Ohio," he said looking confused. "Out hea, we call it Iowa."

I was speechless, except to order chowder at Bartleys Burgers.

Michael and I began an ongoing conversation that threw me for a loop. "Kelly," he said, "don't you know that every person finds his faith or worldview reasonable, intellectually sound, like you do the biblical faith? Every faith can be equally supported both by the human construct of reason and by experience."

I had no idea. I wondered for a few months if he were right. And naturally I was interested in discovering the fruit of such liberal academic insight.

On hallway bulletin boards, da Vinci's painting of the Last Supper was used to promote HDS's weekly social gathering (or "pub"), with Jesus and his disciples drinking Budweisers. *Dames Divinitas* posters

invited "sultry sisters" to evenings of "dancing, drinking, and de-
bauchery, for women only." Though HDS prided itself on its open-
minded tolerance, I had to wonder how sincerely that tolerance was
held when someone conveniently cleared all bulletin boards just before tours for potential donors.

The few evangelicals barely came out of the closet as Christians;
meanwhile, the Full Moon Circle—self-defined as the "Neo-pagan,
Pre-Christian, Eco-feminist Wiccan Society"—packed out the chapel
when it was their turn to host weekly worship. The songs were more
like chants, and some knew them by heart. Several women led the service and had choreographed a dance to beckon the "spirits of the east,
west, north and south." One professor was speaking to a spirit or an
ancestor; I couldn't tell which. *Gee,* I thought to myself, *we're not in
Ohio anymore. I wonder when we sing "Amazing Grace" and "The Old
Rugged Cross."* Turns out it was the day of a full moon, and the wor-
shipers were as uncomfortable with my presence as I was being there,
so I quietly slipped out.

One of the Full Moon leaders and I had mutual friends, and I hoped
that she sensed my kindness to her after that day. She was an environmentalist of sorts and I prayed she'd desire the True Vine when she became disillusioned by the impersonal forces of nature, which shed no
tears for human beings.

Sexual promiscuity, gay or straight, was common; I felt truly sorry
for any white heterosexual male, Christian or otherwise. One man said
he was nearly "burned at the stake" for his comments on gender and
power at HDS as reported by a Harvard College newspaper. His polit-
ically incorrect words were, "The witches are hunting."

Still, I felt privileged living in a university community, meeting the
world and seeing through many eyes. But there was also a joyless cau-
tion about the place. What I had anticipated to be a rich and respectful
exchange of ideas began to feel more like walking on eggshells, or
maybe minefields. Buzz words and empty language masked weak realities. The search for truth had degenerated into relativism and the acceptance of almost anything as true. A celebration of rich "diversity"
had faded into a gray, passive "tolerance" that usually ignored the

ideas and beliefs of isolated others—especially orthodox Christians.

Though I was only a part-time student writing a thesis, I eagerly read the origin texts and sacred scriptures of other faiths, including the epic of Gilgamesh, the Upanishads, the Gnostic Gospels and the Qur'an. I wanted to understand other people and even make new friends. Though there were some prodigious Old and New Testament scholars at HDS, the overall level of biblical knowledge and depth of conversation was underwhelming. My Ohio youth group seemed more earnest.

I was sad that many at HDS didn't know that the gospel was the "good news" of Christ's sacrificial love on the cross that restored us to abundant life in the kingdom of God. When I'd hear the mantra "The Bible is full of contradictions," I learned to say, "Show me where; I really want to know." But students were unfamiliar with the Bible except for hard passages usually taken out of context. I sensed they were merely reiterating what they'd learned from poor college religion teachers, who had learned from incompetent religion teachers themselves.

HDS prided itself on pluralism and tolerance while it shunned orthodox evangelical Christian faith and scholarship. To them Christianity was merely a Western religion led by dead white males. One student explained to me that HDS was "not a denominational seminary where one unquestioningly accepts ancient dogmas and the traditions of our elders. There are nice little Bible colleges for that." Rather, he said, students were studying religion so they could be teachers, journalists, social workers, psychologists, political candidates, community activists or government advisors.

But I wondered if HDS graduates were entering those good callings with a limited education. The more I read eyewitness history (rather than modern revisions of history), the more I saw that the church wasn't only Western, but that it grew in the Middle East, the Mediterranean, North Africa, Turkey, Asia Minor and even China centuries before the gospel came to North America. And the more I read contemporary world news, the more I saw that the church wasn't dead but growing rapidly—not in most Western nations but in Africa, China, South America and Korea. Christianity was neither exclusively Western nor led by irrelevant white males. It was the fastest-growing movement on earth. And it produced the fruit of social justice, freedom, art, science and community.

Feeling reprimanded for still caring about reason as well as emotion and human wholeness, I went back to my friend Michael. "Okay, you're a secular Jew with reason, right?"

"Sure. We thought God was there for us, but then he disappeared. The Messiah didn't come."

"What do you make of the Old Testament Messianic prophecies that seem to have been fulfilled in the life of Jesus?"

"What prophecies?" he asked.

I pointed out some passages: the Messiah would be a descendant of King David (Jeremiah 23:5; Acts 13:22-23), he would be born in Bethlehem (Micah 5:2; Matthew 2:1-6), he would be known by the miracles he performed for others (Isaiah 61:1-2; Luke 4:18-21), he was rejected in the end as he suffered for the sins of others (Isaiah 53:2-6; Mark 15:1-39), and he was subjected to crucifixion, with his tormentors gambling to decide who would take his clothing (Psalm 22:15-18; John 19:23-24).[2]

"And apparently," I added, "archaeologists have dated the earliest manuscripts of Psalm 22, which describes the crucifixion, back several centuries before the Romans invented crucifixion as a death penalty."

"Kelly, you need to lighten up."

"Michael," I said smiling, "you're the one who needs drugs to be happy." We both came to see that few students knew what they believed or why. Few had reasons beyond lifestyle preferences or going with the flow of relativism; often they were shaped by past abuses of love and power. I came to see that Jesus loved the students at HDS. But why God would allow teachers to spread falsehood in classrooms, institutions and pulpits—on that subject I was confused.

When I asked a comparative religion professor this same question about Old Testament Messianic prophecies, he responded with silence and then changed the subject.

Soon after these events our small group of Christians invited a Christian apologist, Norman Geisler, to HDS. He presented a compelling case for the logic and historical evidence of the Christian faith. The HDS chaplain and I spoke afterward and I said that I could only assume everyone found it moving, given the weight of evidence presented. "But Kelly," said Chaplain Krister Stendahl, "students here don't equate logic and reason with truth. They see no connection." That was another lesson in postmodern skepticism.

JOURNAL ENTRY

A widely respected African professor sympathetic to Christian faith, in fact a former Muslim who became a Christian, was mysteriously denied tenure. And then an administrator sympathetic to the Christian faith, whom most students loved, was also mysteriously released by the dean. This time because of an alleged "diversity" issue.

A Korean friend asked me to sit with her in her doctoral defense with a committee of HDS professors. These defenses can be grueling, over the course of an entire evening. One professor consumed a six-pack of beer while critiquing her dissertation and determining her future, perhaps. Though her scholarship is now widely known and respected, they did not approve of her dissertation because she included in her theology the literal, not metaphorical, resurrection of Jesus from the dead. Their a priori bias cost my friend several years of her life before she finally graduated and returned to Korea, now a tenured professor of New Testament.

I began to notice the extent of the disconnect. Those who believed in Jesus were considered quaint at best, enemies at worst. But when I first heard people say "the J word" instead of "Jesus," refusing to use the name that holds power, I knew they were nervous about him— that he might become a real live issue once again. Many wanted to keep that possibility at bay. A living Jesus would threaten the prevailing relativism and deconstructionism, as well as the politics of money, sex and power.

Perhaps HDS merely reflected the world as it was, but I had hoped to find a culture dynamic enough to explore many ideas about reality and hope and honest enough to consider classical Christian faith. Diversity can be wonderful, I thought, because it includes the whole family of God—every set of eyes, every color and culture—who reflect the mind and heart of God. But HDS, and to some extent the secular university at large for most of the past century, has not been known for intellectual diversity. I wondered if worship of God might interfere with the university's worship of itself.

As David French, the former president of the Foundation for Individual Rights in Education, recently said on ABC's *World News Tonight*, "You find more intellectual diversity in most evangelical megachurches than in most universities."

I came to understand the insight of the brilliant journalist G. K. Chesterton: "It's not that Christianity is tried and found wanting, but that it is considered difficult and left untried." I believe that the culture of Harvard Divinity School and the university beyond it found Jesus difficult, and best left untried.

Ironically, everything was tolerated except that for which Harvard College was founded—*In Christi Gloriam*—Jesus Christ's glory.

I came to perceive the spirit of HDS then as postmodern skepticism, irrationality and eroticism—attempts to fill the void that remained in the hearts of those who didn't know God's love. I also sensed a bit of administrative insecurity, since the divinity school was not high profile on the Harvard scene.

I suppose people like me were considered repressed conservatives. I had come to faith as a liberal, and then I discovered realities that were valuable and worth conserving. I'm a conservationist when it comes to clean water and trees in creation for the same reasons I care about truth, beauty and goodness in cultures. Slash and burn is not okay if you care about the future. And I believe that true knowledge is possible not because I'm smart enough to figure it out but because the Author is good enough to have spoken and entered the play—but I'm jumping ahead.

Biblical faith is both romantic and realistic. It is the story of the world's Lover who empowers us to love. It is the story of the value of human beings and the whole cosmos. To lose that reality is to lose intrinsic meaning, romance and joy. My hunch was that the loss of biblical faith at Harvard would naturally end in the loss of everything else valuable. We would see dehumanization, objectification of both men and women, and a culture filling the void with false idols. At Harvard, as biblical truth slipped away, I felt that human beings were being reduced from soul to body, sexualized and commodified.[3] I had once thought liberal academics were trying to solve these injustices, not exploit them.

In fact, tragically, within a few years the dean of HDS (and the founder of the school's Center for Public Values) was demoted by Harvard's president for doing just this—as the press told America, he downloaded a large amount of Internet pornography onto a Harvard computer system.[4] Strangely, he is still a tenured Harvard professor, in religion. This story is both a parable and a painful foreshadowing of our cultural brokenness and desperate age.

I also sensed a dismissal of Jesus in the college and larger university, even though he was the most influential person in history in terms of information, ideas and knowledge. He saw, spoke and acted clearly and with proper confidence. If he were at Harvard now, does anyone doubt that he would magnetically attract the brightest thinkers on campus, as well as those who were most hurting?

The university, though it was filled with bright and well-intended people, was experiencing a rise in binge drinking, sexually transmitted disease, depression and even suicide. The questions of authority, wisdom and what it means to be human were up for grabs.

But I was an unsophisticated and bewildered minority and did not know what to do with my own angst. Though I was at first timid, my

Ohio youth-group-leader operating mode kicked in. It had taught me that we earn the right to be heard, that it's fun to creatively express the gospel and that we all can be redeemed. So I organized a Bible study group, a conference titled "A Mind Awake: The Reasonableness of Christianity," concerts and meals for fellow students. To little avail. A few people came out of the woodwork, but not many.

JOURNAL ENTRY

In the Yard, posters and papers are often about the politics of diversity, for rights with no mention of responsibilities. Posters advocate the use of embryos for research. Notices about hooking up with strangers (the only rule is no names are asked) next to date rape counseling, next to info on rallies for continued abortion rights, next to info on depression, AIDS, and drug and alcohol support groups.

But we can't say "the J word." Does anyone sense a loss of perspective here? That we're rejecting the very One we most desperately need?

I was useless on my own. And daily, hourly, the images and ideas of secular fundamentalism were permeating the campus. An ambient spiritual stupor, like an anesthetic, hung in the air. My faith and vision were beginning to dissolve, making any possibility of true north seem increasingly delusional. I was being subtly reoriented. I was homesick. And I was lonely.

3

Rumors of Another World

A Taste of New Wine

*We do not draw people to Christ by loudly discrediting what
they believe, by telling them how wrong they are and how right we
are, but by showing them a light that is so lovely that they want
with all their hearts to know the source of it.*

MADELEINE L'ENGLE, *WALKING ON WATER*

*The thief comes only to steal and kill and destroy; I came that they
may have life, and have it to the full.*

JESUS, JOHN 10:10

Later that year, I heard rumors of a Christian group in the light beyond the shadows of the divinity school—a fellowship of students
from all the other Harvard grad schools run by a hip Californian
named Jeff Barneson. Jeff was a Harvard chaplain (one of an eclectic
group of about fifteen), on the cycling team, a Kennedy School of Government graduate, an excellent carpenter and an instructor of com-
puter-aided design—a Renaissance-Reformation man who fired on all
pistons. Jeff invited me to a grad student weekend retreat, but I wanted
to go home to Ohio. I also felt a little out of my league with this bright
group, so I said, "Thanks but no thanks." However, my roommate per-
suaded me to drive down with her the next morning.

The drive to Cape Cod was refreshing, but little did I expect what awaited me. I walked into a Bible study with seventy grad students. They were talking naturally and curiously of the relevance of the mind of Jesus to all of life. It ended with singing, after which people introduced themselves to me and to other newcomers. Jeff announced volleyball and Ultimate Frisbee, and we were soon changing clothes and grabbing lunch on the way to the beach.

Throughout the weekend, the reach of the gospel amazed me. Here were chemists, musicians, physicists, historians, artists, athletes, and business and medical students sharing the goodness of God in friendship. We discussed research. We considered our careers as vocation—the voice of God calling us beyond success to significance, where our gifts and joys might match up with the world's need. We learned that we were first called to Christ himself, then to the world he loves—an ecology of first abiding in Christ (roots), then overflowing for others (fruit). He's the Vine. We're the branches.

For the first time since coming to Harvard, I saw joy.

How countercultural for a group of graduate students to be together without excessive twentysomething sexual tension and academic angst but instead to have time for long talks about what matters and why. This was why I attended grad school, and I was thrilled to find a community that felt the same way—a community of like minds, spirits and hearts. We had found one another.

JOURNAL ENTRY

What an introduction to this iconoclastic subset of Harvard's ten thousand graduate students. They are more interested in making a life than in making a living. They are attracted to Jesus because Jesus knows that our danger is not in too much life, but in too little. They come from many cultures to integrate great ideas with lives of service and truth for the art of life.

Students in the social sciences and humanities discover the gospel's inspiration in abolition and civil rights, jazz, women's suffrage, great literature, in the founding of schools and hospitals.

Engineering students create images of the previously unseen—the interior of the human body, or the subsurface of the earth to help archeologists unearth ruins of an ancient Chinese city or biblical site.

Scientists with their sense of wonder are fascinated by the universe. We discuss the genome project, the big bang, entropy and chaos. They find information, order and complexity embedded in living systems. They advance research, ethics and epistemology in their fields.

I've met education students whose love excites classrooms and children about life. Kindred spirits at the Kennedy School of Government see how the humility, creativity and forgiveness of the cross can resolve international conflicts with both justice and mercy.

Like many retreats to come, this one involved hiking, guitars around the fire, stargazing, prayer and laughter among new friends. The retreat marked a turn of seasons. Wood smoke scented the cool air. Inland ponds reflected the white of birch bark and the orange and reds of a fiery New England autumn. Cranberries floated to the surface of watery bogs. Ours was a time-out-of-time to prepare for a world which, we believed, would soon become alive to us.

Living in a Larger Story

Back in Cambridge, Jeff began to ask us, "Where in the world is Jesus' love least felt?" We started planning a three-week mission project in Peru, building schools with Food for the Hungry. The first school would be in a shantytown near Lima nicknamed La Boca Del Diablo, the mouth of the devil. The second school was to be built in the Amazon rain forest. Eighteen grad students signed up, and I was the wimp who sheepishly asked, "Is either of these projects likely to have, well, snakes?" Yes. The Amazon. Right. I almost backed out.

Upon arrival in Lima, we were introduced to the mothers in La Boca who had to leave their infants, some with tuberculosis, in the hot desert while they eked out a living selling crafts. It was heartbreaking. I'd been to a European psychology convention with my family, and to Sarajevo for the winter Olympics, but I'd never been face to face with this kind of poverty. "The poor" were once an abstraction. Poverty to me was statistics without human faces.[1]

The next week, half of us took off for the Amazon where we joined missionaries to work on the second school. In a slight diversion, we triangulated to Cuzco where we caught a train to see the breathtaking Machu Picchu ruins, once the center of Incan religious activity. With the help of trail ropes, we hiked up a mountain above the ruins. The sign-in/sign-out list at the base, we later learned, was to let the locals know whose body they had found in the Andean riverbed two thousand feet below if someone signed in but never signed out. After our hike, we all signed back in.

Exhausted and exhilarated, ten of us walked to a sleepy town called Aguas Calientes a few miles down the road to spend the night. We were told to follow the railroad tracks as they carved a path along the mountainside. I was out in front with a few friends, and we entered a dark tunnel hewn out of rock through the mountain. Less than halfway through, we heard shouting behind us. Andy and Jeff were near the tunnel's entrance, wildly waving their arms and pointing to a train headed for the tunnel.

We quickly surmised that the tunnel wasn't wide enough for the train and us. We raced forward away from the train, helping one another run with backpacks in the dark on railroad ties and rocks. When the sound suddenly escalated in volume, we knew the train had entered the tunnel. My heart raced. I had to tell myself to breathe. I thought, *If I trip, I'm dead. Just don't trip.* We kept moving. As the train closed in on us, its headlight lit our way.

We exploded through the opening and, no longer concerned about snakes, pitched ourselves into a dry riverbed, hearts pounding as the train rumbled by. Soon we were laughing. Over dinner and a visit to the hot springs, our fellowship that night was sweet. Grateful for our friends' vantage point and warning behind us, and for one another on the journey through the tunnel, we realized that we needed each other.

JOURNAL ENTRY

I feel so alive here. How good life can be when we live fully in the present. But I have not yet mastered this since I am a human with memory and with future hopes and fears. Nonetheless, there was always something thrilling about living large in the moment, and a hundred times I've thought, I wouldn't be here without God and friends with me in the journey.

We were soon in an Amazon village called Pucalpa near the richly forested Brazilian border. It was the rainy season, and we worked every day in mud and torrential downpours. After experiencing various skin issues, we found plastic garbage bags to be excellent foul-weather gear—a fashion trend we even revived back in Cambridge a time or two.

Days were spent mixing cement, pounding nails and helping missionaries build a school for children with polio. Many of these children were once outcast but now were welcomed to a loving community run by missionaries associated with South American Mission, Wycliffe and

Food for the Hungry. The kids would drag their withered bodies on wobbly crutches through the mud of the rainy season—signs of the Fall, and yet what a beautiful picture of the kingdom of God at work.

These once-forgotten children now began each day with songs of praise and laughter. They spent mornings learning to read, write, do math and practice life skills. In the afternoons they used practical mechanics and woodworking skills to build crutches, wheelchairs and even artificial limbs for one another and for others. They were grateful to God and to the missionaries; their joy brought us more joy.

JOURNAL ENTRY

For some reason I brought a plastic Twister tarp with big colored dots, which has doubled as a foul-weather jacket and makeshift tent. I once stole Paul Anthony's clothes while he was in the shower and left him only the Twister tarp. An innocent mistake. But not without payback.

Muddy and wet as usual, I was late to lunch. When I walked in Paul and Andy asked me to grab some apples "in the burlap bag." I reached into the bag, but being the rocket scientist I am, paused to ponder, "Hmmm, why is everyone watching me grab the apples?" I opened the bag wide and saw at the bottom a well-fed and therefore "safe" (I was later told) boa constrictor. After my heart failure, the missionaries named the snake Julius Squeezer. Later that week they found another such creature and named him Squeezer Augustus. Missionaries are very hearty.

Through this adventure I came to see how the gospel, rightly understood, conserves rather than wipes out what is true, good and beautiful in people and in local cultures. The children changed us. We saw a ruined community coming back to life. Also, we saw how Wycliffe missionaries preserve indigenous languages by writing them down, teaching the Bible and reading in native tongues and customs rather than in the language of the colonizing elite.

In our camp each night without the distraction of computers, televisions, phones and cars, the most extraordinary thing happened—we grew to know one another. We bonded in the adventure of serving crippled children, and we risked showing one another tears of sorrow as well as silliness. As we lived together, shared our doubts, and explored scripture each morning and evening, we were learning to trust God and each other. That was our real education. Jesus wants each of us to more fully become who we were dreamed up to be by the Trinity before time.

I came back to Cambridge with bronchitis and a changed heart. I returned with a renewed sense of the adventure of kingdom-building with friends.

The anesthetic of HDS was wearing off. I felt alive again, more so than ever.

Going Home, Almost

The grad student fellowship redeemed my time in Cambridge. What a privilege to have met these people. Having finished my thesis and glad to be going home to Ohio, I packed the car. Jeff showed up.

"Where are you going?"

"Home to Ohio," I answered.

"Why?"

"I'm done," I replied.

"Why don't you stay and do what you've been doing with various fellowships around campus, but as an intern chaplain with grad students?" he asked.

"Jeff," I answered, "I'm just a crazy youth group leader without a theology degree."

"Pray about it?" he asked.

"Okay. And Jeff, thank you for everything."

And then I drove past the Yard, down Memorial Drive, paid the toll for 90-West and headed toward Ohio—with fifteen uninterrupted hours to think, to remember and to pray. I thought of going home. I thought of Jeff's offer to return to Harvard. I tried to make sense of the past few years.

Images came to me. Though worn and weathered by nearly four centuries, the imprint of Harvard's first wisdom—Jesus—was still faintly visible in the stonework, seal and early motto. I saw him most vividly in the remnant of a hundred or so believing students, but not as clearly in the remaining thousands, nor in the faculty, nor classroom discussions. Instead, Harvard had become a symbol of human knowledge, of prestige and power, of the ways and kingdoms of the world.

I imagined a tree that adds branches while laying an axe to its own root. I felt the pain of that axe within my own academic family, influenced by the "enlightened" university. We were among an earlier wave of the secular harvest, ourselves reduced and separated by divorce, for we reap in life what we sow as ideas. I wondered how many millions were laid low as well, left wondering, "What happened?" and "How does love last?" I began to understand the insight of Charles Malik, former president of the United Nations General Assembly, when he said, "Change the university and you change the world." I also began to think of his great question, "What does Jesus Christ think of the university?"

Back and forth I debated. Maybe I just needed to lighten up, go home and join the country club. I reminded myself that no one person can get her arms around a university. Everyone sees it from a separate vantage point, differing wildly in philosophy and approach. I'd stay home and forget about it.

But then I wondered whether the university could be any different in a fallen world. Was it, as one college president said, "a multiversity connected only by a central heating system"? If at its worst the university was a collection of dead branches, at its best could it abide again in the True Vine and become fruitful—a tree of life in which the birds of the air were fed and strengthened and sent out to create a better kingdom?

During the following few months, I asked God, parents and friends for counsel. I came to believe that I was to return to Cambridge to explore and share the truth of Jesus, with and without words.

I packed the car and once again headed east to Harvard. This time for a decade.

4

Veritas Envisioned
The Idea of The Veritas Forum

In a world . . . deluged with data, and choked with choices, the abilities that matter most are now closer in spirit to the specialties of the right hemisphere [of the brain]—artistry, empathy, seeing the big picture, and pursuing the transcendent.

DANIEL PINK,
"REVENGE OF THE RIGHT BRAIN," *WIRED*

There is an increasing danger that reason will simply be ignored, and that arguments will become mere shouting matches where the loudest, or most acceptable, voice wins. Granted, the Christian knows that reason by itself is not enough. The Christian gospel highlights one who went to his death for a higher reason, the law of love. Nevertheless, this higher reason, sometimes called wisdom in the biblical tradition, offers rich, deep and coherent answers to the ultimate questions, and we owe it to our contemporaries to wrestle afresh with the questions and articulate the answers in fresh ways, not least to rehabilitate wisdom within a culture that is fast making a virtue of folly.

N. T. WRIGHT, THE VERITAS FORUM AT YALE

Back in Cambridge I was enthusiasm-rich but cash-poor, and so I was kindly invited to sleep on the couch of my Ugandan friend Harriet for a few months while I readjusted to what would become my life at Harvard.[1]

Jeff and I, along with our colleague Kevin Offner, began small group Bible studies in most of the nine graduate and professional schools that made up the university. In a given year, we worked with about two hundred students in the Grad School Christian Fellowship (GSCF).[2] Like campus ministers everywhere, my life consisted of facilitating discussions small and large, preparing dinners with international students, baking bread, stuffing mailboxes, playing squash, mountain biking (much of my hangout time was spent playing sports with students), planning retreats and mission projects, organizing lectures—and doing my best to relieve the angst of papers and exams.

The groups were decentralized for the most part and hundreds of wonderful conversations took place as students explored the mind of Christ in every realm. Every spring the fellowship "ordained to daily work" twenty or more graduates who now saw their careers as calling—the place where their gifts met the world's needs.

For the first few years I felt like a cyclist on Jeff's rear wheel, drafting off his clarity and energy. Then again, we all hoped that we were drafting off the work of God's Spirit who was bringing us along for the ride. Jeff and I sensed that students were less interested in propositional defense of faith (though logic is often helpful, if unusual, in Cambridge) and more interested in finding kindred spirits with whom to share life. They wanted kindness and adventure and fun.

And so, along with gatherings at Harvard, we embarked on many trips into the New England mountains or the Cape and islands. I remember games of charades around the fire—some of the more esoteric being Shakespeare's *Troilus and Cressida* and Immanuel Kant's *Critique of Pure Reason*. One could score more points if popular films were expressed in foreign languages or puns, so *Star Wars* became *Astre Disastre* and so on. And then we were up early to ski or hike. We were in perpetual motion, and friendships deepened with laughter and adventure.

Fireplace Inoperable

In Harvard Yard stands the elegant Phillips Brooks House, which had been funded by alumni a century ago (during a time of spiritual renewal) as a home for the Christian fellowships in years to come. Within three decades, however, the house had been taken over by other groups and was now available to Christians only for occasional meetings. In the main parlor, a sign hangs above the mantle reading, "Fireplace inoperable." That sign struck me as a perfect spiritual metaphor for the lost opportunity of Phillips Brooks House at Harvard.

I had a vision to gather believers like kindling from the shadows and margins of the university to the middle of the Yard for a fire as a unified witness for Christ's glory once again. But the logs for that fire were kept apart, and the spiritual fire that had once been the college's light and heat was now an inoperable fireplace. Though marginalized in many ways, believers were trying to remain a blessing to the university. After all, God had covenanted with Abraham that children of the promise would be a blessing to their neighbors and to the nations. And the nations were now coming to Harvard and other American universities.

The Veritas Forum

The first Veritas Forum at Harvard came together as a confluence of several streams, much in the way I myself experienced Harvard: first as a visiting student, then as one of the university chaplains to graduate students with the Harvard-Radcliffe United Ministry, and later co-teaching senior electives in film, the works of C. S. Lewis, and multiculturalism. My life was an archaeological dig of sorts—an adventure, feeling and looking beneath the surface of things modern. I did not feel entitled to the position and often couldn't believe I was there—this Midwesterner raised in Wisconsin, Illinois and Ohio with a passion for sports, ideas, nature and treasure hunts.

One long winter weekend in 1991, friends and I headed north out of Cambridge for Jaffrey, New Hampshire, the site of our annual sleigh ride and barn dance. On the sleigh ride, huddled together under thick blankets, we glided along to the sound of the horses' bells and our own singing and laughter. When it began to snow, one African friend said, "Oh! I've never felt snow before!" We made snow angels as a spontaneous snow-initiation ritual.

Warming up inside the barn with hot apple cider and homemade doughnuts, I hugged old friends and met new ones. Each year, this was one of my happiest evenings because I loved square dancing and pulling shy students into the dance. Each person was beautiful individually, and even more so all dancing together.

What fun these traditions of sleigh rides and country dancing were for international students from England, Korea and South Africa. Many came without knowing a soul, and here in the grad fellowship they'd laugh and twirl with seventy-five new friends, under the shelter of sky and barn and one another.

Country dancing is more than math in motion with its circles and squares and triangles, its centrifugal and centripetal forces pushing out and pulling in. If you could somehow see our dance from the ceiling looking down, you'd see a room filled with colorful people from various cultures and walks of life, spinning and weaving, promenading and laughing together. Country dancing is not only a lovely metaphor for community and inclusion, it's also just plain fun.

Before midnight, nine of us headed for northern Vermont. We arrived at a friend's cabin (really a renovated barn) by 2 a.m. We were abruptly awakened early when Poh Lian, a brilliant med student from Malaysia, while walking in a sleepy stupor, suddenly descended the loft's steep stairs with a series of thumps ending in a very loud crash. In the silent aftermath, one of our group remarked, "But Poh, we thought you didn't know how to ski." To which she replied, "My experience with sports is limited to chess." Morning had broken. This was Poh's prophetic initiation to her first day of skiing.

I had a best friend within this adventurous Cambridge gang—I'll call him Rob. He was at MIT studying physics, and we'd become friends at a Thanksgiving dinner for international students when we decided it would be fun to take extra food to homeless folks in Harvard Square. Rob and I became each other's touchstones. Studying together, starting Veritas, ski-hiking, playing soccer, baking bread, hosting dinner parties, swing dancing, mountain biking and snorkeling—as he would often say of our happiness (and busyness), our feet never hit the ground.

Our gang made breakfast, chopped wood for the evening and headed for Mad River to ski. When I bought the lift tickets the man behind the counter said, "Those can't be refunded." I asked, "Why would I want to return them?" To which he responded, "Because on top, with the wind-chill, it's eighty below zero." Sure enough, on our way up the mountain we saw more cars leaving than coming. "Cool," we said, "we have the mountain to ourselves."

As we ascended on the four-person chairlift the temperature plummeted. I looked over and saw that Poh had on a lightweight jacket, leather driving gloves and her famously thick eyeglasses. What began as a ski lesson ended with, "Poh, you're going to freeze to death. Hug me around the waist, put your skis in between mine and point them downhill, and let's go." We actually had a lot of fun on the way down. (She may say that I helped prevent frostbite, but I humbly prefer to think that I helped to stem infectious disease around the world, since Poh survived the descent and went on to become a leading SARS expert and the 2005 Malaysian Woman of the Year.)

Throughout the day we'd check one another's faces for frostbite on the lifts. If anyone had it, they had to go inside the lodge and meet us when their nose or ears were no longer white. Sometimes you need a college education to be so stupid. But we survived, noses and all.

Those next few nights in the cabin, at the dinner table and later around the fire, we enjoyed a warmth made warmer by the contrast to frostbite and skiing on ice. We compared wounds, told ski stories, laughed at ourselves and sang. Conversations were often deep and personal, evoked by a day well lived with friends well loved.

The diversity of questions and ideas that arose in our conversations converged when woven into the fabric of the mind of Jesus and the biblical story. One friend, Josh, was a nuclear engineer, Rob a geophysicist, Becky an ethicist. Brian was an economist and his wife, Kay, an English scholar. One was a law student. Two were finishing medical school. I wondered, where is the hole in the gospel? It makes sense to every one of us from wildly different vantage points. The gospel is comprehensive, coherent and full of substance and hope.

As we talked late into the night, a vision of our country dance kept coming back to me. Our conversations seemed to form a similar unity in diversity—the beauty of individual diversity made even more beautiful in the unity of the biblical life view—veritas.

JOURNAL ENTRY

I wish that somehow a spiritually cold university could have joined us around that warm hearth. Though I prefer a cozy cabin, I'm beginning to wonder how we can winsomely invite everyone into the conversations and adventures we naturally have as Christians.

I wondered how we could initiate a grassroots conversation at Harvard about real questions and true life in relation to the original understanding of veritas as Jesus Christ. How, in a spirit of exploration and hospitality, could we invite others to join the dance?

Driving back to Cambridge, I tried to synthesize what I'd learned from the many experiences and conversations I'd had since coming to Harvard—rich with joy and adventure, with people who took themselves lightly but the gospel seriously, who tried to embody the Word in the world God loved, who knew that the Word became flesh and so did not reduce him to mere words once more. I wondered how I could be a steward of what I'd been given.

The appeal to the gospel has at least three advantages in a university town. Many students and teachers still love beauty. Many are aching for community. And some still practice reason. I like Dallas Willard's definition of reason: "the mental power to discern connections in reality. The reasonable person is the one who is devoted to truth, and to finding it and living in it by all available means."[3]

One reason evangelical Christian faith in Cambridge has become so dynamic, even hip—"a big rowdy tent," according to a recent *Boston Globe* article—is that so many at MIT and Harvard are in the sciences. Scientists not only have a sense of wonder and believe in a real rather than imaginary world, but they also understand the value of putting a theory to the test. They test to see if a container holds water or leaks. They test to see if the gold is refined or impure. They test for harmony of the spheres. They look for elegance and beauty in an equation. They look for clear signs of information and intelligence. In short, they ask, "Do we hear the ring of truth here?" They trace out connections in reality.

This is why so many scientists now believe in God. Nowhere else does the universe cohere so elegantly as in the biblical text and in the person and story of Jesus Christ. Astronomers are finding the cosmological alignment of Genesis 1 and the big bang.[4] Microbiologists can now see that information is encoded as DNA beneath the human genome as if a Word was intending life itself. Quantum chemists are intrigued by signs of intentionality and vitality at the subcellular level.[5] Archaeologists no longer mock the Bible as mythology; rather, they use it in the field as factual history along with ground-penetrating radar and shovels. Physicists marvel at the constant speed of light in an accelerating universe, both realities described in the Bible.[6] Oceanographers and biologists are only beginning to discover the vast biodiversity of species generated after the Cambrian explosion and after a global flood.[7] Few M.D.s or psychologists deny the health benefits of monogamy, forgiveness and prayer in the path of healing.

Other disciplines and experts are also finding God on the far side of complexity. Educators are exploring the brilliance of Jesus as a teacher. Parents and grandparents are empowered by the mystery of sacrificial love for a child. Linguists marvel at symbolism, correspondence and the human capacity for shared meaning. Economists see how faith in the creativity and intrinsic value of humans (made in God's image) energizes an economy, a nation, a world. Political advocates with that same sense of human value work for social justice and freedom for the common man. Sociologists are understanding the wisdom of human-scale communities, farms and businesses. Cultural analysts sense a social evolution from the information age into a "meaning age," with a growing desire for synthesis, pattern and wisdom. This shift will help many move from success to significance, and from information to transformation.

It's rare for three academics to agree on anything, but here in the Grad School Christian Fellowship were chemists, astronomers, philosophers, lawyers, doctors, researchers and teachers all seeing the face of God in Jesus Christ, the One for whom Harvard was founded nearly four centuries ago. I was struck by the overwhelming coherence of the biblical worldview, and I wanted others to overhear the conversations I was in on all the time.

The next week in Cambridge, Rob and I were invited to a concert by a dear friend, Kristin (Brunner) Thurlby, a sophomore oboe player in the Harvard Bach Society. We loved listening to Kristin on her own, but that night at the *St. Matthew Passion* it occurred to us that the rest of the audience would likely not have come to hear a performance of the woodwinds alone, nor the percussion section by itself, nor the strings alone—but we came to hear them together, in concert, symphonically. Each instrument was tuned to a fixed reference point—the first violin. Together the musicians played in the same key, in melody and harmonies. For a college orchestra, it was exquisite. The orchestra of course had a human conductor on whom each gaze was fixed, but more importantly, behind the symphony was a composer. A master.

With these recurring images of unity in diversity—the meaning of "uni-versity"—I started to ask people to write down their stories. As contributions started coming back to me, I was impressed by the candid accounts of changed lives and the sense of true life that students and alumni were expressing. Rarely did we see such honesty and vulnerability in the academy, with people speaking honestly of pride, addiction, despair and salvation.

This project was originally meant for our fellowship group, but it eventually became the book *Finding God at Harvard: Spiritual Journeys of Thinking Christians* (Zondervan, 1996). I began by asking friends to write, and I eventually summoned the courage to contact people like Elizabeth Dole, astronomer Owen Gingerich, Nobel Prize-winner Aleksander Solzhenitsyn and Pulitzer Prize-winner Robert Coles, asking for their stories. One week I sent out a batch of ten letters. The first response was postmarked "Calcutta, India." I opened it nervously and read:

Dear Kelly,

Thank you for your letter. If it is for the glory of God and the good of his people, you may use the talk I gave at Harvard in 1982 in your collection. Keep the joy of loving Jesus in your heart, and share this joy with all you meet. Let us pray.

God bless you,
Mother Teresa, M.C. (Missionaries of Charity)

I'd been nervous about raising the name of Jesus so publicly within the Harvard community. Mother Teresa gave me the courage I'd been lacking. More than forty alumni eventually wrote for the book, and I wanted others to meet these humble and bright believers in person.

Dance. Coherence. Symphony. All streams of thought came together as one compelling idea: Why not gather as a vibrant community in one location for a few days and invite the whole university to explore its questions, ideas and hopes in relation to Harvard's radical vision, its first light—veritas, knowable in and through the life and mind of Jesus Christ?

The Veritas Forum Proposed

I first mentioned the idea to our ski gang.[8] We had been in a Cambridge Bible study together for three years. "Hey guys, so let's call it the Veritas festival, or treasure hunt, or forum." Kay Hall and I agreed on "forum."

"It's Latin, and a tad dull," someone said.

"Yeah, but it gets to the heart of things; it's why we're even here. We'll make it fun."

Heads nodded. Vera's blue eyes sparkled, "I love it!" That was it.

Vera Shaw was our seventy-five-year old friend who imparted both youthfulness and knowledge of God. At a campus "tea" in Sparks House, she and her husband Jim, faculty advisors to Harvard's Inter-Varsity Christian Fellowship, had befriended me. For more than five decades they'd spent their Friday nights with students in Harvard Yard. When one would say, "God is good," the other would reply, "All the time." Vera and Jim often shared Harvard's history with us and made us see that if not for Jesus, there would be no Harvard.

Barely over five feet tall, Vera was a vivacious dynamo. She was a chemist, a lifelong lover of creation, a mother to two children and a spiritual mother to hundreds more. With fire in her heart and joy in her eyes, she would lead us in prayer for hurting people, for alumni around the world, for a remnant of faith to be revived not only at Harvard but in the Ivy League and countless universities beyond. Prayer and joy were her weapons against the world's power. When difficulties seemed overwhelming, Vera would say, "Honey, the future is as bright as the promises of God."

Her enthusiasm was contagious. She launched me on a treasure hunt, opening my eyes to the real Harvard.

JOURNAL ENTRY

I am captured by the elegant craftsmanship of the European immigrants who built the college. I find beauty in the lovely worn-ness of marble stairs, of leather chairs, of John Harvard's brass shoe rubbed by countless students and tourists in Harvard Yard. In Phillips Brooks House I gaze through the perfect imperfection of old glass in leaded windows bending the image of red autumn leaves, or wood smoke, or snowfalls. I feel as if an artist were behind the university, as well as the universe, speaking to me.

I began to spend time in the archives of Pusey Library and in the Houghton Library rare book collection. In the lobby of Houghton, visitors could view the only remaining book given to the college in 1636 by John Harvard himself. All the other books were consumed by the fire of 1764, but this one was "borrowed" by a student (before books were meant to be borrowed). The book's title was *The Christian Warfare Against the Devil, World, and Flesh . . . And Means to Obtain Victory.*[9] Though the contents were inaccessible behind glass, I took the title as mysterious inspiration.

I loved walking in and around the university—into Widener Library to see the Gutenberg Bible and up into the lonely stacks to read the writings of those intellectual giants who finally came to Christ—T. S. Eliot, Malcolm Muggeridge, C. S. Lewis and Charles Malik. I spent rainy days in the Fogg Art Museum with its treasure of transcendence come to earth and history long undervalued. I'd sense God in the German lyrics of Bach concerts, in archives and old seals. In the Yard gates and stonework I found encoded references to Jesus Christ as veritas.

I thought of the story of the sculptor who asks his friend while looking at a block of wood, "Do you like this eagle?"

"Eagle?" says his friend. "It's only a block of wood."

To which the sculptor replies, "But soon I'll remove whatever doesn't look like an eagle, and then you'll see it."

For those like Vera and Jim with the eyes of faith, Harvard was essentially, though dormantly, Christian. It was my hope that Veritas Forums might draw attention to the eagle at the core of Harvard—and more importantly, at the essence of all of life.

I spoke with friends, leaders of Christian fellowships such as Campus Crusade for Christ, InterVarsity, Navigators and others. We met monthly to visit and pray together. I proposed the Veritas Forum as an interdisciplinary gathering for the whole university, exploring our questions together in relation to Jesus. I saw it simply as a vision of creative hospitality, a party with a purpose—to welcome all in love, especially the seeker. Veritas would be a safe place to doubt and to question. With rising rates of drug abuse and depression, we wanted people not only to think but also to *feel* the truth of God's love. We wanted students to have a place of belonging and acceptance and dialogue, even before belief.

But everyone was already doing great things, and no one needed more to do. And the value of such a large event was not always clear. For over a year we grew in friendship, trust and vision for a witnessing community in the middle of the university. But we didn't know what to do about Veritas.

In the meantime, wanting to play by the rules, I made an appointment to ask permission of the appropriate Harvard administrative office to use the ancient *Veritas: Christo et Ecclessiae* shield for our grad fellowship and to contextualize the Veritas Forum. The request was denied. I was told that they couldn't even find the plate in the archives. It had disappeared.[10] I was sure there was some misunderstanding.

I went in a second time with a photograph of the shield but met with the same outcome. Feeling dejected I thought, *Who am I to ask this question? Is it appropriate for one of the college chaplains to be rocking the boat?* Jeff, Vera and Jim encouraged me, but I at times felt afraid. Harvard had become silent about Jesus—"the J word." It was a bit dicey to raise to the forefront the name that others avoided and to gently make known to a post-Christian university the reason for its very existence.

After many months I was still unable to generate consensus for a united Veritas Forum. I considered throwing in the towel, but the support of friends like Mark Gauthier, and sermons by my pastor, Todd Lake of Cambridgeport Baptist, kept me going. Hearing of my difficulties, good friend and law student DJ Snell suggested, "Let's just go ahead with the forum and the Law School Christian Fellowship will host it."

"Really?"

"Really."

JOURNAL ENTRY

Perhaps we're not overtly persecuted so much as we assume constraints. Press on.

On my third visit to the same administrator, I asked once again to use the *Veritas: Christo et Ecclessiae* shield and banner on our programs to be given to students as invitations to the forum. I brought in examples of altered uses of the shield. The Ultimate Frisbee club (with whom I occasionally played) had replaced the books in the shield with discs. The bisexual-gay-lesbian group turned the shield pink and replaced *Veritas: Christo et Ecclessiae* with "BGLSA." I placed these on the administrator's desk and simply said, "I have one last question. Why is it that the only students denied the right to use the Harvard shield are the ones who don't want to change or mock it?" I thanked him for listening once more and left his office.

Oddly, the administrator followed me down the plush green hallway and over to the teak-paneled elevator. I was expecting the same outcome, but perhaps in more vivid language. Instead, he said something I've never forgotten. As we watched the elevator numbers descending to our floor, he said quietly, almost in a whisper, "This reminds me of the book of Acts where the Sanhedrin officials released Peter and the apostles who had been speaking in public. They said, 'If it's not of God, nothing will come of it. But if it is of God, we can't stop it anyway.'" He continued, "I'll send a letter allowing you to use the shield."[11]

Shocked as the elevator doors slowly closed between us, I simply said, "Thank you." I walked home in a daze, realizing that in the halls of power, though constrained by pressures, there are people of integrity—quiet Daniels who still care for justice and truth. I would thank him here, but those pressures still remain.

Encouraged, I spoke again with the leaders of the various Christian fellowships. By then they were on board as well. In the spring of 1992 we gathered in Memorial Church for a worship and prayer fest for the campus. Andy Crouch led us in singing the chorus: "I will build my church, and the gates of hell shall not prevail against it."

Jeff and I scanned the ancient shield into a computer and spent hours digitally cleaning up the scratches. The *Veritas: Christo et Ecclessiae* shield soon began to appear on GSCF T-shirts, Veritas Forum invitations and programs, and even a law professor's letterhead (Mary Ann Glendon, a female Daniel, who also reminded me of the Old Testament Deborah). We invited the whole university by stuffing mail-boxes with invitations to a Veritas Forum at the law school.

We began to pass the hat for funding, and friends chipped in what they could. The biggest help came from a friend I'd met at the business school, a fellow Ohioan named Jerry Mercer who offered financial support and ideas such as inviting an unknown-to-us Indian apologist, Ravi Zacharias, as the keynote speaker. Other individuals and foundations later supported Veritas as well. (It is amazing what can happen when you place a few dollars in the hands of enthusiastic and resourceful students.) The other twenty presenters would be student and alumni contributors to the ongoing *Finding God at Harvard* project. They would respond to questions as a multicultural and interdisciplinary Christian community.

I hoped that at least a hundred people would show up.

After praying together in a room off Ames Courtroom at the law school with Ravi Zacharias, we were shocked when we walked into the auditorium. My law school friend DJ Snell whispered in amazement, "Kelly, this is incredible."

5

The Veritas Forum Begins at Harvard

Unless we establish the possibility and the necessity of truth and of how one arrives at the truth, any belief system can be mocked at will or off-handedly dismissed as cultural. For the Christian this is where the battle must be fought, for no worldview suffers more from the loss of truth than the Christian one.

RAVI ZACHARIAS, *DELIVER US FROM EVIL*

If truth is dead and knowledge is only power, all that remains is a world of lies, hype and spin. . . . But truth matters supremely because in the end, without truth there is no freedom. Truth, in fact, is freedom, and the only way to live free is to become a person of truth. Living in truth is the secret of living free.

OS GUINNESS,
THE VERITAS FORUM AT STANFORD

The elegant academic law school courtroom was stirring with excitement and was so crowded that even the massive windows were filled with students.

DJ and I welcomed everyone from the podium. Student ushers had handed everyone a program that read,

> For nearly two centuries the University shield combined "Veritas" with the name of Jesus. The University motto, Veritas (Truth), was followed by an explanatory reference to John 8:32, "And Jesus

said, 'If you hold to my teaching . . . then you will know the truth and the truth will set you free.'"

The shield suggested to students that truth and freedom were found in Jesus Christ. In the display of three books on the shield, two open and facing up refer to the knowledge revealed by God, and the third open but turned down acknowledges the limits of human reason. (The third book is the Book of Life, which God will one day reveal, and in which we hope our names will appear by grace through faith in Christ.) In the tradition of Augustine, Galileo, Newton, Pascal and Bach (and Abraham Lincoln, John Muir and countless others) humility yielded wisdom and purposeful action. Hard critical thinking was only deepened by a humility that recognized that truth was sought—heart, mind and soul—by a whole person in restored relationship with God.

But much had changed. Harvard's popular Veritas shield no longer makes reference to Christ or the church. The book once facing down has been turned up, as if to assure us that it is only a matter of time before we know it all. The Veritas program posed the questions: "We see in our world a discouraging correlation between reason apart from God and human unhappiness. The frequency of suicide, crime and broken relationships indicates that ours is a crisis of meaning. Is there any real hope? If so, what is it? Can we believe it with our minds as well as our hearts? How?"

The Veritas Forum was created to be a place for hard and real questions, along with honest answers—so we might know the truth and the truth would make us free.

That first night at the law school, hundreds of students packed the auditorium to hear Ravi Zacharias speak on the question "Is Atheism Dead?" More came the next night to hear "Is God Alive?" Ravi explored the insufficiency of the world's systems and promises. Given the alienation and human evil so palpable in the twentieth century, in which "God is dead," now known as the bloodiest century in human history, many students seemed to agree with Dr. Zacharias that man cannot live without God. Ravi made the case that the human heart yearns for God and that a world without God is too small for our dreams. He said that God wants us to dream and has made us for a purpose.

Ravi asked, "What is your passion?" He explained that

light was the passion of the Hebrews. Knowledge was the passion of the Greeks. Glory, the passion of the Romans.

To the Corinthians, Paul wrote, "For God who said, 'Let light shine out of darkness,' made his light shine in our hearts—to give us the *light* of the *knowledge* of the *glory* of God, in the *face* of Christ Jesus."

Light. Knowledge. Glory.

St. Paul tells us here that everything we most deeply desire is found in the face of Jesus Christ. That the gospel alone is perpetual novelty, and the hope of our hearts.

Ravi was joined by a panel of four articulate students from four disciplines and cultures.[1] Questions emerged from the audience such as, "How do we know anything to be true?" "What are our origins, and what does it mean to be human?" "Do faith and science align? What about DNA? the big bang? chaos? quantum theory?" "If God is loving, why is there suffering?" "Where is there hope for racism and sexism?" "It's my body; why can't I do whatever I want with it?"

We also heard slogans and secular claims such as "There is no truth," to which a speaker might respond, "Truly?" Others were, "All religions are the same," and "The idea of one way to God is ridiculous." The speakers attempted to decalcify minds and hearts and open them up to oxygen, and to test their ideas against reality. New questions began to arise. For instance, "Why is there crime?" moved in sequence to "How can I have virtue?" The question "Why is there injustice?" became "How can I forgive and be forgiven?" "Why is there despair?" became "What is my hope, and why?" The slogan "Whatever!" became "What matters and why?" The question "Does beauty mean anything?" became "How can I enter into beauty?"

As the forum unfolded, Jennifer Wiseman, a graduate student in astronomy and star formation, spoke on the growing friendship between science and faith. She was joined by Ian Hutchinson, a professor of plasma physics at MIT and soon to become the head of MIT's department of nuclear science. Joined by a biochemist and medical doctor, we began to see new levels of detail, elegance and beauty in creation within the now-visible extremes of the "very large" and "very small."

Any question was fair game.

All together the panelists helped us sense life as a much greater wonder than we previously imagined. More than a thousand students participated in our four-day weekend of seminars, performances and coffee house conversations.[2] Yale students came for football and parties and ended up discussing their deepest questions.

Christianity Today reporter Tim Morgan happened to be in Cambridge and covered the opening events. The keynote talks and stu-

JOURNAL ENTRY

A Veritas Forum, in both the planning and participation, is an intriguing communal apologetic. Students might wonder, "There's an Australian physicist, a Sri Lankan economics student, a Malaysian medical doctor, an artist, a janitor, an African theologian, an elderly art historian, there's a grandmother, an astronomer—why do all these people agree about reality? Maybe not about all things, but about 'first things' like God's genius and his love showing up in the person of Jesus. And why do they seem to love each other and us? Why do they seem joyful even though they've suffered? Why do they sing together? Why do they laugh at themselves but take us seriously?"

dents' questions and insights were like a prophetic sparkplug, and thousands of copies of the first few events went around the world by audiotape. Word about Veritas began to spread beyond Cambridge.

Speakers' vision of reality fit together in a comprehensive whole. We saw a point of unity in the diversity of cultures, disciplines and generations. Some found a new starting point for living life.

We were learning that the truth claims of Jesus were not marginal but central to human history—starting in the Middle East and spreading into Asia, Africa and Europe by the end of the first century A.D. We were seeing that every real scholar wrestled with the challenge of Jesus Christ; it is intellectually more honest to question him, and be questioned by him, than to ignore him.

An intentional conversation about Veritas, after nearly a century of amnesia, was reborn in the heart of what had become known as the godless academy—an incubator of "knowledge" and cultural leadership in the world.

A Treasure Hunt in the Yard

To end the first Veritas Forum, my good friends Kay Hall and Todd Lake led a tour through the Yard for more than fifty people. Students discovered early Christian symbols in the Yard and noticed inscriptions on buildings such as, "What is Man that Thou art mindful of him" inscribed over the front door of Emerson Hall, the philosophy building. "Is that a Bible on John Harvard's knee?" students asked, referring to the landmark in the center of the Yard. "I never noticed."

We walked from the Yard into the Fogg Art Museum where our tour was led by a lovely elderly German guide. The week before she had told me, "No one has ever asked for a tour like this. Even if only one person comes, I will do this for God." (I'd found yet another Daniel.) During the tour she stopped our group in front of a beautiful Italian Madonna and child. "You want to find veritas?" she asked, pointing to the sleeping child as a foreshadowing of his death—"This is veritas."

Like light released centuries ago from a distant star, we were beginning to see Harvard's first light. It's true north. It was as bright and joyful as the ache had been dark. We felt its warmth because it answered a longing for intimacy, for meaning, for glory. This was not abstract and unembodied truth. It was alive. "It" was a "him," a great love who wanted to live within us, and us in him. It was a kingdom to build and to gain. Ordinary people like us were changed. We had found a story worth living in.

Follow-Up

New friends were welcomed by sponsoring fellowships and churches. They were invited to join summer mission trips and retreats or just hang out in coffee shops. It was fun to see career choices, minds and hearts begin to change. To see eyes brighten.

The morning after the first Veritas Forum, I received a phone call from a guy I'd never met who asked to meet for lunch that day at the Charles Hotel. I arrived a bit wrung out after a squash match with Rob. Not long after we greeted one another, he cut to the chase.

"I was there this weekend at the law school. Are you and all these others serious about this?"

"About what?" I asked.

"Do you really mean to say that, well, that it's all real?"

"Umm, yes. That's what we're discovering for ourselves and we're also inviting others into the conversation. No kidding. For real."

He became quiet. I could tell he was bright enough to imagine the awesome implications, and he may also have been thinking that this possibility was too good to be true—or too difficult to try. I suggested that if the nature of truth was goodness, then this was too good to be false. And that life with God is not too difficult since it's his life in and through us. In fact, I said, "I'm having fun." We began to talk through some of the questions Veritas was exploring in detail: epistemology—how we could know anything to be real and true. We talked about the accuracy and authority of the Bible, new physics, the implications of DNA, moral law as an invisible wall that we kept bumping our faces and bodies into, and our desire for sustainable joy—which my new friend said he'd been searching for his whole life.

He looked like someone who had seen too much. Looking for light, he had found mostly heat. He was young but weary, and deeply kind.

He said something about a meeting with the Senate Foreign Relations Committee and I thought, how odd for someone so young.

"What are you doing for Thanksgiving?" I asked as we were leaving.

"We were going to Colorado, but I think my family is boycotting the state because of an anti-gay rights bill being proposed." He mentioned his very visible and political Boston family, and I believe that the gospel was presenting itself to him as a comfort in the midst of a fast-paced life full of sound and fury. He was a truth-seeker.

Later he and I joined a monthly book and conversation club run by law student John Kingston in a funky grad student café called Gato Rojo. In comfortable chairs around a coffee table, above the din of Latin jazz, our new friend was taking a turn reading aloud from Augustine's *Confessions.*

"Our hearts are restless until we find our rest in Thee."

And then, in mid-paragraph, he stopped and whispered, "This was sixteen hundred years ago. But this is my life."

Someone else said, "I think it's the journey we're all on. Welcome."

6

Road Trip
Living in Skin

The flat soul is what the sexual wisdom of our time conspires to make universal. . . .

Are we lovers anymore?

ALLAN BLOOM,
THE CLOSING OF THE AMERICAN MIND

Perhaps it is no wonder that the women were the first at the cradle and last at the cross. They had never known a man like this man. There never has been such another.

DOROTHY SAYERS, ESSAY, "ARE WOMEN HUMAN?"

The worldview that supports the highest aspirations of the human heart is Christianity. It gives a basis for believing that love is real and genuine because we were created by a God whose very character is love. . . . Love is not an illusion created by the genes to promote our evolutionary survival, but an aspect of human nature that reflects the fundamental fabric of ultimate reality.

NANCY PEARCEY,
THE VERITAS FORUM AT OHIO STATE UNIVERSITY

The same year that we started Veritas at Harvard in 1992, a serendipitous event occurred that encouraged my thinking about the value of Christians (other than myself) speaking in secular universities. I was discovering that angst and confusion were not unique to Cambridge but common in other university towns as well. I sensed an extreme conformity to the spirits of the age—cynicism, loneliness and demoralization.

I was home in Cambridge, cozily avoiding the morning's nor'easter snowstorm, when the phone rang.

"Kelly, hi, it's Mardi Keyes."

Mardi and her husband, Dick, ran the Boston L'Abri study center thirty miles from Cambridge.

"Kelly, I'm really sick and I hate to ask, but could you fill in for me tonight by speaking at SUNY Albany on 'The Bible and Feminism'?" She really did sound awful.

I was tempted to say, "You have the wrong number," or in broken Spanish, "*Lo siento, Kelly no esta aqui en la casa no mas, y no comprendo ingles. Adios.*"

I felt truly unqualified to speak on the subject, so I asked, "Did you talk to Becky or Poh or Kay?" She explained that they were all working. She seemed desperate, and Mardi was one of my heroes. I was honored that she even thought of me, and I didn't want to let her down.

"Sure, Mardi. And I hope you feel better soon."

Having received the necessary info, I was soon packing for Albany.

Becky and I had just presented at L'Abri a "slide show" on the gospel and women in impoverished cultures. Set to indigenous music, Scripture and photos, we spoke of women we'd met on our mission journeys. I figured that's what Mardi had in mind. Anyway, I hoped it was something that everyone could appreciate.

Not wanting to face this unknown crowd alone, I called the one friend I had near Albany. Josh agreed to come as a comrade offering support. I felt better knowing there would be one smiling face I'd recognize.

What was normally a four-hour drive took nearly seven hours through the heavy snowstorm on 90-West. I was driving my trusty red Isuzu Trooper nicknamed "the Lunch Box" for its nonaerodynamic squareness. (All it needed was a large handle on top, a big thermos and some Buzz Lightyear decals on the sides.) Trying to stay on the road, I imagined the multitudes of sleepy suburbs across the snowbelt of

America in which cozy couples with small children were tucked in by the fire reading *Winnie the Pooh*. Self-analysis drifted into self-pity. *I'm thirty years old. Why am I not in one of those homes drinking hot chocolate and snuggling?*

Eventually another thought woke me from my snow-induced semi-hypnotic state: how inspired I was by students whose passion got them out in the cold, such as those who held weeklong prayer vigils by candle-light to end Communism in Eastern Europe; seminary students and pas-tors who attempted against all odds to thwart the plans of the Third Reich; nineteenth-century graduates who became missionaries and built hospitals in China; students and friends, even tonight, who were trying to end slavery and sex-trafficking of children in Southeast Asia.

Feeling like a whiner in comparison, I imagined how God must love people who risk so much for a kingdom beyond themselves. I also was certain God loved those students at SUNY Albany who'd be coming out in the cold tonight to hear an unknown replacement speaker from Cambridge.

Despite an early start and all-wheel drive, the weather slowed the Lunch Box's progress so that I was my customary ten minutes late. Time didn't allow me to change clothes in the parking lot—I arrived in Timberline boots, blue jeans and a Celtic sweater looking like a preppy lumberjack. I was glad I'd left my pearls at home.

Fumbling for directions, I saw the building in the distance. In eerie incandescent light, it loomed as a forbidding monolith—a gloomy and unfortunate Marxist construct.

I entered and immediately saw familiar posters in the hallways—the same poster I'd been faxed this morning: "God's Word Speaks to Fem-inism, Room LC21, 7:30 p.m. Sponsored by the Southern Baptist As-sociation for Bible Awareness Week."

"Good, I'm in the right place," I said to myself.

Then I noticed, attached to the posters, larger pink notices that screamed, "Counter-Protest. Don't let them contribute to the already sexist atmosphere on campus!!! Tonight. 7:30 p.m. LC21." The protest was sponsored by the International Socialists Organization, the SUNY Bi-Gay-Lesbian-Transgendered Rainbow Coalition, and the Albany chapter of the National Organization for Women."

Huh, I thought. *There must be a mistake. I think that's the room in which I am speaking.* Entering the large auditorium I saw that every seat was occupied and the aisles were full.

"What's going on tonight?" I asked a student trying to squeeze in.

"Some Bible-thumper is talking about feminism," he answered.

I often feel that the earth is spinning too fast for me, that I'm not quite there, I should say here, now, in the moment with everyone else. I talked to myself. *Kelly, this is real. You're not in Kansas, or Ohio, or even Cambridge anymore. You've just driven seven hours through the snow to speak at a university in Albany, New York, where you know no one. The whole student body has been invited, and they already don't like you. You're to speak about the Bible and feminism. You know—women. You are one, after all. You can do this.*

I saw a small group huddled in one corner and thought, *One of these groups is not like the others.* They were the only folks without chains, tattoos, hair-color-not-found-in-nature and visibly pierced body parts. So I went over and said hi to the Southern Baptist organizers. They looked wholesome but a bit nervous.

"Welcome," they said. "We'll be praying for you."

"Thank you," I responded.

One woman in her late twenties was in the middle of the room and seemed to be a ringleader. She was chanting loudly—Lord knows what. Her tattoos indicated a hybrid of Gothic and Wiccan spirituality complemented by black lipstick, jet-black hair and various metallic additions to her face. Morticia Addams would have been proud.

The Marxist club looked more civilized in chic New York black. Maybe they were still mourning over the recent collapse of Communism; I don't know.

I looked for my friend Josh. He'd not shown up yet. The room was loud. People were angry, all shouting at once. I wondered if I had enough aspirin in my backpack for all of us.

My first hope was that no one would get hurt, especially not the speaker. Since gang violence looked possible, I first sat off to the side, in an aisle along with the crowd, facing forward and looking down to the empty podium. They probably thought I was with the L.L. Bean Workers Against the Oppressor Club. I was simply trying to envision what would become of the speaker.

"Situational Awareness 101," I thought. *Right. What's in the room? More than three hundred angry students, ten Southern Baptists off to the side in mild shock, and me. A chalkboard and chalk. And no security trained in crowd control.*

Mardi had said that some students from Smith and Amherst colleges were planning to come, and I found irony in the thought that their grandmothers probably still imagined them in cashmere and pearls wanting to marry Ivy League men, or wanting to marry men of any kind, and raise families—but back to the story.

At first the ranting sounded almost intelligible, something like this: *Who the whatever the sexist we want pigs not teach women men no authority out of our rights women churches not submit man Eve abort right was framed to my f—— body!*

"Lord," I asked, sitting with the chanters. "I'm just curious; what are YOU planning on doing tonight? I can barely wait to hear what the speaker has to say."

He shared the thought, "We're going to scrap the slide show about women around the world with the pretty music."

"Right," I replied. "And then what?"

"Go to the chalkboard and start writing down what they're saying. Listen to them. Show them how to listen, how to take turns speaking, that I care about what they're saying and feeling."

"Right. Then what?"

"I'll tell you when you need to know."

So I went to the chalkboard and started to write.

The room got louder still. One of the Baptist leaders attempted an introduction.

"Hello, everyone. Thanks for coming out on this snowy night. We've had a slight change in our Bible Awareness Week series. This is not Mardi Keyes but Kelly Monroe, a chaplain to graduate students at Harvard . . . "

It became obvious that their strategy was to simply shut down the speaker who, I kept reminding myself, just happened to be me—the sexist bigot du jour. They wanted to stop the event altogether so that no one could hear anything the Oppressor would say. I briefly wondered, *How does anyone learn anything around here?* The shouting continued: *My body beration of we want who the whatever the f—— sexist women not our God rights teach women no authority church women gay rights God submit out of our crotches Eve to God was framed abortion right to my body!*

I began to write down the sequences of words I heard, such as, "Whatever we want," "Women not teach men," "Authority," "Abortion," "Right to my body."

"Sorry, but could you speak your concerns so that I could hear them one at a time?" I said at the board. "I'm sure I'm goofing this up and not really understanding what you're saying."

They looked confused. Some started to leave, but then decided to stay. Gradually people began to speak sequentially, some even raised their hands and waited to be called on. The volume decreased to the point where actual words were audible.

"Who the hell are you to tell us how to live?"

So I began to write, "Who the hell tells us how to live?" "Thanks very much. Next?"

"We can do whatever the f—— we want."

I wrote, "We can do whatever we want." "Next?"

"The Bible says women should not teach men or have authority over them and women should submit to their husbands."

"Thanks. Next?" I said.

"If you don't like abortion, don't have one."

"Right. This is really cool and interesting," I said. "Let's do one more thing. Could you introduce yourself before you express your concern? That way we'll get to know one another a little better. Next, in the back there, in black."

"I'm Jeff, the president of the socialist club," he said with a serious demeanor atypical of a twenty-year-old. "I think God is a construct of the capitalist oppressor."

I began writing, "God a construct of . . . " "Okay, thanks Jeff. Next, in the middle?"

"Question authority," someone said.

"Amen," I said while writing. "Next?"

The Gothic-Wiccan woman didn't seem to like the way things were going. "I'm Adrian, a teaching assistant in women's studies here. I think it wasn't Eve's fault. She was listening to the wisdom of the serpent, but then she was oppressed by men and blamed for the problems in the world."

Writing "Eve was framed" on the board, I said, "Wow, that's a lot to think about. Thanks, Adrian."

And then she started in on me. "Did some men pay you to come here? You're being used. You are a subjugated tool of the white male hegemonic power structure, a repressed homophobic Westerner, disconnected from goddess wisdom and the rhythms of nature."

She sounded like a women's studies textbook. I said, "I'm sorry, but I think you're a lot smarter than I am. Could you repeat that in terms I can understand?"

Several students broke into laughter. "Some of us are in her class and we've been asking her that all semester," one said.

She tried again, but when asked for her own thoughts what came across was a lot of hurt. And loneliness. She hid behind clichés and academic jargon, muttering about choice. How could I reach her, tell her she'd first been chosen by God, that she was loved, that her Creator found her beautiful and she no longer needed to externalize inner darkness in order to achieve a sense of integrity and authenticity? I wanted her to connect with the Creator behind the impersonal forces of nature she worshiped, to realize that God not only creates but re-creates us into our truest selves.

Another woman spoke up. "I'm Suzanne with NOW. Every child a wanted child."

I began to write, "Every child . . . " "Or else what, Suzanne?" I said.

She looked shocked. "What?" she replied.

I responded, "It's an incomplete sentence. A wanted child or else what?"

"I don't know," she said.

Someone yelled, "The Bible says women must not speak in church!" Another yelled, "Wives submit to your husbands!"

As I wrote those down I made a mental note to suggest that they read those passages in their larger cultural contexts, given that Paul was saying that women were now allowed to learn in church for the first time and that men were commanded to give their lives for their wives "as Christ loved the church." The husband had the harder job. I later would share that I felt more respected, more befriended by Christian men than by others. Jesus is the great liberator of women, of men, of all of us if we'll let him.

"Get your churches out of our crotches. I'm Heidi."

"Thanks, Heidi, I've seen that on a bumper sticker," and while writing on the board I thought to myself, *Huh, I don't know of any churches in bed with anyone. I do know that many Christians volunteer with AIDS patients and in foster care for mothers and children.*

"What do you mean by this, Heidi?" I asked her.

"Abortion has already been settled by the Supreme Court," she said, "and that ended the matter. We don't need to continue to talk about it."

"I'm not arguing abortion with you, but I'm curious: do you really want to live in a country in which citizens aren't allowed to talk about the loss of millions of small but living beings?"

"It's already been decided by law," she said.

I wondered how her proposed scenario was any different from Stalin's Russia or Hitler's Germany. I asked God to comfort those in the room who'd had abortions and to bless them tonight.

And so on it went until the room was quiet. I must have written down slogans and complaints for over an hour. The anger subsided. I think I wore them out.

With their comments as the backdrop, an actual conversation began. I sensed the Lord asking me to share some of my own story.

"Well, thanks for participating," I began. "I'm Kelly. I live in Cambridge now but grew up in Wisconsin, Chicago and Ohio. I was a tomboy with lots of uncles and older brothers, whom I love. I broke some bones playing sports, trying to fit in, trying to keep up. My dad became a psychology professor at the University of Chicago and then Ohio State at a time when traditional ideas and norms were being tossed aside for newer ideas. The culture invited exploration of autonomy, the sexual revolution and learning to become one's own best friend when other friendships ended."

I told the now-quiet audience how in the sixties new liberations in psychology promised abundant life and freedom. Like other marriages in my father's psychology department, my parents' marriage ended in divorce—it dissolved in the cultural tidal wave of the sixties and seventies. Within a few years my brothers moved to colleges far away. I wanted all of us to move to a farm somewhere back in time. Our home went from five to two people—my mother and me. My parents, whom I really love, became disillusioned. What was taught in the classroom didn't work in real life. The culture, shaped by the university, had lied to him. To us. We bought it. We were no longer drinking from an endless wellspring.

"Some of you may feel hurt, angry, homesick for a place to just be and to belong," I said. "To be accepted without having to perform. To be taken care of and to care about others. To be in the shelter of one another.

"But I see women reduced to sex objects, to conquests. We buy into the idols of beauty and status. Sometimes we do it to ourselves and sometimes to one another by the way we dress and talk and think. Sometimes we feel victimized by a sexualized culture. I've even known college profs who thought of themselves as women's libbers while they were into pornography. But I also see men dehumanized and reduced to success objects, used for their performance, status, security and income.

"Life is difficult. We need to know what's true in order to make good choices. To find real life. I know that we long for intimacy, real connection with people. And with the God who has placed that desire in our hearts."

It got even quieter.

What now, Lord? I thought. *I'm all ears.*

"Tell them about my heart by telling them about my Son. They don't know."

I'll try.

I continued, "So, there I was, a lonely teenager hiding in a church balcony. I'd been invited by friends to watch a musical play about Jesus.

I said 'no thanks,' but I went anyway. Well, I was blown away by what I saw and heard—not dead religion but a person. I had no idea what he was really like. That he was at the heart of Christianity. Strange as it seems, it was as if I fell in love with this guy Jesus. I fell in love with his personality, his tenderness, his brilliance and humor and sacrificial courage. And for the way he treated, and loved, women.

"In some ways I agree with what you have been saying tonight. A lot of religions do oppress people. They teach that we need to work our way to God, to salvation, to perfection, to nirvana. Some of you might believe there are many paths up the mountain. But each path is still an impossible climb. One person was different. Only Jesus came down the mountain to love us where we are, at the bottom, and then to lift us up and carry us with him. Together, we enjoy the beauty of the journey as well as the destination.

"He hated the false religion of hypocrites, power brokers and oppressors—those who condemned and suppressed others in order to maintain their own advantage and position. Jesus harshed on them, calling them a brood of vipers and whitewashed tombs."

A hand went up. "What do you mean he loved women?" the young woman said. "I thought the Bible was sexist."

"The Bible *describes,* not *prescribes,* sexism, racism and horrible injustice. But when you read the first two chapters of Genesis, you'll see that God did not make a broken world; it's what happened when we turned our backs on God. It's sometimes called 'the Fall.' Sure enough, things fell apart.

"Adrian, you said the serpent spoke wisdom to Eve, but I believe the serpent lied. Any claim that we can be our own god, I believe, is a lie. And I think we all know in our hearts that we are not God.

"Yet to help us in the midst of our pride and rebellion and shame, God promised a savior, not a myth but a real person in a real place, a better Adam, a seed who would come from the lineage of Eve, born of God's Spirit—the 'son of God.' The savior came as a real person, his name was Jesus, the one who reconnected us with God's love. He was the better Adam who didn't blame his bride but died for her—we are the 'her' for whom he died. We are the ones he loves.

"How does Jesus show us God's heart for women? Take the stories home and read them yourselves: the outcast Samaritan woman at the well who finally felt loved. The woman caught in adultery who experienced life-changing forgiveness. The 'unclean' woman whom Jesus touched and healed of constant bleeding. Mary, and many women, who were invited to learn along with the men. The women who were first to witness the resurrection.

"In each life, Jesus ignored the power constructs and cultural norms. He humbled the exalted and exalted the humble. He honored women. He honors all who love him."

I was surprised that the students were silent. Many were actually listening.

An older male, maybe a grad student, asked, "What do you, what does the Bible, say about gender and same-gender sex?"

"God says that our primary identity isn't gender. We are first of all human beings, made in God's image—an image beyond gender. John chapter 1 says that those who believe in Jesus have the right to be called the children of God, innocent, free, creative, full of life again—isn't that cool?"

He wasn't impressed. I continued with a personal story.

"In college, my roommate got pregnant. Her boyfriend took off. The night before her scheduled abortion over Christmas break she called me. It turned out that she really wanted the baby but her father and ex-boyfriend didn't. She decided to have the baby, Jonah. Friends and I helped her raise him early on. A few years later she told me that her mom had a drinking problem and she had been looking for a long time for someone to take her mother's place. 'I want a mother,' she said. After college she became a lesbian, moved several times, looking for a mother, and when her dad died, perhaps she longed for her heavenly father too. In the meantime, her son Jonah is the joy of her life. She named him 'Jonah' because God saved him from death and for life."

"What about homosexuals?" he repeated angrily. I sensed I was being baited, and that he was looking for a sound byte.

I asked him a question. "Have you ever lost a very close friend to AIDS?"

"No," he replied.

"I have. My friend Scott's father died in an accident when he was young. Scott and I were friends in high school and went off to college together. (He was named the American playwright of the year in 1994.) Maybe Scott didn't have time to bond with his father. Maybe he didn't feel masculine, or accepted. I don't know. But in college he began to consume maleness, and though he had once been a comic genius, his eyes went dark. In the end he was consumed himself, though I believe he felt the love of Jesus. I was too 'tolerant' to ask questions or say much to him even though I could see it happening.

"Was that love?" I asked this student. He didn't answer. "I miss him like crazy," I said.

"Please don't raise your hands," I continued, "but has anyone here been sexually intimate with someone, giving yourself totally, and then been forgotten? Has anyone suffered pain and regret because you were used for sex and then discarded?" Silence and downward glances followed.

"The body is a gift. It's good to live in skin, but 'free sex' is expensive. It can cost your life, and the lives of children you may never have. Sex is like fire. Fire is wonderful in the right context, like a fireplace that gives off warmth and light for a long time. But fire can be a bummer in the wrong context, like in the middle of the living room. It gets really hot for a few hours and then burns your house down. You're left in ashes.

"God wants to save our hearts and to encourage them with hope, not deflate them with despair. So it helps me to listen to what God says about sex—after all, he invented it. He could have made us reproduce by binary fission or something less enjoyable." I spied at least a few smiles.

"Maybe," I mused, "the 'body' we most desire is the body of Christ, which is the community around the world in which he lives. Those are places of intimacy, worship, acceptance and belonging. You are wanted and needed in that body, and there's no shortage of opportunity to love and be loved in that revolution.

"But some of you still want a sound byte to fuel your sense that

Christianity is oppressive. I wish you could see that lies are oppressive and that Jesus is freedom.

"I'm not pushing morality on anyone. The point is that God, like a loving father, doesn't want his children used or exploited. His Word says that we're not meant to love and then leave, or to be left, repeatedly. Regarding gender, if you think about our anatomies, there's a rather obvious, um, design there. Like pieces of a puzzle fitting together. Naturally, we'd see disease and confusion when design is repeatedly abused, and we'd see wellness where design is respected. God wants us to live well in the body. He wants to heal our minds, hearts and bodies, and for us to become merciful healers. That's why so many Christians in Cambridge are into medicine and hospitality and prayer.

"Let's listen to our hearts beneath all the noise of college life. How many here do *not* want children?"

Only a few hands went up.

"How many here envision themselves with children reading *Winnie the Pooh*—okay, or Freud or Derrida—by the fire?"

They laughed sheepishly. Several snuck a hand out for me to see.

"I think that many of us want a legacy of love and family. It's nothing to be embarrassed about."

My inquisitor suddenly rose to his feet, tripping over others as he headed for the door. Once in the aisle he shouted, "I'm the editor of the school paper, and tomorrow morning the whole campus will know that Christians hate homosexuals."

"Go ahead," I replied, "but you'll have one problem."

He stopped and looked at me. I continued, "Everyone in this room will know that you're a liar."

He left. The next morning, no story appeared in the paper.

I sensed that most of us were really listening to one another now.

"Someone was supposed to talk tonight about the Bible and feminism. Well, I guess all I have to say is that it wasn't until I saw communities of friends living the gospel that I experienced men and women, together, in a different way. Mistakes happen, but for the most part people are accepted for who they are, not how they perform or their popularity or looks. People aren't considered conquests, objects to control or products to consume. They are souls with bodies. Virginity is possible because we care about one another's dignity and we want to cultivate our capacity for faithfulness in marriage. I'm discovering that romance is more a way of seeing and living than it is about sex. I want to squeeze every ounce out of life. I want my life to count for something. I want to love and be loved.

"My Christian friends and I spend time helping the poor, sleeping under the stars, singing, having mud fights and going on five-hundred-mile bike trips. We're too busy to pay much attention to how the world and the media tell us to think. We're at least somewhat unbranded—where people are free to become themselves.

"Feminism started as a Christian movement to value women and men as equal image-bearers of the Creator, not as an effort to degender women or emulate a male model for success. Rather, the early Christian view honored the uniqueness of women and acknowledged their stories, including the curse to Eve: that we'd be tempted to take our identity from a husband rather than the Lord, that we'd know pain in child-bearing and child-raising, that thorns would pierce our hearts. Christian feminism looked to Christ as the redeemer of that curse. Early feminists worked for opportunities for women to vote, to express our personalities and to use our gifts in the culture and at home—equal to serve with men.

"Feminism once celebrated the nature of women to give life. Eve's name means 'mother of all living.' Women and men worked for proper conditions in which to raise children, and most early feminists could not have imagined what the movement would become. They would not understand the modern emphasis on rights over responsibilities, individualism over community, competition over cooperation. They would not have defined freedom as doing whatever 'the hell we want with our bodies,' but as the power to do what is good, true and beautiful.

"In Eastern Europe under Communism, women who heard of 'the women's liberation movement' assumed it was the right of women to stay home from the factories and be with their children. As you travel or read world literature, you'll find that many women in undeveloped countries find abortion primitive and barbaric. The right to abortion didn't come out of feminism but out of the sexual revolution, which set women up to be used, vacuumed out and used again.[1] True feminists would not depend on men who profit from an industry that destroys life.

"As for the Bible and feminism, my assigned talk tonight, I've read many origin texts that attempt to tell the story in which we live: Native American, Hindu, atheist, humanist, Buddhist, Islamic, pagan and Wiccan. I'm suggesting that only one story has the ring of truth—a personal, loving God created men and women equal. They are equal in his image to love him but have secondary differences in order to love and serve one another. They also have a unique purpose: through an act of love, they continue to create and nurture life in his image.

"Jesus' offer of forgiveness and new life is the answer to sexism, racism, consumerism, injustice and cynicism. Where there is forgiveness and love, the cycle of evil is broken. Bitterness dissolves and gratitude emerges. With Jesus as our best friend, the world begins to look new and full of possibilities. Full of hope.

"God is for us. He breaks down the walls that divide us. Kind of like tonight. We're here on a cold snowy night, discussing what's important to us. I had a long drive, but I'm glad I came. Although that wasn't my first thought when I walked in the room."

We all laughed.

I thanked everyone for coming and we applauded one another, grateful for what everyone sensed was a gift of mutual understanding. Afterward some students came up to hang out and to talk some more.

Amazingly, the Wiccan teaching assistant came up to apologize. "I didn't really mean everything I said," she told me. "It's just that there's a lot of pressure in my field, and I'm trying to get into grad school, and I had a different image of Christians."

"No problem; I'm glad you came," I said. "You added a lot to the conversation."

Since the Baptists had given out Bibles on the way in, she asked, "Where do I find those stories?" I marked some passages in John and

Luke. I don't know what she did after that, but I was proud of her that night.

The socialist club president, Jeff, was waiting in the background. "My club is having a hard few years," he said. "I am, was, trying to build our numbers. I came with a thesis, looking for an antithesis—Christianity—but didn't find one. I'm sorry I was somewhat harsh at one point. I didn't really know about Jesus."

I said, "Jeff, the Communist revolution is likely over. It lasted less than a hundred years. Would you be willing to consider following a greater revolutionary? One whose movement has gone from a few friends to more than two billion? One who died to forgive and to love the least, the last, the lost? People like us?"

He looked at me over the top of his sophisticated Euro glasses, and I saw the eyes of a boy who wanted little more in life than justice, kindness and a cause to live for. He nodded and quietly said, "Yes."

"I know how he loves you already," I said, and then introduced him to a student who helped organize the event so Jeff could connect to believers who would welcome him with open arms. He had been found by Jesus. We hugged goodbye.

What began at 7:30 p.m. ended with students lingering to talk until 11:30 and then dashing to catch the last shuttle bus back to the dorms. A few stayed a bit longer, and when security showed up to close the building, we brushed the snow off the Lunch Box, piled in, and I drove them back to their dorms.

"Where's Josh?" I wondered again, as we were leaving. It turned out that my friend did make it, but only to the parking lot where he lost his car keys in the snow and spent most of the evening trying to find them. I saw him the next day.

"How did it go?" he asked.

"Fine," I said. "The students were awesome."

I stayed with the planners and thanked them for their faith, and for the seed of faith the event placed in my heart and mind. I was again reminded that we aren't persecuted so much as we assume constraints, that the gospel belongs in the middle, not the margins, of the most secular incubators of cultural leadership—the universities. I learned that we don't need to be brilliant, wear black or have a Ph.D., but that the gospel and the grace of God are sufficient for every question, argument and situation.

As I'd seen with the Veritas Forum at Harvard, I began to imagine the value of introducing Christian scholars to students around the country. They would know to listen first, to share their research and personal discoveries, and to speak clearly of Jesus, the anvil who wears down every hammer—or better yet, the watchful shepherd who waits for every child to finally come home. Or better still, the relentless lover who searches for us in the cold darkness and finds us wherever we are.

7

Veritas Beyond Harvard

First Flight

One word of truth outweighs the entire world.

ALEKSANDR SOLZHENITSYN,
NOBEL PRIZE SPEECH, "ONE WORD OF TRUTH"

You mean this is a place I can really bring my criticisms and ask whatever questions I have?

UCLA STUDENT COMMENT CARD

[Veritas] helped me to see the world beyond the narrow scope of my mind, and to venture out into a world of truth far more elegant than I could have imagined.

GORDON SIGLER, BROWN UNIVERSITY STUDENT

Rob asked why I was leaving town at midnight and I said that it was to talk to professors at Ohio State about Veritas. I had been invited by my new friend Jerry Mercer, who owned AirNet, a network of zippy cargo jets. I'd met Jerry the night he shared his remarkable spiritual journey at a Harvard Business School Christian fellowship gathering. He had offered to help with Veritas. It was rather mysterious, preparing to board a strange aircraft at midnight for my hometown. Someone handed me earplugs and pointed to a small plane on the runway. I hopped in, tried to avoid boxes marked "biohazard," strapped myself into the jump seat behind the pilot, and we were off like a rocket.

I had been surprised that another school would care about Veritas, but upon my arrival it soon made sense. Jerry and a gifted faculty ministry leader, Howard VanCleave, gathered together a group of Ohio State professors and Christian leaders who desired to help students think beyond grades, football and parties and to explore their deepest questions of truth, purpose and hope. My father had been at Ohio State for several decades so I was familiar with the culture. But I felt unqualified to speak to twenty academics at the faculty club. They asked if I would share a bit about what we were doing at Harvard. So, on little sleep, I simply stood up and told some of our story.

"Billy Graham asked a recent Harvard president, 'What is the biggest problem of college students today?' The president answered with one word: 'emptiness.' Unwittingly, he had offered an explanation for the rise in depression, sexual confusion, transmitted disease, drug use, binge drinking, pornography and even suicide.

"How did our great universities become places of emptiness? They didn't start off that way. Harvard, Yale, Dartmouth, Princeton, Northwestern and hundreds of other colleges were founded for students to pursue a life of meaning and truth, to discover the fullness of life in Jesus Christ that we might advance his kingdom of love. Harvard's particular vision and motto was 'For Christ's glory' (*In Christi gloriam*) and was later changed to 'Truth, for Christ and the church' (*Veritas: Christo et Ecclesiae*). To Harvard's original founders, truth (veritas) wasn't an abstraction or a nice word for T-shirts and diplomas; it was a person—the Life-Giver.

"The Harvard College bylaws read, 'Let every student be earnestly pressed to consider well that the main end of his life and studies is to know God and Jesus Christ who is eternal life—John 17:3—and therefore to lay Christ in the bottom, as the only foundation of all sound knowledge and learning . . . seeking him for wisdom.'[1]

"Nonetheless, the name of Jesus was eventually deleted from the motto. Today's students are invited to a university dedicated to the pursuit of veritas, but upon arrival they often feel that no real truth is worth pursuing. As one student quipped in his commencement speech in HarvardYard,'They tell us that it is heresy to suggest the superiority of some value, fantasy to believe in moral judgment sounder than your own. The freedom of our day is the freedom to devote ourselves to any values we please on the mere condition that we don't believe them to be true.'[2]

"The mind of the One for whom Harvard was founded has been expelled from nearly all classes and subjects. As a visiting grad student and then a chaplain, I felt the confusion on campus: this year four students killed themselves, one after murdering her roommate.

"I began to wonder, along with friends,'What if the ancient veritas still holds a secret? What if veritas is timelessly true, a wellspring for hope and progress in an otherwise dying culture? Maybe veritas is coherent and testable and holds water at every angle.'We thought,'Let's find out by asking our hardest questions.' After all, if God can find us at Harvard or Cal Berkeley, he can find us anywhere.

"We pressed on in the belief that knowledge is possible not because students are smart enough to find veritas, but because veritas is loving enough to find us. For this reason, humility with a listening heart, not arrogance, yields wisdom and true life.

"In 1992 we began theVeritas Forum at Harvard as a creative exploration of our hardest questions in relation to the person and story of Jesus. The weeklong forum is rooted in the lives of real people and real communities. It's a party with a purpose. It's a way for us to process our deepest concerns together. By restoring an essential conversation to the university,Veritas creates a way for colleges to be what they were meant to be all along.

"That's all we're trying to do."

I then shared specific ideas about content and form, about hospitality and how to build unity and critical mass. Howard passed around a list for people to sign if they wanted to beginVeritas at Ohio State.They unanimously agreed to give it a try, and I caught the next cargo plane back to Boston, sleeping bag and earplugs in place. Before sunrise I was in bed in Cambridge. That's howVeritas started to spread.

National Interest

Students, professors and ministry staff workers are not only bright and courageous, they are also semi-nomadic and networked together by shared experiences and dreams. Their energy is contagious.

Content as a busy chaplain to Harvard graduate students, imagine my surprise when I started receiving phone calls and e-mails. "Hi, I'm from the University of (fill in the blank). What happened in Cambridge? We're interested in starting a Veritas Forum here. What do you think?"

I first thought to myself, *Sounds great, but I'm just filling in for the person who's eventually going to come along and actually know what they're doing.*

But after admitting my sense of inadequacy, I would then say, "Okay, let's dream about this together." From my apartment, I would simply share with anyone who asked what God was doing at Harvard—against the odds. I'd suggest that a local champion on their campus begin by gathering Christian professors, students and ministry leaders to explore and pray about becoming a unified witnessing community. Before long Jerry Mercer and some Ohio friends set up a nonprofit organization to support interested groups anywhere in the country.[3]

Rather than the semi-nomadic life I was developing, I preferred the idea of staying in New England and settling down with the person I loved. Rob and I had recently visited the Boston L'Abri community and had walked down Lover's Lane—literally. Without mentioning marriage, we wandered into the shell of a post-and-beam house under construction, and we dreamed of our own home. We'd been dating for several years but were often so busy with school and hospitality to others that we had a way of forgetting about each other and ourselves as a couple. We didn't understand the centrifugal forces pulling us apart in the age of the almost-marriage.

In 1993 a counselor suggested to us that I was distracted and that Rob might be a perfectionist and may find it hard to marry. Rob, who seemed nearly perfect in some ways, agreed. He mentioned something about God also wanting our perfection. I said, "Yeah, with his help, perfect at loving." I also asked him, "Gee whiz, why are you dating me? Maybe you've got the wrong girl."

But I kept trying to be all things to all people, balancing life and love and opportunities to advance the kingdom beyond Cambridge. But the more I gave to others without first drawing from the Vine, the more exhausted I became and the less I gave to Rob. The longer he labored with the question of marriage, the more I traveled for Veritas. And the more I traveled, the longer he labored. It was a downward spiral.

Without specific plans to build a life with Rob, I continued to do the good in front of me, which was to help with Veritas at other universities. If grassroots enthusiasm blossomed on a campus, I'd hop into the Lunch Box, either alone or with friends, and drive to Brown or West Point or Penn. Or I'd head to the AirNet tarmac at midnight, where I'd dig for the earplugs and hitch a flight to Madison or Chicago or Dallas.

I was unwittingly becoming a part-time consultant. And we all know the definition of a consultant—anyone from at least fifty miles away carrying a briefcase. In my case, it was a backpack.

I began to meet kindred spirits in Bloomington, Gainesville and Ann Arbor. By word of mouth, a few news stories, and the help of Jerry and Howard in Ohio, Veritas Forums emerged at leading universities, drawing thousands of participants. Some forums were mostly lectures and others were more artistic, depending on the questions and interests of each campus.

A second-year graduate student at the University of Virginia wrote that Veritas "was a great introduction to UVA. I appreciated novelist Larry Woiwode's call that people surround themselves with beauty in all areas of their life. It was the first time I'd seen people look at Christianity from an intellectual perspective and really use their minds to engage their hearts."

National Media

My travel increased in 1995 when Peter Jennings and ABC's *World News Tonight* aired a clip of the Veritas Forum at Indiana University during a feature on academia's intolerance for faith. One Indiana student said in an interview, "College shouldn't require me to abandon everything my parents tried to teach me growing up." Another student added, "When I asked a professor about God's possible role in evolution, he told me that my questions were not helpful."

Against the image of a crowded Indiana Veritas gathering, the ABC reporter said, "Hunger for answers runs deep. When Veritas Forums happen . . . thousands of students pack auditoriums to listen." The feature progressed to Princeton's Robert George, professor of jurisprudence and ethics, saying, "Students who are taught that there is no such thing as moral knowledge graduate with no sense of moral responsibility—and that is a recipe for disaster."

ABC's final image showed two hundred Harvard students praying for their professors and university. Rather than complaining about widespread prejudice against the Christian faith, these students took turns at a microphone and spoke of God's faithfulness, his goodness and how he was changing their lives.

I later learned that ABC almost canned the feature, saying, "Where are the images of angry students protesting?"

The feature's executive producer, an impressive Jewish woman, stood up and said, "I've never seen anything like it. These students don't protest—they pray. The more they are persecuted, the more they pray." The feature aired.

On the Road: Wrinkles in Time

Being the national director of Veritas meant a lot of time talking on gas station pay phones (this was the age before cell phones—at least for me), typing on e-mail and flying on cargo jets. This was a strange variation on my life as a college chaplain and summer missionary. I soon needed a better grasp of road maps, Dramamine, IRS regulations and flexibility about where I might eat or sleep. When visiting a campus, friends and I needed to multitask, which often included time with professors, fellowship leaders, administrators and even archivists who could tell us the history of the school. Since administrations rarely helped with funding, and since forums often cost more that ten thousand dollars to host, we'd occasionally meet with a foundation, church, alumnus or community member who would provide matching funds to make Veritas a possibility.

Logistics were often a challenge. One travel adventure—a wrinkle in time—happened during a coastal monsoon at the University of California, Santa Barbara. A retired chemistry professor, John Kennedy,[4] had asked me to introduce their first Veritas Forum, so I flew into LAX on a commercial flight a hundred miles south because the fare was cheaper. Delayed by the weather, I arrived with two hours to rent a car and drive a hundred miles in pouring rain through Los Angeles and up the coast. I parked in a large puddle, ran into the auditorium three minutes late and soaking wet, and introduced the first UCSB Veritas Forum to nine hundred students who had to avoid the first five rows because they were under water—it was like a moat around the stage. The speakers, Jim Sire and Walter Bradley, may have wondered if the moat contained alligators.

This turned out to be the mother of all El Niño storms, and UCSB was shut down for the first time due to natural disaster. What could have been a disaster for Veritas proved to be a gift—several thousand students without classes, beaches or sunshine were free to attend, and the forum relocated to churches and university buildings higher in the hills. Hundreds came to hear speakers such as chemist Fritz Schaefer and philosopher Peter Kreeft—who had brought his surfboard all the way from Boston. In an effort to limit the mortality rate, we postponed the Veritas surfing workshop even though monsoon-surfing might have been a vivid way of experiencing truth.

Some moments in life, the moments we most live for, are less like *chronos* (measurable time) and more like *kairos* (timeless moments). From Santa Barbara I drove down what was left of the highway to pick up author Madeleine L'Engle in Montecito. We were planning to attend a one-man play, *Tales of Tolstoy*, performed by our mutual New York friend Bruce Kuhn. Heading back to Santa Barbara we saw that people were traveling Highway 1 by kayak and canoe. The roads were under water.

Down the creek without a canoe, Madeleine and I began to look for shelter. We turned back and, through the driving rain against the windshield, saw a small French restaurant. We hurried inside and entered a different world. Greeted by kindly servers and subtle jazz, we sat at a cozy table by a warm fire and happily holed up for the evening. I had read Madeleine's books as a child, and so time with her seemed surreal. A robust and powerful woman at seventy-eight, she was an innate storyteller with a vivid memory. Over hors d'oeuvres we batted around our common fascination with physics, adventure and theology as woven into *A Wrinkle in Time* and her other books.

Over dinner and a glass of Merlot she shared about falling in love with her husband, a stage and television actor. She spoke of family life as a wonderfully "irrational season." And then moments later, with the warmth of the fire in her eyes, she spoke of her husband's death and how she missed him deeply. "A friend said, 'Madeleine, the Word of God is like seed upon our hearts. But only when our hearts break does that seed fall inside.'"

I felt God impressing this on me but did not then know why; nonetheless, I was grateful for the insight given my own frustration with love back in Cambridge. When I took Madeleine home to her friends, she reminded me that "a hot bath at the end of the day is one of the answers to the world's problems."

The next day we made it to Santa Barbara and she engaged over a thousand students in her Veritas Forum talks on "Getting to Truth Through Fiction." When she spoke of her fascination with God's creation, she said, "Albert Einstein felt that anyone who isn't lost in rapturous awe at the wonder of the universe is as good as a burned out candle. When I read that I thought, *Aha, I've found my theologian!*"

Nurturing Unity

I've often discovered that Christians at various universities do not really know one another. Though they are kindred spirits, they are often separated by age, ethnicity and varying Christian associations. So before visiting a campus, I would often ask the various group leaders to gather and listen to one another, pray and begin new friendships.

I remember a call from Chuck Roeper, who was on staff with Christian Leadership Ministries at the University of Michigan. Chuck was planning a Veritas Forum on his own and I suggested that he might befriend and invite other ministries to be a part of the process. Within several months Chuck was coordinating twenty-six student and community organizations who welcomed over a thousand students each night to a five-day Veritas Forum in 1995. Speakers included Hugh Ross, Ravi Zacharias, Eleonore Stump, Os Guinness, Walter Bradley and local scholar Peter Payne. After each evening's event, planners gathered in a local church and divided up fifty-six hundred comment cards so they could follow up on student requests and ideas. Outside of the large auditorium, I noted Michigan's seal inscribed on the building: *"Artes, Scientia, Veritas."*

J O U R N A L   E N T R Y

Increased Christian unity is a silent victory of Veritas. Students are so encouraged just to find one another. But then, when they learn to welcome the university with the gift of hospitality, the victories are even sweeter. Veritas is only as strong as the partnerships, creativity, hospitality and follow-up work of fellowships such as Campus Crusade for Christ, InterVarsity Christian Fellowship, Chi Alpha, Navigators and many others.

Encouraging Creativity

Little did we know what our "party with a purpose" might become—a model for a unified witness that would catch on with students who wanted to change the world through love, truth and beauty. It was wonderful to meet such caring people who bloomed where they were planted.

I loved hanging out with students in dorms, dining halls, coffee shops. There we would back up to the basics with creative naiveté and discuss, "What are we doing here?" "What are students experiencing and struggling with?" "What's this school meant to be about?"

We often asked student leaders and Veritas planners to describe their university from three vantage points. First, we'd draw the university as if from an airplane at ten thousand feet, looking at the layout of academic buildings and campus facilities, and the school's proximity to water, mountains, cities and farms we might incorporate into Veritas.

Second, I'd ask, "How does this school look and feel at five feet—on the ground—to most students? What are their concerns and dreams?" Third, we'd look beneath the surface at the university's roots, origins and intentions: what purpose the founders had envisioned, its motto and seal, its bylaws, its endowments. And we'd consider what the university was doing that was true, good and beautiful—and how we could support those efforts.

We wanted each Veritas Forum to respond to the unique needs and questions of each campus. No two forums were the same. They were filled with local questions and local color, raising up indigenous believers from many departments and cultures and hosting presenters who would serve as mentors and encouragers. Our lively brainstorming and prayer sessions with students shaped most forums.

I loved working with college students. They said things like, "The problem with changing the world is that it takes *weeks* to get anything done." I was in awe that so few could do so much with so little when inspired by the love of the Holy Spirit. They reminded me of a group of once-cowardly and barely functional friends—some fishermen, a doctor, some hospitable women, a tax collector, a tentmaker—who later shaped the course of human history after encountering the resurrected Jesus. This movement continues today as an expanding kingdom. Veritas is just one small subplot of the story; we try to play our part in our time, learn from others and enjoy the journey.

Hard Work

When it came to an actual forum, Veritas was (and is) a lot of work. The national Veritas organization has only two or three paid staff members, a few interns and hundreds of volunteers to host thousands of participants. The volunteers plan and work hard, pull all-nighters and are the unsung heroes. One of my favorite e-mails was from a Harvard student who fired a late-night request to the list of thirty planners: "Help! Who can run mics and set up for Tom Key's 'C. S. Lewis on Stage'?" After a few hours of sleep he woke up with new energy and signed onto his e-mail account. Unaware that he was reading the same e-mail he'd sent out before falling asleep, he responded, "I can!" He soon realized he'd responded to himself. That was one of many exhausted laughs the planners shared that week.

Interesting Inroads

Veritas speakers, scientists and artists are invited not only into lecture halls but often into classrooms, faculty clubs, labs and departmental gatherings. Philosophy departments have hosted world-renowned philosophers Alvin Plantinga, Nicholas Wolterstorff, Dallas Willard and Eleonore Stump. Science departments have asked to hear chemists, microbiologists, physicists and engineers, including Fritz Schaefer, Michael Behe, Hugh Ross, John Polkinghorne and Walter Bradley. Condoleezza Rice spoke at the Veritas Forum at Cal Berkeley while she was the provost at Stanford.

Artists began composing original music and plays for Veritas Forums. We were moving closer to the heart of the university both in mind and heart.

Aha! Moments

As forums emerged across the country, reality-seekers experienced countless moments of insight and grace. At Arizona State University in 1996 over a thousand students turned out for a dialogue between philosopher William Lane Craig and Douglas Jesseph, a professor of philosophy at North Carolina State University, on the question "Does God exist?" Their debate centered on the problem of evil and human suffering. Dr. Craig's argument moved logically from the wild improbability of life on our planet to the anthropic principle (which asserts that the universe and earth are conspicuously hospitable and fine-tuned for human life) to the person of Jesus Christ and evidence for the resurrection. In the midst of evil and pain, Dr. Craig said, God literally entered our world. He took the world's evil and pain into himself, died, and rose again to defeat death and give us the hope of eternal life.

His "opponent" (I don't like the word, but the students wanted to host a debate), Dr. Jesseph, argued the opposite. He said he was an atheist precisely because of the needless suffering in the world. He argued that a powerful and loving God, such as the God portrayed in the Bible, would prevent evil and suffering. He believed that, given all the apparently needless and random suffering, this God could not exist, and that such a God was a product of our imagination. One could read the headlines of any newspaper on most days to sympathize emotionally with his argument.

I think the crowd was divided—until one question was raised. After nearly ninety minutes, a tall and earnest undergrad finally got his turn at the microphone. Addressing both professors he asked, "Can you tell us what difference your worldview makes to you in your own personal lives?"

Dr. Craig said that as a philosopher (with two Ph.D.s), he had searched in vain for meaning, for hope, and only found it when he finally came to believe in Jesus Christ. He said that Jesus changed his mind, his heart and his marriage. "I came to know joy for the first time," he said. "I can't help but want to share the wonder of Jesus Christ whenever I am welcomed to give reason for the hope within me. I just can't keep him to myself."

All eyes were on Professor Jesseph after Bill Craig's compelling response. He said, thoughtfully, that if he had to share his hope with someone, he wouldn't have much to say. "I'd probably just go home, put on the Grateful Dead, and play chess with my computer."

In the pregnant pause that followed I heard several gasps from students who understood, perhaps for the first time, the connection between beliefs and the living of life. It's not gracious to say there was a clear "winner" in this debate, but when Bill Craig and other Christian philosophers and scientists are allowed to use reason and to include their personal experience, it is hard to find a willing opponent, and there is rarely a contest.

A combined Veritas Forum at Carnegie-Mellon and University of Pittsburgh included a tour through an art museum and various science and engineering labs. An engineering team demonstrated their impressive remote-controlled reconnaissance helicopter. After hearing about their multimillion-dollar grant, and seeing what it had produced, a student asked, "Do you study and learn from flight in nature, such as bees and birds?"

One of the engineers said they did try to learn from nature but that they had to accomplish a lot more than pollinating a flower. Another student asked, "Could you replicate a hummingbird?" The team looked at the project leader. Slowly he answered, "No, a hummingbird is extremely complex." She then asked, "How about a sparrow?" The capable research team was left in a humble silence.

Sometimes in such a moment of newfound humility, in a re-enchanted world, we would move from our questions of God to God's questions of us. In Genesis he asks us, "Where are you hiding? Who told you that you were naked? Where is your brother?" In Job 38 and 39 he asks us, "Where were you when I laid the earth's foundation? Can you bring forth the constellations in their seasons? Do you know the laws of the heavens? Did you give the horse his strength? Does the eagle soar at your command? Have you seen the gates of the shadow of death? Have you ever given orders to the morning?" Jesus asks us in the Gospels: "Are you thirsty? Do you want to be healed? Have I been with you so long and still you don't know me? Who do you say I am? Do you love me?"

Sometimes upon thinking of these things we would be stunned into silence and a new place of hearing and of seeing. Of cooperating and not competing. Of reconnecting and belonging. Of resting and perhaps even trusting, for "the mind that comes to rest is tended in ways it cannot intend," as poet-farmer Wendell Berry says.[5] Slowly, we begin to care less about holding truth and more about loving the Truth who holds us.

JOURNAL ENTRY

I've begun to realize that this is the journey I am on as well—a journey neither of blind faith nor of total certainty, but of growing assurance. This journey requires a continual conversation with the story's Author and Completer. His story challenges me more than I could have imagined, and it requires my submission and trust. It is a story that I can understand only as I walk forward into its unfolding.

8

Searching for Clues

A True Vine in the Ivy

Truth is not only that which awaits discovery, but also that which was once known and is now threatened by forgetfulness.

ROBERT FONG,
"WHY I TEACH," *FINDING GOD AT HARVARD*

The best two hours I've spent in a long time.

PRINCETON STUDENT COMMENT CARD

Rob and I were driving to Princeton, his alma mater, cramming along the way for his doctoral exams in nuclear engineering and physics at MIT. Approaching Princeton in rural New Jersey, I was impressed by the fields, farms and distant spires. Upon arrival I was struck by the university's subtly elegant architecture. To spend time at Princeton was also to be impressed by the students' brightness and energy. A remnant of old-school cheer made Princeton feel more like a small liberal arts college than a big-city university. But the pressure to perform was apparent, and timeless values of character, ethics and truth had morphed into modern values of image, competition and success.[1]

We ordered Philly cheese steaks at Hoagie Haven and found our favorite picnic spot—up in the branches of a tree behind the president's house. Getting up and down without being caught was a challenge. Late into the afternoon Rob showed me Princeton's original building, historic Nassau Hall. We entered a dark and musty wood-paneled gallery, the last of daylight barely illuminating the room through windows. He flipped some light switches and suddenly before me were the framed portraits of Princeton presidents and statesmen, theologians and scholars going back to Jonathan Edwards and the founding of what was then "the College of New Jersey." Here in front of us were torch-bearers of the Puritan belief in the advance of God's kingdom, now waiting in the darkness of Nassau Hall for others to be animated by their passion.

I was in awe. Gazing into their faces I absorbed the majesty of the room and began to imagine the greatness of these lives, and of what else might lie in shadow.

Curious to learn more, I visited the archives to discover Princeton's reason for existence. Many alumni assert that the school's motto is "God went to Princeton," but I discovered that the current motto was *Dei sub numine viget*, "Under God she flourishes." A lovely phrase, but I wasn't convinced it was the original motto. Digging deeper I found Princeton's founding records and ancient seal. I learned that for the first hundred and fifty years, the College of New Jersey's motto was *Vitam mortuis reddo*, "I restore life to the dead." This was a vision powerful enough to explain the emergence of a great university: the resurrection of Jesus Christ—eternal life for believers and the power to build his kingdom of love in the world.

How ironic the juxtaposition, I thought, when I attended an annual memorial service for deceased alumni in Princeton's chapel. The minister's sermon offered hope for salvation and eternal life. How? By means of one's Princeton affiliation as an eternal fellowship.

"No wonder this school is so expensive," I whispered to Rob. "It comes with serious perks."

The minister failed to mention the cross of Christ that atones for our sin before a holy God or the resurrection of Christ that defeated death itself.

The Christian students I met were concerned about a growing culture of death rather than life. In particular they spoke of the dehumanizing influence of ethics professor Peter Singer, the Jack Kevorkian of the academy, with his moral reasoning that humans, animals, reptiles and insects—all living creatures—are of equal value. According to Singer, not to believe in species equality was to be "a speciest." (This insight could belong to your child for only $140,000 in tuition and fees.) The very people who advocated such teachings often wore leather belts and shoes, and I believe they would save their own child at the expense of several deadly snakes.

Before long, Veritas Forums emerged at Princeton and the nearby University of Pennsylvania. They were led by Scott Luley and Dave De-Huff with Christian Leadership Ministries, and events primarily focused on questions of origins, humanness, bioethics and science.[2] I returned not only for forums but also to speak at Princeton Theological Seminary about Veritas and the *Finding God at Harvard* book. The next time I sat in the portrait gallery in Nassau Hall, it was with friends to pray for Princeton.

Dartmouth

That same year I visited Dartmouth College in Hanover, New Hampshire, at the invitation of Craig Parker with the Navigators ministry.[3] Craig gave me a tour, and when we entered Rollins Chapel in the center of campus, I said, "Wow, it's dark in here. I can't imagine why anyone would build this chapel like a catacomb."

There were windows in the back, but the sides and front of the building were solid and dark. Craig said, "Walk around the outside of the chapel and see what happened."

Outside looking in, I realized that priceless Tiffany stained-glass windows had been covered by drywall inside. I traced the leaded outlines in the windows, trying to detect a pattern. The concealed windows featured a robed man—healing someone, teaching, hanging on a cross, emerging from an empty tomb—who was now obscured. No light shone through to illuminate the students within. The chapel resembled a tomb.

"Why was this done?" I asked Craig.

"Some students who wanted to use the chapel as a meeting space were offended," he said.

"Aren't there other meeting spaces available?"

Craig shrugged as if to say that was never their point. I wondered how Mr. and Mrs. Rollins would feel if they knew their chapel was now quiet and dark in the middle of a college dedicated to being *Voces clamantium in deserto,* "A voice crying in the wilderness." This motto was a vision of bringing the gospel to native Americans and others who hadn't yet heard of the love of God in the life of Jesus Christ—who claimed to be the light of the world.

Driving home to Cambridge through the White Mountains, I wondered if Dartmouth was hiding Jesus or hiding from Jesus. Or both. I felt sorrow and anger and pity. I wanted to ask whoever was responsible, "What if, just possibly, the eyewitness authors of the New Testament were accurate and speaking truthfully—since people don't normally allow themselves to be martyred for a known lie? And what if modern astrophysics is accurate, and what if archaeology confirming the biblical record is trustworthy, and what if two billion human beings today just happen to be right about Jesus? What if Jesus is who he claimed to be—God in flesh and blood, here for us and for our salvation? And you board him up, trying to erase him from the minds and hearts and longings of students. How is this good pluralism or intellectual diversity, which you claim to uphold? Did you have the honesty to cover Christ's image with your own

JOURNAL ENTRY

Grad fellowships are established in seven schools at Harvard (Jeff and I are wearing out tennis shoes and bicycle tires) and we had a retreat on Martha's Vineyard with particularly good worship and volleyball. Afterward, Rob and I found a sailboat and explored an inland pond on Cape Cod.

hands, or did you force an employee carpenter to do it for you?"

It's probably good that I was alone in the car.

Harvard

Back in Cambridge, we had a great autumn semester. We continued to be affirmed in our belief that good play, as well as good work, is part of the "lightness of being" afforded by the gospel. We told people that although Paul says we have the ministry of reconciliation, we also have the ministry of silly recreation. Silly recreation often leads to reconciliation, or just plain fun in a world that takes itself too seriously.

On hikes throughout New England, we sensed that "in him we live and move and have our being" (Acts 17:28). In college I had volunteered for the Lake Placid Olympic Organizing Committee and fell in love with a little hideaway called the Adirondack Loj. Friends and I rediscovered it.

JOURNAL ENTRY

We skied Whiteface before the snow entirely melted and rushed down the mountain faster than we could race it. We sang Scottish ballads on the chairlift as we rose up through the fog and the verdant crags. That night our sing-along drew in other lodge guests. A stranger asked, "Why do you sing like this? I haven't heard such singing since I was a boy." We had late-night readings of *The Little Prince* and *Winnie the Pooh* with six grad students piled on my bed.

The next day we hiked Mt. Joe, inventing funny tunes to Pooh's song, "Sing, ho, for the Life of a Bear." Between snowball ambushes we discussed bioethics, luge, just-war theory, the nature of true romance, geophysics, landscape painting and the beauty of the earth. I ran my hands and face down a sunlit ice sculpture against a cliff in a white birch forest. Rob lingered also. Winter. A strange time to celebrate the birth of Christ, but such may be God's nature—life and birth in what seems to be the dead cold of winter. As at Harvard, maybe the seeds are merely dormant.

I thought of Wendell Berry's line "the standing sabbath of the woods" and the complete reordering of life that can freely flow from the love of God. Any seed knows that obedience to the earth and sky is life and fruit—for it is rooted in the source of life, just as branches draw from the vine, just as a child nurses from her mother. Rebellion and autonomy are death. As J. S. Eliot said, "Man without God is like a seed upon the wind."

Living Without Fear

We were learning the freedom to live without fear of all that death can touch, though not without sorrow. Each spring we'd leave Cambridge for other U.S. cities or other countries and work alongside Haitian slaves cutting sugarcane, eight thousand people living in a garbage dump in San Salvador, Bolivian prisoners, widows and children in war-torn Guatemala where entire villages were burned down, leaving no living husbands or fathers.

Mission trips resulted in interesting choices after graduation. Andy Webb decided to decline a high-paying engineering job to reforest sections of the Dominican Republic with a mission called Floresta. Heather Ruhm welcomed many Central Americans to Boston and

JOURNAL ENTRY

Haiti and Dominican Republic

After work, we rested on our bunk beds, also trying to avoid a few tarantulas of unspeakable size. Jeff was reading Scripture about God's love for the poor. Suddenly the room began to shake as two men pounded through our door with rifles. They entered. I'm not sure who was more surprised, we or they. Very drunk, they were simply looking for a place to sleep.

When faced with desperate poverty, I still feel that I have more questions than answers. I can only try to feel along with people, to learn from the poor and reciprocate their generosity as they offer us the shirts off their backs. They laugh and love, despite their poverty. I can see the nature of my own poverty, which requires at least some pretense of security for a presumed future. What matters, Lord?

then began medical school. Harvard business students John Sage and Chris Dearnley began a gourmet coffee company called Pura Vida with all profits going to the Costa Rican workers and at-risk kids. Katie (Smith) Milway became the liaison for Food for the Hungry in Africa. Steve Radelet helped lead the world's "Jubilee" campaign of debt-forgiveness to African nations, and he also invited Bono to Africa to help in the AIDS crisis.

Gary Haugen, joined by Harvard Law grad Sharon Cohn, began International Justice Mission, which legally intervenes to liberate children and the poor from sex trafficking and slavery around the world.

In Cambridge, I kept looking for ways to engage and add vitality to the university.

For the 1994 Veritas Forum we rented Harvard's largest indoor space—Sanders Theater.[4] Set into the massive stage wall facing the audience were three identical shields: *Veritas: Christo et Ecclessiae*. Unfortunately, the shields had been hidden in shadow for years and most students were unaware of their significance. We asked the lighting crew to illuminate these shields for the attending twelve hundred students, even if for one night. Against the background of the now clearly visible shields, Harvard's seventy-person gospel choir, Kuumba, took the stage and rocked the inside of that "giant rolltop desk," as Sanders is often called.

Time magazine senior correspondent David Aikman then spoke on "Truth, Consequences and History," tracing the fruits of atheism versus Christian faith through the twentieth century, often called the bloodiest in human history. Fourteen scholars joined Aikman on stage, taking students' questions about gender, race, suffering, evolution, chaos, deconstruction, pluralism and the reliability of the Bible and the resurrection.

HARVARD VERITAS 1993-1995

- *Treasure hunts for veritas in the museum labs and the Yard*
- *John Stott, "Jesus: Truth for the Twenty-First Century"*
- *Ron Sider, "The Whole Gospel for the Whole Person"*
- *Peter Kreeft on philosophical evidences for the existence of God*
- *A film festival showing* **Babette's Feast, Shadowlands, Chariots of Fire** *and* **Teresa**
- *Handel's* **Messiah** *sing-along in Dunster House*
- *Increasing unity and friendships as the different fellowships came*

When *Finding God at Harvard* finally came out in 1996, fifteen of the writers gathered as speakers for a very personal, creative and "symphonic" Veritas Forum again in Sanders Theater.[5] Actor Tom Key gave a powerful performance from *The Screwtape Letters*. Then medical student Brian Foster walked up to the podium. He opened his *Finding God* book and began to read the story of his brother

Brent's battle with bone cancer. Many of the twelve hundred students were Brent's classmates.

> Here I am an accomplished Harvard student and athlete, the world seemingly at my feet. However, there is one little catch to all of this success: I have widespread bone cancer and only several weeks to live.

I had asked Brian to read because Brent, after eleven surgeries, passed away before the book's publication. Brian continued reading.

> God himself suffered more than even I could imagine when he became a man, and can therefore understand our deepest sorrows. I am always moved when I read the account of Jesus visiting the tomb of Lazarus. After seeing the considerable grief that death had inflicted on his people, Jesus himself wept. And then he faced death head on and defeated it.
>
> That is my hope—to be found in Christ—to see the light of life again because of him. I have always placed my hope in the promise that, just as Christ revived Lazarus, he will come and fix our brokenness also. I hope that you who hear this will remember their Creator "before the days of trouble come," so that when forced to confront the horrible abyss of death, God will be able to lead you back to safety, sanity, and an eternity of glory with him.

There was a palpable silence in the room. Many students remembered the last time they'd seen Brent. He had spoken in the Freshman Union on suffering before he left school. To get the attention of students in the noisy dining hall, he removed his artificial right leg and put it on the table by the microphone. His classmates were all ears, as they were again tonight.

We ended the evening with more than a thousand participants standing and singing "Amazing Grace," led by speakers and students who joined us on stage in front of the illuminated Veritas shields.

The graciousness, coherence and brilliance were vivid. To my delight, my own father came from Ohio. Afterward he said, "Kelly, they're so bright. And their eyes are so bright."

"Daddy," I said, "they're forgiven, and free, and grateful." It meant the world to me that he came. My father has a precious heart.

One student planner, Elisabeth Overmann, told a reporter, "When I arrived as a freshman, I was confronted by professors and students who questioned the possibility of knowable truth and denied its relevance to higher learning. They cast shadows of doubt on Christian belief. Ironically these professors would often speak from the stage in Sanders Theater, against the background of three dimly lit shields reading, 'Veritas: Christo et Ecclesiae.' I never thought that two years later I would see that same stage filled with members of our various Christian fellowships, united in worship and prayer two hours before a Veritas Forum began. On that stage we welcomed a thousand people to three days of exploration and dialogue about the Person who claimed to be truth."

Yale University

Not only were Harvard, Princeton and Dartmouth originally rooted in Christ, so were most other Ivy League and early colleges. Yale's founders sensed Harvard's early wanderings from veritas and the human tendency toward darkness and deception, so in 1701 they dedi-

---

JOURNAL ENTRY

I met with Christian students who felt the student body had been reduced to sensual experience as seen in Yale's annual "Sex Week," which dehumanized students by normalizing pornography. They also spoke about a recent law school bombing and the rise of depression and suicide. Still, believers want to build in the ruins of a devolving culture. Things are fermenting.

cated Yale to *Urim v'Thummim,* which translates from Hebrew into Latin as *Lux et veritas,* or "light and truth."[6]

At Yale I learned that the best reason for my visit was to help very busy students finally meet one another. The dorm elevator was out so our group of ten leaders climbed to a student's room on the thirteenth floor of the Tudor dorm. We sat in a circle on the floor beneath posters of U2 and Albert Einstein. I soon realized that I was not the only stranger in the room. They were mostly strangers to each other.

They introduced themselves: "Welcome, everyone, I'm Donald Dacey, former business executive and now divinity student."

"I'm Dave Mahen with Campus Crusade."

"I attend InterVarsity."

"Hi. I'm with the Law School fellowship."

"I'm Lauris Kaldjian, medical doctor and researcher."

"I'm Eric, doing a doctorate in theology."

"I'm Greg Ganssle with the Rivendell Institute."

And so on.

By the end of the meeting I was reminded not only of my favorite symphony metaphor but also of spontaneous combustion. The horsepower in the room was explosive.

J. Donald Dacey, the leader of the leaders that evening, later led a *Lux et Veritas* Forum at Yale.[7] Renowned New Testament scholar N. T. Wright explored the possibility of knowing truth in a postmodern world where there seems to be no overarching story, only power plays, revisionist histories and our own small stories. He addressed the loss of truth by asking, "What story do we live in?" and "How do we know what's true?"

> Implicit in our questions, in our search for an "absolute truth," is the deep, conscious awareness that we each personally exist with a past, present and future, we have a soul, and every life is important. That despite the best efforts of the cynics, we continue to be drawn to the universal idea that we're living in a "grand, overarching story" that gives meaning and purpose to our lives.
>
> Combining with our strong grasp of personal identity exists an

appreciation of the beauty and design of creation, the ongoing ethical struggle between good and evil, and our understanding of imagination and love. These universal features of human life create a testimony that overwhelms the postmodern worldviews of naturalism, reductionism and hopeless despair—exposing them as the nihilistic, rebellious acts of foolish, unhappy people.

In contrast to this cynical view of life, we sense, and at times would go so far as to say we truly believe, that we live in the great narrative of a Father-God, a life-giving Creator, who has revealed himself to those he loves, to and through his creation.

JOURNAL ENTRY

Yale 1996

Friends are encouragers as a path unfolds.

Kelly—

When we produce from the impetus of God's call in our lives (menial as it may seem on certain days), we can neither predict nor control what he will do with our actions—isn't that marvelous? So here we sit listening to the brilliance of our Christian brothers and sisters, like a symphony, who have been invited to New Haven because of Veritas' efforts to instigate and inform this style of forum in these places in this time. Thank you. Moreover, of course, thank God.

With love,

Ruth Allderidge

Nearly a thousand students participated at Yale despite a February nor'easter ice storm. Several came from California and took their experience home with them.

We began to see that seeds of faith had been planted long ago in many universities. Perhaps they still contained hope for the future.

Before long I was regularly hitching rides from Boston to towns such as Charlottesville, Chicago, Toronto and San Francisco. In each city were kindred spirits who were also looking for clues, who were also wanting to find life.

9

East to West
From New England to California

The growth of evangelical fellowships is because students are
"attracted to the joy of Christian students and the way they live.
It's less about eternity and more about today." Many point to the
Veritas Forum as an indicator of spiritual interest.

THE HARVARD CRIMSON INTERVIEW

There is no apology for God's long silence, no word of consolation
for Job in his distress. But nor does God crush and humiliate him.
Instead, God takes him on a whirlwind tour of the universe.

VINOTH RAMACHANDRA,
THE VERITAS FORUM AT CAL BERKELEY

I headed to the subway in Boston and then to the train station on my
way to Philadelphia. I had agreed to "debate" the existence of God at
Haverford, Bryn Mawr and Swarthmore with the president of an East
Coast secular humanist society. This woman was also a caring neonatal
nurse who attempted to disprove God's existence given the fact of the
world's suffering. She didn't accept that God himself entered into that
suffering more deeply than we ever could. Nor did she accept that suffering had meaning. We eventually became friends.

It was strange to be so near to Rob's hometown without him. My patience with our relationship had waned and turned to resentment, and after six years we parted ways. It was an act of the will to advocate God's reality when I didn't really see his hand at work in my own life. At least not in my love life.

JOURNAL ENTRY

"I love you, but I don't know if marriage is God's will," Rob had said in anguish after six years. He wasn't sure either way. But I was more interested in my own will than Rob's version of "God's will" just then. And besides, I wouldn't have stuck it out for six years if I hadn't believed it was God's will. No one is perfect—which is why marriage is so beautiful. The choice of love, unconditional agape love, alone perfects us. This is what friends are for. This is what Jesus shows us, I thought, true love.

The Rockies and Pacific Northwest

I kept moving, carried forward by momentum and the need to stay busy. I went on to the Veritas Forum at the University of Western Ontario and worked with Michael Veenema, who led extraordinary forums there. I then flew out to meet wonderful planners at the University of Colorado. Friends from Ohio came to Colorado for a Veritas board meeting, which was a great encouragement. Afterward I spent a Sunday alone skiing up in the high country outside of Aspen.

After my time in Colorado, I caught a 6 a.m. cargo plane to Portland, Oregon. I rented a purple Neon and drove to Corvallis through mild

JOURNAL ENTRY

Waking at Deanna's under a glass dome ceiling in winter. Silent but for birds and wind. A January hike down the valley, ending up at Snowmass Lodge where I swam alone in a heated pool in the snow. Stroking the white and blue reflection of the mountains, water like liquid sky. The pines my friends in that moment. Wanting to live in the moment but floating into memory of hikes up that mountain in snowshoes with Rob and others, crossing log jams, cycling. Memories washing over and through me. I am trying to understand, to make sense of my own life, to forget. To live forwardly.

Water and snow, wood smoke and steam, pine and eucalyptus, the best of creation pouring into me in those hours. Remember the lesson of my skis: "Trust the fall line, center, and go." Freedom and form. As my Cambridge housemate Heather used to say, "Relax and accelerate."

Various friends suggested that I cut my losses and move on without him. But it's hard. Maybe it's all my fault. I'll try again, hoping this time to get it right with Rob. He still talk occasionally, and he's never said it is definitely over. Both with Rob and with Veritas, I'll do what God gives me to do—again.

rain and lush farmland. Again, I found the love for students to be strong among the Oregon Veritas planners. They were led by Gary and Pam Hough, who welcomed students into their home, Logos House. What fun we had with students and New Testament scholar Catherine Kroeger, environmentalist Cal DeWitt and philosopher Alvin Plant-inga. Catherine surprised people with the gospel's ennobling of women. Cal spoke and led a river tour called "Jesus, Salmon and Creation." And Alvin gave his ironic and thoroughly logical talk "The Evolutionary Case against Naturalism." We all visited past midnight. And then on to California.

California

Historically, the vision of a Christ-centered life and education was carried like a torch from England to New England. Within two hun-dred years this same impetus had swept across America from east to west. The University of California at Berkeley, for example, was founded in the model of Christian education. In fact all the Cal schools have the motto from Genesis 1, "Let there be light." Veritas planners in California wanted to fan that flame back into light and heat once again.

Stanford University

Northern California Veritas Forums began in 1996 when Kurt Keil-hacker, Libby Vincent and Dave Dettoni called to talk after hearing about Veritas and *Finding God at Harvard*. Libby and Dave were on staff at Menlo Park Presbyterian Church (MPPC) serving Stanford students as well as at-risk kids in East Palo Alto. Libby and Dave had been at the Yale *Lux et Veritas* Forum in New Haven and, despite the unwel-coming ice storm that week, they loved what they had experienced at Yale. They returned to Stanford with a vision of a unified community of believers hosting a university-wide forum.

They invited me to visit balmy and pleasant Stanford. Another friend, pastor Steve Zeisler of Peninsula Bible Church in Palo Alto, also invited me to be a writer in residence for a month. I liked the idea of thawing out on long hikes in the redwood forest, and possibly even regaining some emotional ballast in the wake of heartbreak. So I agreed. Before long, the Bay Area felt like home.

Driving up the palm-lined entrance to Stanford, I felt drawn to Memorial Church as the heart of the campus. The exterior of the church was a large mosaic of Jesus with his friends. Inspired by the tragic death of her son, Jane Stanford had filled the chapel walls with signs of her own deepening faith, which she wanted to impart to future generations. Carved into the interior sandstone of Memorial Church walls, the words spoke to me: "We need something outside of and beyond ourselves."

And then I saw, lit by sunlight, "Remember, you are not your own—you are bought with the precious blood of Jesus."

As I exited the church to enter the Rodin Sculpture Garden, I read, "It is by suffering that God has most nearly approached to man; it is by suffering that man draws most nearly to God."

As I'd seen before, Veritas at Stanford began with an interfellowship gathering of twenty leaders. They wanted to hear this strange story about New England students and professors considering truth. And they wanted to work together to explore Stanford's hardest questions in relation to the biblical worldview and the person of Jesus. Veritas took as a subtheme Stanford's motto, "Let the winds of freedom blow."

While in San Francisco, I enjoyed getting together with new friends across the Bay in Berkeley. Cal Berkeley and Stanford planners had decided to cross-pollinate—to team up and share speakers and ideas for their creative forums. Planners included a wise fellowship of local pastors, alumni, students and professors.[1]

I drove back and forth across the San Mateo bridge between well-manicured Palo Alto and cluttered urban Berkeley, marveling at the change of ambiance and wondering what was beneath the surface of each. To dive into the University of California was to be in awe of its heritage of genius.

The vice chancellor of Cal Berkeley warmly introduced the Veritas Forum at Cal, followed by Condoleezza Rice, who was then Stanford's provost. Many on these campuses were surprised to learn of the Christian roots of their universities as seen on thousands of Veritas invitations.

I asked several planners to reflect on their experience creating a unified Veritas witness in challenging places. My friend Susan S. Phillips, executive director of New College Berkeley, wrote the following letter:

> Inspired by the work of the Harvard Veritas Forum, a group of us gathered in the mid-nineties to pray about creating an open conversation about the truth at Cal. Most of us served churches or ministries that reached out to the university in a variety of ways, but we did so independently. The work of Veritas became for us a work of *caritas* (loving care), as we prayed and worked side by side, month after month, year after year.
>
> Sitting at my desk today I look at stacks of folders several feet tall that record the work of cultivating these conversations at U.C. Berkeley. Kelly Monroe visited us early and often in the process of hosting three full forums and numerous freestanding lectures on campus. She encouraged us to think of the work as symphonic, exploring faith's relationship to culture, art, science, worldviews, and life as it is and can be lived in the light of God's love.
>
> The motto of the University of California, like that of many long-established American universities, is taken from the Bible: "Let there be light." Founded in 1872, its charter reads, "The College of California is an Institution designed by its founders to furnish the means of a thorough and comprehensive education, under the pervading influence and spirit of the Christian religion." For its first quarter-century, even after it was secularized, the university required daily chapel attendance of all students. This is a heritage unknown to most students at the Berkeley campus today.
>
> Without arguing that a public university ought to endorse a particular religious faith, we lament the loss of religious literacy at the highest levels of education. What a travesty for the United States to be turning out scholars familiar with Marx and Jefferson, but not King David and Jesus. How do we as a nation presume to

draw on faith as a guide for policy-making and the restoration of families and communities when we have banned critical, scholarly teaching of religious faith and values from our schools and universities?

We leapt into that educational vacuum with more enthusiasm than calculation. The work of coordination for each forum was immense. Thousands attended from the university, the adjacent Graduate Theological Union, and local churches. The only unifying attribute of the speakers was their faith in Jesus Christ. Their politics, genders, ethnicities, nationalities, professional disciplines and denominational affiliations were varied. The audiences were similarly diverse, and even more so, as many who came were not Christian. Christian students brought friends with whom they desired to discuss faith. Faculty without faith commitments came to see how Christian colleagues explained their work in light of faith—conversations not easily entered into in classrooms and faculty meetings.

In a conversation I facilitated about holding a faith in transcendence while immersed in the human-focused social sciences, a graduate student said, "I haven't thought much about truth. I've thought about validity, data, and justice, but it's interesting to try and bring my religious understandings of truth into the same room as my sociological thinking about facts and legitimacy." Over and over again we on the steering committee heard reports of these epiphanies as the false divide between faith and reason was breached.

In the years since we began this work at Cal, I've thought frequently about the way Jesus Christ knows no borders. Focusing on him enabled us to gather and listen to each other across distances ordinarily difficult to traverse. The work of the Berkeley Veritas fellowship shed some light on the Light that shines in every darkness—be it in a wayfarers' inn or an ivory tower. Let there be light, indeed.

Likewise, Veritas at Stanford gathered dozens of student groups and, over the course of several years, thousands of students. Broadway actor Bruce Kuhn performed *The Gospel of Luke* and *Tales of Tolstoy*. University of Southern California philosopher Dallas Willard spoke, despite his brother's death the day before, on subjects including "Jesus Versus Nietzsche: The Rematch." Hundreds came to hear Stanford astrophysicist Michael Strauss on the wildly improbable confluence of the big bang, of chemistry and the forces of physics, and of modern cosmology with the biblical story. British composer-conductor Jeremy Begbie gave wonderful multimedia performance-lectures on music as a metaphor for our wanderings and the hope of coming home. Students jammed into Os Guinness's powerful address "Truth in a World of Lies, Hype, and Spin" in Stanford's majestic chapel. Posters everywhere on campus read, "Care for a Guinness? Come to Veritas."

Local professors came out of the woodwork. Medical doctor John Dorman spoke and later wrote, "What a great experience! Walt Gerber, senior pastor at Menlo Park Presbyterian Church, said he thought it was the biggest gathering ever to happen at Stanford in relation to the gospel."[2]

Another speaker, author and former priest Brennan Manning, recalls in his book *Ruthless Trust* walking across campus toward the auditorium where he was to speak. A student walking near him said, "I like your voluminous, baggy jeans. For an old goat, you're cool, man."

With an in-your-face pretense of indignation he responded, "If you ain't cool, what's the point of going on? I mean, give me one good reason you should go slogging through the molasses of the dark, dreary, dismal world . . . if you're uncool in a cool world?"

The student said with alarm, "Geez, it ain't that bad, man. Why don't you go talk to the chaplain or something?"

Brennan laughed and revealed his identity as a chaplain of sorts speaking that night at Veritas—on the radical love of God. To his delight, the student came to the talk and hung out afterward to talk with Brennan. "The academic load is heavy here," the student said. "I used to have a vibrant prayer life in high school, but I've gotten so busy here with studies, fraternity life and wanting to fit in that I've grown careless in my relationship with God. I miss him."

The young man wiped away tears with a surreptitious gesture. "I want to feel his presence. Life in the fast lane keeps me so distracted that sometimes I wonder if I trust God at all. Then I get scared. But I keep doing the same stuff out of habit because I can't imagine any other alternative. I wish I were closer to God," he told Brennan.

The following morning a faculty member visited Brennan. "At one point in my life," she said, "I had a faith so strong that it shaped the very fiber of each day . . . even in stressful situations. The fire of Christ burned inside me. Slowly, and almost imperceptibly, I stopped sitting at the fireplace. The academic competition is fierce here, all-consuming."

With an expressive sigh she sank back in her chair. After a moment she continued, "After you spoke on the love of God last night, I cried for an hour. My life is so empty. I see so much pain and suffering both on and off campus, and sometimes I feel a deep resistance to a loving God. I still have faith—I know I do—but I can't feel it, I've lost any sense of God's presence. I long for the relationship I used to have."

Brennan pondered the conversations:

> Now look at this student and this faculty member and pretend that you are the God of love bodied forth in Jesus of Nazareth. The young man is sad because he misses you . . . and close to panic that he does not trust in your love anymore. The woman is in tears because she cannot feel your presence as she once did. Ambushed by academics, she fears that her faith is fading and that she has lost you, forever. Still supposing that you are God for a moment, what are your feelings towards these two? . . . Is your heart overflowing with compassion for their feelings of exile from you? Do you see their whole life as a prayer of longing? Will you sweep them up in your arms the moment they call to you?[3]

Precisely. Veritas is best seen in a Person whose nature is love. It is precisely this relentless-lover God of the Bible, father of the prodigal son, Jesus friend of sinners who we want to introduce to students and professors again. This is the One for whom their colleges were founded. The only sufficient Cause for our universe is the only sufficient hope for abundant life before and after death in a broken world.

10

Forgiving

Pain, the Color of Crimson

I knew I'd disappoint you, if I showed to you this child,

Who is crying out inside . . . lost in wild.

Now inches from the water,

About to disappear.

I feel you behind me,

But how did you find me,

Here?

DAVID WILCOX, "HOW DID YOU FIND ME HERE?"

I flew home after my month out west. Though Rob and I had been broken up for several months, I was still thinking about being faithful to both Veritas and Rob. I would continue to love both—at least to try. Approaching my house on Dana Street in Cambridge, I thought I saw Rob's car in the driveway. "Thank you, God," I whispered in excitement. "He's changed his mind."

It turned out that it was not my driveway but the driveway of my next-door neighbor and close friend. She had also been a friend of Rob's since college, almost like a sister. She'd joined some of our camping trips as a chaperone of sorts so we'd avoid compromising situations, honoring God and the meaning of marriage. She was energetic and fun. I loved them both. The three of us had been quite a pair.

So after seven years, and having been broken up for nearly a year, Rob had trouble getting our driveways straight and could not look me in the eye. That's when I decided to disappear to a remote pine cabin near the ocean on the North Shore of Boston, close to a seminary I was attending part time. The cabin was less than an hour from Cambridge but it was a safe place—and another world away—almost.

JOURNAL ENTRY

Lord, a life without him? And with a decade of sketches, photographs and future hopes? Memories of hikes high above a school of breaching whales off the coast of Maui. Sunrise on the cratered lava summit of Haleakala. Feeding hundreds with bread we kneaded. The long endurance of graduate school. Kayaking by fire and moonlight. Beginning Veritas. A million words and years working on Finding God at Harvard. The making of an elegant dining table upon which we'll not eat; the making of quilts under which we'll not sleep. Camping with friends on Mt. Washington and above Yosemite in squalls and snow and lightning. The islands off Vancouver. The magic of the Cape and its dunes and winds and pines. A thousand quiet kindnesses that made every place and time a diamond in the mountain of my memory.

By 1998 Veritas had a presence at more than forty major universities and involved more than a hundred thousand people. *Finding God at Harvard* was a *Boston Globe* bestseller and a Christian Booksellers Association Book of the Year. *Christianity Today* named me one of the "up-

and-coming" Christian leaders in America. And that same year I was in a cabin in the woods, barely breathing, feeling abandoned and wondering where God was.

I was still going into Cambridge each week to facilitate senior electives in film and in C. S. Lewis. I remember wondering whether Veritas was anything more than what I could see backwards through the beveled glass door as I exited the Harvard Faculty Club: satireV.

The satire felt like an ironic mockery of my own heart and mind. My own life.

Being a bear of small brain—and big heart, I suppose—I was still unclear whether I should show undying love or cut my losses and move on. I tried to begin dating a friend I respected, but Rob, who was very hospitable, befriended that fellow while I was traveling (strangely enough), and before long that new relationship ended as well. It was rather bewildering.

I ran from memories in Cambridge. I avoided him. But he began coming up to the North Shore with her to visit friends. One day he asked to meet me in the chapel of the seminary I was attending. In that chapel, he told me that he was going to marry her. That it was "God's will."

And so, after a decade in Cambridge, that cabin in the woods was where I began to enter into the pain of the world. A world in which even well-meaning and otherwise decent people can wound one another deeply.

I sensed more deeply the realities of human pride, injustice and horror in the world. I thought of the women and children on our mission trips whose husbands and fathers had been murdered. I felt the fact of children sold into prostitution. I imagined the deceit that inspired terrorists. And then I felt the brokenness of a friend whose wife had recently left him. Another friend, a Veritas planner, lost a son. A girlfriend had just died of cancer at age thirty-four.

I felt the unromantic realities of a planet out of order with hurricanes and earthquakes and famine, and I began to question more deeply the gospel's sufficiency for the problem of pain. I was feeling sorrow from the inside out. Veritas might hold water at any angle, I thought, but how about at any depth?

My empathy for others grew. What wonders we humans were to just keep going. It must be easier for a turnip or a chipmunk in the woodpile, but to have memory and fear and unfilled hope, and just keep going?

"Each heart knows its own sorrow," the writer of Proverbs tells us. A broken relationship, a lack of intimacy, an undistinguished career, financial stress. To live in a fallen world is to die a thousand deaths. I wondered for the first time if the spiritual life was an uphill battle worth fighting.

Lifelessness. Betrayal. Wasted time. Ashes. I remember reminding myself to breathe because it was no longer a natural inclination. I not only lost him—and my future, including the children I'd always imagined—but I retreated from my circle of close friends in Cambridge who were also in shock. I reeled, seeking answers. If God treats his friends like this, I wondered, how does he treat his enemies? Maybe it was all my fault. Or it was all Rob's fault. Surely someone would pay. Maybe it was the Fall. Worse yet, I considered, maybe it was no one's fault and life is just random chaos and ashes and thorns that pierce your heart. Maybe the cynics had it right. Get what you can while you can. Then you die.

The phone rang and it was Jerry Mercer, who had supported many Veritas Forums beyond Harvard with years of generosity and board leadership. Jerry called to say that he himself was hurting and needing to slow down, which we felt was wise given his altitude and speed for so long. And so Veritas no longer had a chairman or financial backing, though we had commitments to about fifteen universities that year.

With enough pocket change for gas and fast food, I'd still climb in the Lunch Box and visit schools on autopilot. Because of the stellar planners, and despite my confusion, Veritas Forums continued to gather many students around life's big questions. The same questions I was now skeptically asking.

Several Harvard undergrads came up to the cabin.[1] They offered to lead the Harvard Veritas Forum, sensing that their former leader had disappeared into the woods. When I next went into Cambridge, I asked several administrators if Harvard would allocate a few thousand dollars to cosponsor the upcoming Harvard forum so students and friends and I wouldn't have to continue to foot the bills. Since the university did have twenty-two billion dollars, including many unused endowments given for the gospel by now-deceased Christian alumni, it seemed like a fair question. I and others had been asking gently for seven years. Again no answers, no funding. But this time a divinity school administrator said, "Kelly, this is how officers of the university lose their positions. Do you really want to be asking?" Things were not going well.

I was having a hard time concentrating and felt drained of enthusiasm and hope. Before long doctors discovered that I'd been bitten by a deer tick carrying Lyme disease. The disease is a viral invasion whose mission in life is to attack the central nervous system. Symptoms included physical fatigue, mental fog and partial paralysis, which was bad enough, but they were expected to worsen over time.

Slowly, achingly, my questions of God were changing. If I talked to God at all, which was rare, my tone was shrill and bitter. "Do you know how dark it gets in a cabin in the woods? Do you know how cold the winter is, and how the handle of a woodstove can burn your skin at 420 degrees in the middle of the night? You, senior member of the Trinity's eternal community of perfect love, what do you know about being alone? How much beauty hurts, alone? That it begs to be shared? That skin aches when not touched by the one you love? That the soul is not designed to be rejected?"

This same year, my mother called to say that my stepfather, to whom I was an only daughter, was in the hospital with lung cancer. When the cancer worsened, I conjured up my residual strength, flew to Columbus and sat with him for ten days in the hospice as he lay dying. I read to him favorite stories from The Chronicles of Narnia, borrowing the brilliant faith of the books' author who knew grief but who suffered as one with hope. Rob's fiancée called the hospice to say, "I'm sorry." I responded, "Me too."

After my stepfather's funeral, I returned to the cabin, lifeless.

Life on that boundary of land and water began for me as an escape—from my exhaustion and sense of lost life. There I questioned with anguish my past choices and failures. I faced the fact of wasted time, having squandered various opportunities for marriage and children while waiting for Rob and in a small way trying to change the world. I questioned my frail faith in God's sovereignty, his love and his very presence in my life.

Stretches of beach and small islands served as sanctuaries for artists as well as piping plovers. In a vast expanse of estuary and ocean, summers were full of wildflowers, bumbling bees and tidal currents that challenged my sea-kayaking skills. During fiery autumns and frozen winters, hikes, books and the scent of wood smoke spoke to me, "Breathe and rest."

The Red Barn Run

I liked to go for runs in the snowy salt marsh at low tide. With worsening Lyme disease and heartbreak, the runs became occasional walks. One day the sunlight was getting away from me and I thought I'd catch the last of it. I put on some Gore-Tex and hiking boots and was off on what I remember as "the red barn run."

I had a routine for these outings: put some wood in the stove for heat that night, either bring or hug the dogs, go down through the woods, pass the neighbor's chicken barn, greet the sheep, skirt the big red barn, hike into the marsh to the tide's edge, and be back home in under an hour.

Tonight was different. A shining planet rose like a jewel beneath the crescent moon. Stars slowly emerged as members in the choir. Songbirds in their snowy pine trees became a timbered chorus of complex and lilting harmonies. The ocean tide slowly rose to the occasion. Earth and sky became the colors of bread and wine, flesh and blood. The setting sun turned the barn to orange and, later, to crimson.

Something about it seemed too good to be false.

I felt inklings of a symphony behind which might be a score and a conductor.

I sensed a story with a wooing Author. I felt something like Tolkien's enchanted vision, but the rightful owner of the one ring was the lord of light, not of darkness. The bearer of that ring to rule the spheres was some sort of wild and relentless lover, one who could find me anywhere.

Moon and tides danced together. Creatures changed shifts—some were off to sleep, others waking. It struck me that this, in fact, happened everywhere, every day, every year. We live on a life-giving planet, in a vast solar system that's just a small part of a vast and finely tuned universe. And we have minds and hearts that are free to reject or to receive the gift and the giver of it all—to join the dance, or to wait it out.

In that hour there was too much beauty to be comfortable, to pay the weak compliment of aesthetic pleasure. It all seemed orchestrated, conspicuous, too overtly fine-tuned for me to do anything but be still and silent. I felt it all as con-spir-acy—a breathing together—inviting me.

But I could not respond. What stopped and then sickened me that night beneath the starry host was the feeling that I could not participate. Except for me, all creation seemed to be joining in an exquisite cosmic chorus. The more I listened and watched, the more it seemed like worship. Yet I was on the outside, wanting in but standing against it in rebellion.

The beauty was too painful to bear alone. But I was the one who had chosen aloneness, the one who had run away after a great loss. The universe could sing and dance the night away for all I cared. My own story was flat and cold, the midwinter bleak and unending.

How could I enter back into God's presence with this enchanted symphony of the creation around me? How could I trust the One behind it all? The answer came unbidden and clear: I was to choose life, to join the dance, by forgiving. Only by doing so could I enter into the abundant reality I deeply desired.

I had been dismembered from life by my unwillingness to forgive. I was now invited to be remembered to life by choosing forgiveness.

Whether I bent my knees or my legs were broken for me, I don't know. I fell to the wet earth, forehead down in mud and snow, fighting nausea, trying to breathe. I was my own inquisitor. In what story had I been living? Was it the story of life in the garden before the Fall, or after? Was it a story that accepted, even expected, the epic movements of creation, fall and redemption? Was it a story with time-depth and future hope, or was I stuck in the too-small cell of self and moment?

I began by asking for mercy for myself, and even for the gift to see my own need of mercy. I began to forgive a person, two people, who'd inflicted my heart with a primal wound. I even felt the desire to forgive God for allowing it.

Bitterness is like saltwater at high tide, forcing us to shrink back, to retreat into safe places and sorrow, but someone changed the tides in me that evening on the ocean. He welcomed me back in. I rose and slowly began to rejoin that symphony of worship, of gratitude, of life.

When his light and love floods us, it shifts the boundaries of our being. Our hearts are enlarged. Our minds begin to heal. I was grafted back into the tree of life, brought back to the land of the living.

Sometimes, when the sun sinks low enough, when the glow of crimson captures my attention, I behold its light, its glory, if you will— its face.

On the hike out to the tide that night, I saw the world in the warm light of the sun setting behind me. On the way home, I saw the sun itself.

Before entering the dark woods and then the warm cabin, soggy and content, I looked back across that sanctuary. And the red barn was lit from within.

11

Knowing and Believing

True North

The elegant mathematical forms encoded in nature, the nineteen universal constants that are exactly what they must be, and the multitude of initial conditions argue persuasively for a universe that has been carefully crafted for our benefit. . . .

God purposely gave us strong evidence to "know he exists" from what we see in creation. Therefore, we shouldn't go on ignoring the implications of this evidence and what it means. This Creator has a purpose for our lives and has revealed himself to us so we might have a relationship with him.

WALTER BRADLEY,
THE VERITAS FORUM AT PRINCETON

Nothing I feel is outside the reach of your arms.

JILL PHILLIPS, "GRAND DESIGN"

The Word became flesh and lived among us . . . full of grace and truth.

JOHN 1:14

I was now able to breathe again, and to rest. Slowly I began to think as well. I began to ask myself, *how can I know anything? What do I believe? What lasts? What matters and why?*

Life had humbled me, and I figured humility was the best place from which to discover if anything was knowable or real. I tried to give every possibility a chance. Everything was to be opened up and reconsidered. I was asking old questions more deeply. I tried to imagine anything better or truer than the gospel. Veritas is for Christians too.

How do we know what's real? What should we be for? What's the best compass to guide us? Coolness? Prestige? Wealth? Sex? Past hurt and lost expectations? Or is there something unchanging outside ourselves to help us?

If there was some higher truth, I wondered, was it even knowable? Knowledge of the real story at times doesn't seem possible. The world tells us that we have many small and often wonderful personal stories, but no large story, no grand narrative to which we all belong. No deeply connecting truth, only our own separate and subjective truths and spiritualities. No epic, only myths. No Creator-Lover God who spoke and got messy in our world, only our own authority.

Without a transcendent truth breaking into our world and revealing reality, we're left to our own imaginings, despair and power games. The power brokers thrive in a world without truth, for they invent their own, and few have the moral verve to stop them. A world without truth is a recipe for disaster—our small personal truths simply don't cooperate. Hitler's truth was not the Jews' truth. The suicide bomber's truth is not his victims' truth. Your neighbor's truth may not be your truth. Rob's truth was not mine.

Our current postmodern culture is a condition of being against, rather than for. But what can we be for? And why?

I wanted to find a better way of being in and belonging to reality. It was time to shift into a higher gear. Things were different now. I cared more deeply about truth. I needed it. I used to ask academic questions out of curiosity. I now needed to be transformed, not just informed. I needed hope. I needed to reenter the living. I was asking myself to do what I'd requested of others in Veritas Forums: to be open, to seek rather than be cynical, to consider belief, to keep growing.

So how was I to discover the real story? How would I know true life from false? I began to journal and systematically think, feel and talk it through. I thought again about the question of knowing. In the original Greek, the meaning of *philosophy* is the act of loving wisdom. And

JOURNAL ENTRY

Materialism/naturalism: An insufficient explanation of mind, memory, conscience, imagination, the "moment" before the big bang.

Secular humanism: Its own religion (a faith-held commitment) pretending to be objective, and a social construct with a weaker basis for human value than Christianity. Sees no need for redemption, which is ironic and self-defeating given the broken lives of humanists in Cambridge alone.

Consumerism. Very American, but not very human. Plugged into the media matrix. But we are created to think, to create. To be free. To have spirits as well as appetites.

Eastern mysticism: Denies suffering—which is easy to do until you suffer. Pain isn't an illusion. I have no scientific evidence for reincarnation and cycles of self-atonement (karma). The evidence points to a real world, and I'm in it.

Relativism: Can be relativized ad nauseam. Every deconstructionist will be deconstructed. Even the slogan "there is no truth" is itself a truth claim.

There must be a truth, as C. S. Lewis said, against whose face all questions will die away.

central to philosophy is the question, how do we know anything at all?

In the cabin I was surrounded by books. Kim, the cabin's owner, had offered me anything in his "representative library" of the world's literature, so I read many books. After several months of biographies and philosophical and scientific texts, I came to sense, again, the insufficiency of the world's ways of reasoning apart from a transcendent word and authority.

Logically it seemed that the world's philosophies offered no convincing answers or solutions apart from the mercy of a loving God who redeems those incapable of redeeming themselves. But if a merciful God were real, why would life so disappoint us and seem so cruel? I wondered, *Kelly, on this side of complexity, in your pain, do you believe God is there and loves you?* I needed to know if the gospel was in fact true—for me.

I realized that in my wounded condition (but even in my best condition), I could perceive only imperfectly, incompletely, and that I could know truth only if truth made itself known. If God spoke my language. If he condescended. I saw beauty in "nature," but that same nature could wash us out to sea, sting us with poison, and care less.

I learned to sea-kayak off the coast and between the islands near the cabin. I occasionally got carried off course by strong currents or disoriented in the fog. I learned the benefit of having a friend with me who knew the coves and the ocean, who knew how to navigate in relation to true north. If you ask a sailor or a pilot about navigation, they'll look for a fixed point of reference.

What in the world is not mediated by humans but is immediate, unchanging and clear? How is it possible that a finite person can know the infinite? I could think of only one way: the infinite would have to be self-revealing; the Author of our play would have to show up, come to us and speak our language. Anyone from outside our world, like a Creator, would have to reveal his mind and heart.

So where did the evidence lead? Had anything or anyone beyond us ever made himself known? Had anyone with actual authority over time, space, matter and energy ever broken into our world? Ever spoken or shown his hand or face? Who witnessed it? Could we believe those reports? How?

From what I could observe, three realities answered those questions and seemed unique in all of history, compelling, confluent and deeply true to life: one, the fact of the universe itself; two, a book unlike any other; and three, a person eyewitnesses sensed was, in fact, God in the flesh.

Each of these three realities is said to be a "word" of God—his coherent mind and plan at work undergirding and guiding the universe.[1] Each word is testable as either false or true. I realized that no serious scholar had disproved any of these words.

In my fog of confusion, I listened and reconsidered the presence and harmonies of three powerful realities—these three words unlike any other words.

The First Word: Creation

Though painful at first, I allowed myself to remember a recent event in Cambridge. The night was perfect for a spring dance. In formal attire (we clean up once in a while) a group of friends went to the Dudley House Ball and waltzed the evening away. Afterward, we closed down the Gato Rojo café with coffee and jazz. Saying goodnight, almost good morning, someone commented on the clarity of the starlit sky. Aaron, a doctoral student in astronomy, responded, "The night is still young; follow me."

We exited the Yard through the north gate and entered a nearby courtyard. Aaron had a key to a building. He motioned for us to wait quietly at a distance as he showed ID to a groggy security guard. He then snuck us through the door and down a dark passageway. We piled into an elevator, giggling like teenagers playing hide-and-seek.

We rode to the top and entered a dark, musty chamber. Aaron began to pull cranks and levers. The ambiance was Frankenstinian, and then, above us, the roof rolled back to reveal a glorious galaxy of stars. We had just snuck into the old Oxford Street observatory. Kicking off our heels, the guys loosening their bow ties, we climbed up a ladder and onto the roof for a panoramic view of the Milky Way.[2]

We each waited impatiently for our turn to climb into a wooden chair attached to the telescope. Through the eyepiece and huge lens, our moon's craters appeared close enough to touch. We found Saturn, marveling over its stunning rings and storm clouds that looked like stripes. We saw the spiral storms of Jupiter, its red spot and its moons. We found Polaris, the North Star.

Slap-happy and sleep-deprived, we sounded like six-year-olds. "It's my turn," I said in the dark. Someone dropped a hint: "I want one of these for my birthday."

A growing wonder took us beyond observation to enjoyment and gratitude. For late-night conversation starters, nothing tops staring into the night sky with bright, inquisitive friends. We asked ourselves if we could really know truth by observing the actual world—what simply is.

Galaxies far, far away. Nebulae, supernova, planets and meteor trails. Why do the planets orbit with the "harmony of the spheres"? Are we a unique miracle or are we an accident, wandering aimlessly through a vast space on a really lucky planet that just happens to sustain life? How and why are we here at all? What's going on?

Thanks to technology, in the past few decades scientists have made observations that have afforded an unprecedented understanding of the universe's origin and complexity. Carl Sagan in his 1980s PBS series *Cosmos* spoke for the science community when he stated that "the universe is all there is, was or ever will be." His speculations of a universe without a beginning influenced millions. But cosmology has since accepted the evidence that the universe did have a beginning, ex nihilo, out of nothing. Sagan would have been more scientifically accurate if he'd simply read the first verse of Genesis: "In the beginning God created the heavens and the earth."

"So what," I asked my friends on the roof, "do we make of a universe with a billion billion stars?"

"To look further out in space is to look farther back in time," explained a physics grad student.

"How so?"

"Because we know now that space, stars, whole galaxies are rapidly expanding outward, and we just learned that the speed of the expansion is accelerating," he said with the excitement of a frontier explorer.

"Calculate backwards, rewind the clock, suck it all back in, and you learn about the universe's beginning—its 'big bang.'"

I shared with the group a favorite cartoon quip. "A physicist, with $E = MC^2$ scribbled across the chalkboard behind him, says to his students, 'Now, class, *time* is what keeps everything from happening all at once.'"

The physicist added, "The discovery of background radiation affirmed the big bang hypothesis, the creation event described at the beginning of the Bible."

"The Bible?" someone asked.

"Yep. It's the only origin text in the world that matches what we can now see—a beginning that implies a Beginner. Someone who, out of nothing we can detect, apparently, willed the universe into existence."

"Looks like random luck to me," someone said tongue-in-cheek, gazing skyward.

A new friend added, "It could be luck. With enough chances over time, the right energy and matter, you've got a universe, or several universes."

An M.I.T. student replied, "The only problem with that theory is that there was no time, energy, matter or space before the big bang. It's all a consequence, not a cause. The first cause had to be immaterial, omnipotent and genius."

Like a will, perhaps a word, of the Creator. There was a pause in the conversation. Everyone looked up at the sky as if for the first time. A medical student broke into a witty song by David Wilcox. "Back in science class, through the looking glass, we were magnifying little ancestors of our ancient past," she sang.

We joined in with enthusiasm. "Watch 'em break a couple chromosomes, wait a zillion years or so, and get an ostrich, a jellyfish, a kangaroo and a Romeo."

Together we sang, laughing and swing-dancing in the observatory and on the roof to the chorus. "It was a big mistake, to have eyes that see, to have love like this, inside of me. To have lips that smile, as I sing your kiss, to have minds that will forever, every part of this. All the moonlight shrouded in the clouds above and the autumn leaves and the falling love; the still reflection in the moonlit lake, all they said, it was a big mistake, it was a big mistake."[3]

Given new scientific discoveries we were amazed that so many students and teachers clung to what technology analyst George Gilder called a "19th-century materialist myth." We began to sense the wonder of even one human being. Each human cell (of our trillions) is not a simple lump of protoplasm but rather a complex processor of information (at a gigahertz pace), "comprising tens of thousands of proteins arranged in fabulously intricate algorithms of communication and synthesis," Gilder continued.[4]

We didn't have enough blind faith to believe that DNA wrote itself by dumb luck. Rather, Someone wrote the code.

And so we understood why Professor Henry "Fritz" Schaeffer, nominee for the Nobel Prize in chemistry, explains in Veritas Forums at Rice, Yale and Harvard how new discoveries in chemistry and physics reveal the brilliance, glory and love of God.

In the months and years to come, we blew through intellectual barriers and moved on to wonder and awe. Our gatherings often ended with singing, laughter and worship. We were excited to be alive and to know the one who made us. We didn't just think and talk, we also rejoiced.

I also remembered the "Veritas Institute" for professors, kids and friends. Every few years, several hundred new and old friends headed to Michigan and a cove on Lake Huron called Cedar Campus.[5] I'd drive with my best friend from Ohio, Susan, and her nine kids. We'd first catch up on sleep. Then we'd kayak or hike to Narnia, a cove with mossy green trails and limestone caves. We sailed on the camp's J-22, the Dawn Treader, between islands. A delightful seventy-year-old physicist named George Lebo and I took on college kids in Ultimate Frisbee on the beach. Miraculously victorious, George and I jumped into Lake Huron chanting, *In discus, veritas!*

Eventually the fog in our minds cleared with the energy of new friendships and fresh inspiration. We held Bible studies on loving God with our minds, hearts and hands; workshops on excellence in scholarship and loving students holistically; and creation tours with scientists Walter Bradley and Steve Simmons. After dinner a doctoral student in math played a bowed psaltry, which was much like a dulcimer but from the zither family. After dusk, some of us hiked deeper into the woods and howled for wolves. No doubt the wolves were amused. Only later in the week did they resound, after we gave up trying.

On the evening of July Fourth, a pickup full of us bounced to the nearest town in hopes of finding fireworks—to no avail. Mildly disappointed, we bounced back home and, as usual, headed for the hot sauna on the lakeshore. When we couldn't take the heat any longer, we'd dash out of the sauna and into frigid Lake Huron. When we were sufficiently frozen in the water, we'd run back into the sauna, then back into the lake, and so on until we were as relaxed as invertebrates. After our last dash into the lake, we came up for air and found the sky aflame with shimmering gold and crimson raining down on us. It was my first experience of the Aurora Borealis, or Northern Lights. In that breathtaking moment, that immersion into God's first word—creation—it was as if he said to us, "You want fireworks? I'll give you fireworks."

He was also saying, "Don't just think—rejoice! Swim beneath the stars like children. Be buoyed by the water. Rest in me. Join the dance of creation and re-creation." We were held by truth.

As I relived these memories in the cabin, I began to remember what was truly good in my past. But I also wondered what I should make of this world with its inexhaustible wonder as well as its undeniable, inescapable suffering?

I was coming to see that the story was larger than my imagination. The same Creator behind time, energy, matter and life was the always-present Creator and re-creator of human beings. This active presence of a Creator in my life meant that although my questions began with "Whodunnit, when and how?" my heart's questions ended in, "Do you love me?" "Are you here for me now?" and "I'm sorry; please help me."

Perhaps, I thought, we care less that we're *designed* and more that we're *desired*. We want a place, and a knowing Person, to whom we belong forever. We want him to tell us who we are. And so it is that the very words the Creator speaks to us in his second (written) word are the words we've longed since childhood to hear and to believe: "I have loved you with an everlasting love" (Jeremiah 31:3). "You are precious and honored in my sight, and I love you" (Isaiah 43:4). But now I heard these words with reasons to believe, and to live for, the One who spoke them.

The Second Word: The Bible

If God could create a universe, it would follow that he could also manage to write and distribute a book. He could even care for its translation into many languages and cultures. Unique among sacred texts and origin stories, the Bible emerges as God's Word in print like a treasure map, preserved over millennia yet always fresh. It is open to investigation, inviting the reader to test it by experience as false or true, leading to death or life. It is not a book of human mythology or vague spirituality but of power for real and abundant life.

At a Veritas Forum at Hope College, education professor Mary Poplin said, "After years of secular philosophies like constructivism and radical feminism, and after years of New Age ideas, I began to write the New Testament out by hand, word for word. As I did, I felt my mind begin to heal. I felt clean, and I was healed."

This Word is a hitchhiker's guide to the whole cosmos—especially life on one amazing blue planet. Its Author refines our vision of himself and ourselves. Not only does he reveal himself as the maker of the heavens and earth, but even more so as the lover of our souls.

In all the literature I'd read, it was the Bible that described with piercing precision my human heart, my angst and the pathos of the human condition. "Where can I run from your Spirit?" I asked along with David in the Psalms. Jesus taught his disciples to pray, "Forgive us our debts as we also have forgiven our debtors" (Matthew 6:12)—he knew my secret desire to condemn. He knew I could not forgive on my own strength. The Author knew I needed more than an abstract veritas, I needed a human one, living with and in me. "The Lord is close to the brokenhearted and saves those who are crushed in spirit" (Psalm 34:18).

Though the Bible is calming and lovely, I knew it was not primarily a book of poetry and literature but a book claiming to be the real story in which we live, asking the reader to taste and see that the Lord is good, offering to prove itself true. And so it is full of verifiable information, useful to every person as well as to archaeologists, historians, scientists, healers, artists, lovers, parents and so on. If it is false, we can find out and go on to something else. But if it is true, we have sufficient basis for wise choices and for hope in this world.

At the University of Michigan Veritas Forum, astrophysicist Hugh Ross had explained that he was a precocious kid who became a skeptical scientist. He used the facts of history and science to test each of the world's "holy books." To his surprise, he found the Bible noticeably different—simple, direct and specific.

"Not only did its author correctly describe the major events in the creation of life on earth," said Dr. Ross, "but he placed those events in the scientifically correct order and properly identified the earth's initial conditions. Not only in Genesis but also in Isaiah and the Psalms I found accurate descriptions of how the universe is continually expanding, of its beginning in space and time, how it is getting older and colder—concepts scientists didn't begin to comprehend until the twentieth century."

He continued, "I determined there were over three hundred statements in the Bible with no contradictions. As a scientist, I had to figure the probability of such accuracy; it was less than one in ten to the three hundredth power. Why such accuracy? Because the Bible and the universe have the same Creator."

Like Hugh, I was finding reasons to believe that both the Author and the story were good, even when things were dark in the moment. That he was our light on the journey.

Often while flying or driving through the night to a university, I'd trade my yellow earplugs for portable CD headphones and sing along with Amy Grant, "Thy Word is a lamp unto my feet and a light unto my path." Hiking in the Incan ruins of Machu Picchu in Peru I sang along with John Michael Talbot on my Walkman: "The Word is living, the Word is life. The Word delights my soul, preserves my mind."

On our summer trip to the Amazon jungle where we built schools for kids with polio, we flew with a missionary pilot into a Brazilian base camp of linguists and missionaries. There in the lush forest we ap-

proached the small camp. Before long we were greeted by two beautiful American women in their seventies, clear-eyed and strong, who
had been living among native Incan tribes—for forty years. Their
hands were weathered and worn. Though they and the other missionaries were helpful in many ways, the Amazonian tribes wanted them
to stay for one specific reason—to finish translating the New Testament into their native languages. The tribal leaders wanted to learn, in
their own symbols, God's second Word to us—the Bible.

The flight home to our base camp was thick with clouds and turbu-
lence. After an hour in the single-engine Cessna pounding like a tin
can through the massive storm front, friends and I were wishing for an
"eject" button. I was turning green. Jeff pulled out the pocket Bible
that he carried next to his switchblade, compass and water bottle. He
began to read, in our own native language, from Isaiah.

Do you not know?
    Have you not heard?
    The LORD is the everlasting God,
    the Creator of the ends of the earth.
    He will not grow tired or weary. . . .
Even youths grow tired and weary,
    and young men stumble and fall;
but those who hope in the LORD
    will renew their strength.
    They will soar on wings like eagles. (Isaiah 40:28-31)

The Bible is about real life and how to connect to God in the thick
of our real world. The writers, guided by God's spirit, faithfully and
carefully recorded the deeds, lessons, prayers and prophecies of God
and of his people. They recorded the progress of history as God's story.
They offered future generations a faithful guide for living life.

I found the "ring of truth" in the Bible at various levels: its con-
sistency with modern scientific discovery, the journalistic details
and integrity of the text, the surprising fidelity of the transmission
of the Bible over time, the unique coherence of its many books
though written by forty people in three languages on three conti-

nents over fifteen hundred years, the clear fulfillment of many specific prophecies, and, finally, the sense that the text is true to our human nature and desires for love, mercy, connection, meaning and glory.

In its diversity we discover unity, coherence and truthfulness. In its pages we find three-dimensional people like ourselves with wavering faith, mixed motives, pride, jealousy, humility and regret. The stories are gritty, honest, surprisingly unedited and filled with real-life detail. It's full of the stuff we're full of.

Examined for lifetimes by countless scholars. Cherished by children. Presented as hope to the dying. We read it, study it, marvel at its layers of depth, coherence and wisdom. On a good day we'll even do what the Author says.

In reading the Bible, one senses not only God's plan to redeem all creation but also his active love and presence in our living. In times of exhaustion, heartache and confusion, it's the place to turn.

I came to love this Word of God like I love treasure hunts, like I love opening a love letter. It is a story worth living in. And a Word that is alive.

More than anything, I love the Bible because it tells me about the heart of God himself, seen most clearly in his third word, his living word—the person of Jesus.

The Third Word: Jesus

I remembered another Harvard mission trip, this one to inner-city Atlanta. We met a woman named Mrs. Rodero who opened her home to kids as a safe place in an otherwise rough neighborhood.[6] We were repairing and painting the outside of her home. In the morning, a nine year-old boy I'll call Pablo came up to me and asked if he could paint too. "Sure," I said. I gave him a brush and we worked side by side and talked. After four hours in the heat, a lunch break, paintbrush wars and a water fight, I got up the courage to gently ask him a question. When he had unbuttoned his shirt in the heat, I noticed a perfectly vertical two-inch scar on his chest over his heart.

I asked him, "Hey, Pablo, how'd you get that scar?"

JOURNAL ENTRY

Fighting back tears my mind was reeling. What a graphic picture of human sin. Ugliness and brokenness internalized. One person's sin sets in motion a chain of destruction. Even self-destruction. God hates sin precisely because God loves us, God is for life. I saw how sin must break the heart of God.

Yet in a strange twist, didn't God do just this—bleed because of our brokenness? Didn't he take sin out on himself by becoming flesh and blood and allowing himself to be cut, pierced, slain? The only one without sin "became sin" that we could be free of sin before God. How was Pablo's sacrifice different? God has the power to forgive sins. Pablo does not. But is the impulse the same—to bleed for those you love?

He lowered his head and said softly, "I cut myself."

"How come?" I asked.

"I was mad."

"At who?"

"My father," he said, "for beating my mama."

"Oh," I said. "I'm really sorry."

Pablo could have hurt his father or joined a gang and hurt others, but—not to excuse any kind of violence, even self-inflicted—he didn't because love takes the hit. Precisely why Mel Gibson's film *The Passion of the Christ* had to be violent. The cross of Jesus Christ is God taking all our violence on himself. He is sacrificed. We are ransomed.

Something exists at the core of evil that requires judgment and atonement—someone must pay the price. Evil and atonement are messy and deep, true to the way life is. Without mercy, the cycles of vengeance and bitterness go on unbroken. Fortunately, something exists in the heart of love that chooses to suffer on behalf of another. Ask any good parent. Ask any true lover.

Most religions reach for God. Only one God reaches for us. Some religions sacrifice others for their idea of God. Only the God of the Bible sacrifices himself for us.

The Cross

The cross of Jesus is deepest at the heart of life. The cross is integral, radical, crucial as blood. Jesus set his face toward Jerusalem, toward the cross. "The Son of Man was born to die," he told his friends. Jesus would obey his Father's will—he would choose to become the lamb of God sacrificed to take away the sins of the world. The Son of Man would take our sin on himself that we might become sons and daughters of God. In our place of guilt and brokenness, Jesus substituted himself. The deeper magic, and ancient prophecy of Genesis 3, was fulfilled—from the seed of Eve one came to crush the serpent's skull.

The blood of Christ—that is, the mercy of God—is the only way by which we can be restored to an intimate, innocent relationship with God the Father and thereby to others in human community.

God the Father so desires us that he provides a way back to himself. The gift is priceless to God—unutterably precious—his only begotten Son, Jesus Christ. As the old gospel song puts it, "What can wash away my sin? Nothing but the blood of Jesus. What can make me whole again? Nothing but the blood of Jesus."

What is required of me? The humility to know that I can't stand before a holy God on my own merit, no matter what my test scores, pedigree and resume. Without Christ I don't make the cut. So I say, "I'm sorry, help, please—Lord," and follow where he leads.

What do we receive? We receive forgiveness, love and God's Spirit.[7]
That sets us on a lifelong adventure of a renewed heart, mind, eyes and
art of living. Our culture is open to vague spirituality, but Jesus offers
us the Holy Spirit who reconnects us to God himself.

At the cross the epic battle between God's glory and the one who
wanted to usurp God's glory for himself came face to face. At the cross
Satan thought he had defeated Jesus—but Satan was foiled. Jesus
chose the cross not as victim but as Victor, trusting that God the Father
would raise him from the dead, fulfilling the prophecies of his death
and resurrection.

And so it came—the day that not only changed the world but that
changes lives one at a time. The day of new birth. God the Father vin-
dicated Jesus by raising him from the dead. Neither the Roman guards
nor the Jewish authorities could explain it. More than five hundred
people on thirteen occasions saw him in the days and weeks after his
brutal public death. Their testimonies could not be suppressed. At a
multicultural gathering during the festival of Pentecost, God's people
gathered from every tribe and tongue. God's Word was now written in
human hearts. The rich and poor shared all things in common as each
one had need. The Holy Spirit was given and the church was born.

In Atlanta, I saw Pablo come alive around adults, particularly men
he could trust. The church became his new friends and larger family.
So it is for all of us.

In Cambridge we were learning that Jesus is not only Savior but also
the master, the expert, in living. He is brilliant, vivacious and utterly
competent. Wise apprentices logically follow him.

Jesus demonstrated physical and psychological healing, including
the relationship between forgiveness, prayer and healing. He taught a
culture how to value children and women. He understood agriculture
and the natural world, ethics and human relations. He taught how a
life of gratitude yields the fruit of health, joy and purposefulness. He
taught about the gift of a body, that we don't belong to ourselves but
to God himself and that our bodies are temples of his Spirit. He was a
skilled carpenter. And he even taught Peter a few things about fishing.

He also lived with authority. He didn't teach chemistry; he turned water into wine. He didn't teach weather patterns; he calmed a storm. He didn't teach medicine; he healed hurting people and instructed his followers to heal in his name. He didn't teach moral philosophy; he forgave and enabled us to forgive. He didn't teach a course on world hunger; he fed the multitudes and commanded his followers to feed them also.

Jesus fired on all pistons. He had it goin' on. If he was meek and humble, laying down his rights, should I not do the same?

I love the vivid personality of Jesus—his laughter, his tears, his courage. How he saved the woman about to be stoned to death. How he saw people who were hiding or ashamed. How he healed and reached the woman who was bleeding and unclean. I love his tenderness to the outcast—the least, the last and the lost. I love his pure embrace of men, of women, of children. His humility to empty himself of power and self-defense, his confidence in God's love even while dying on the cross. I'm grateful for his eyewitness knowledge of the Father and his promise to prepare a place for us with him in heaven forever.

During Dallas Willard's talk "The University and the Brilliance of Jesus" with professors and graduate students at the Ohio State University faculty club, a humanities professor said, "I'm confused. You, one of the world's prominent philosophers, believe in Jesus Christ as the hope of the world?"

To which Dallas gently responded, "Who else did you have in mind?"

The professor was silent.

In his light we see Harvard's first light. What is veritas? Veritas is a Person. The Healer. The Lover who empowers us to love—the Life-Giver. How do we know? He has spoken and shown his face in three words:

Creation. God speaks the universe into being and reveals himself.

Scripture. God puts his Word in print—a unique book, a treasure map.

Jesus. The Word becomes flesh and lives among us, loves, dies and lives again, filling his children with the same indestructible life.

And so I came to believe that truth was knowable, not because I was

smart or virtuous or strong, but because the Creator of reality is loving
enough to reveal himself to me. He speaks not only through the brokenness and insufficiency of the world but also more clearly through
the wonders of Creation, his written Word and his living Word, Jesus
Christ. All questions lead back to him. Life coheres in this rich understanding of reality. He is good. He is at heart lovely and a Lover.

I entered into veritas by trusting God, again—this time letting his
words dwell in me more richly. By believing that God means to call us
his beloved. By entering what Veritas speaker, historian and theologian
N. T. Wright calls "a freshly storied world."

It's life-giving to get the real story straight. To breathe the best oxygen, to be planted in the richest soil. I'd been given a clear basis for
knowledge, for hope and for confident action in the world God loves.
He did for me what he does for all of us as a lifelong, dynamic journey.
We need to be awake for it and pay attention.

My pain had been a gift. In some forests, certain seeds break open
and germinate only in the heat of a forest fire. Pride, self-reliance, control and bitterness had been my shell. A crisis forced me to open and
fall into a deeper place of trusting in God's love. As Madeleine L'Engle
had told me, the Word of God is like seed upon our heart; only when
our hearts break can that seed fall inside.

12

Healing and Friendship

True Vine, New Wine

Run off to meet Jesus. Tell him the problem. Ask him why he didn't come sooner, why he allowed that awful thing to happen. And then be prepared for a surprising response. . . . Jesus will meet your problem with some new part of God's future that can and will burst into your present time, into the mess and grief, with good news, with hope, with new possibilities. And the key to it all, now as then, is faith. Jesus is bringing God's new world to birth.

N. T. WRIGHT, THE VERITAS FORUM AT YALE

I consider that our present sufferings are not worth comparing with the glory that will be revealed in us.

ROMANS 8:18

Love is patient, love is kind. It does not envy, it does not boast, it is not proud. It is not rude, it is not self-seeking, it is not easily angered, it keeps no record of wrongs.

1 CORINTHIANS 13:4-5

For me, there was another word, another clear evidence of God's truth—the Spirit of Jesus in the lives of those who love him. This word is seen in human hearts, in flesh and blood. I hurt because I'd lost something good. But the good still lived in my community of believers.

Forgiveness allowed me to reenter many Cambridge friendships. The reentry yielded a process of healing that reconnected me to my calling to restore a conversation of true life in university communities. Without that healing, I don't know what would have become of me other than a life of disillusioned reclusiveness in a lonely cabin.

Some friends came to the cabin to visit the beach, ride horses or just talk. One was Steph Powers, who worked with AIDS and nutrition research in Boston and then Africa. Her laughter alone was life-giving. Others were Eric Convey, the "Christopher Robin" of our hundred-acre woods, and Carole McMillen, an artist.

Another friend was Brenda, a brilliant doctoral student doing cancer research, and who often led times of worship with Jeff and the Grad School Christian Fellowship. We'd talk for hours, and at night she'd sing at my piano in the firelight. Her beautiful voice and the words of Scripture were healing to my soul. I absorbed her faith and friendship like a dark hole absorbing light. I'd watch the sparks rise from the wood-burning stove and mingle with snowflakes and stars just as Brenda's singing merged with God's promises and healing Spirit.

Sharing Sorrows and Borrowing Faith

I was discovering that the people I'd asked to speak at Veritas Forums had also suffered. Our conversations became more real.

I was challenged by the faith of a Harvard law school professor, William Stuntz. Before four hundred students in the Harvard Science Center, he maneuvered his wheelchair to the microphone. Once an athlete, he shared his journey with spinal injury and chronic pain. He ended his talk by expressing gratitude for pain because it drew him nearer to God.

Every few summers a wonderful conference called the C. S. Lewis Institute takes place in Oxford and Cambridge, England. Many of the speakers are also Veritas presenters and planners and we all enjoyed time together. At this conference, however, I was in my mental bog, a big mush really, not only from heartbreak but also from Lyme disease. After dinner in a charming rural pub called the Trout, I walked with Dallas Willard and Kirstin Jeffries Johnson a few miles back to Oxford.

Dallas told me that relationships change but they don't vanish. With God, we have eternity to work things out, so we trust him for what we cannot yet understand.

Dallas shared a bit about his own life, especially the loss of his mother when he was a little boy. Carrying a shovel and a pickaxe across the Corn Belt, he had walked from farm to farm seeking work, and over time he saw the Lord gradually unfold the blessings of a stepmother, and later a wife, and a love of truth and God himself.

As we walked by the Thames river, Kirstin, a vibrant theology and arts student who lives with rheumatoid arthritis, recited the conversation between Jill and Aslan in C. S. Lewis's *Silver Chair*.

"Are you thirsty?" said the Lion.
"I'm dying of thirst," said Jill.
"Then drink." said the Lion. "There is no other stream."

I saw the loveliness of Jesus in the eyes of both Dallas and Kirstin as we walked and I managed to recall some favorite lines of poetry by Gerard Manley Hopkins:

As kingfishers catch fire, dragonflies draw flame.
For Christ plays in ten thousand places,
Lovely in limbs, and lovely in eyes not his
To the Father through the features of men's faces.

Also in Oxford, novelist David Aikman shared with me that God knows our mistakes in advance and that he allows them because he uses them for our growth and for his kingdom. He delivers us from prison to praise.

Wonderful friends Martha and Dellynne included me in dances, concerts and "punting" on the river Cam. Punting involves pushing a flat-bottomed boat along the water with a pole. We formed a flotilla of three boats, more often bumping into oncoming boats than staying in a straight line. Together we watched Dane, who was pushing our flotilla, "stay with the pole" rather than our boats when his pole stuck in the river bottom. In his eyes we saw a moment of panic and then laughter as he and the pole plunged into the river. I began to remember that life could include laughter and even delight. I was beginning to feel once again.

Back in Boston, friends came to the cabin and I experienced the kindness of strangers who became friends.[1] I was touched that my father and brothers called to encourage me to trust God, and my mother visited. Vera Shaw was my constant prayer companion, whether I called her or not. It was a surreal season of feeling alone and yet loved and prayed for by many. It was a time of breaking my idolization of one person and Eve's curse in defining myself in relation to that one almost-husband rather than the true bridegroom who came to reverse that curse—the better Adam who did not blame his bride but died for her.

After several months, I attended a church near the cabin. When I went forward to receive the wine and bread I saw, across the altar, a woman I'd admired since reading her books in college—Elisabeth Elliot Gren. Her first husband, Jim Elliot, was murdered by Auca Indians four decades ago when they were missionaries in Ecuador. Elisabeth had suddenly found herself alone with her infant daughter in the Andean jungle. Her advice to anyone suffering? Abide in Christ, and "do the next thing." Through her witness, the men who killed her husband came to faith in Christ. At that altar we sang, "Heart of my own heart, whatever befall, still be my vision, O ruler of all."

We need one another, especially the wisdom of those who have suffered with hope, whose faith emerges true at the far side of complexity. That gospel is the hope of the world.

I came to sense God's will as a deeper magic beneath the surface of my mistakes and idolatry.

God was asking me to live forwardly, to be reestablished in love. The God who calls himself "I Am" rebirthed in me a childlike love of beauty and a desire to live again in present-tense promises. I sensed him asking me to take him at his word, to believe in his sovereignty and power beyond my own mistakes. I began to believe like a farmer lives—sowing, nurturing, resting and working. I asked for myself what Paul asked for all believers: "I pray that out of his glorious riches he may strengthen you with power through his Spirit in your inner being, so that Christ may dwell in your hearts through faith" (Ephesians 3:16-17).

JOURNAL ENTRY

Wellspring of living water. Sky of oxygen. New blood. True Vine. Best wine.

What a gift to be on a farm. Given hands and legs to work, given imagination, vision, eyes in the front of my head. So, cast off every dead branch. Take the trash to Golgotha. Recycle what I can. Trust. Fall forward. Walk.

Cut the lesser vines in which I am entangled. "These are not my heart. You are."

I finally see something about a healthy mind and life, and a way to live in a world where people go away, both by choice and by death—a world in which hearts are broken. A world where photographs are painful or perishable, flowers wither, pianos lose their tuning, skin ages, appointments disappoint. Things fall apart.

Courses at Gordon-Conwell seminary help me see new layers of depth, the ancient typologies of Jesus in the Old Testament. God has spoken. Is he still speaking and creating? Faith like yeast somehow activates God's will, his healing power, his kingdom. God's will is organic, in process, rising. The Holy Spirit is brooding with mysterious chemistry. Strange magic. Enchanted world.

Veritas Sustained Nationally

I soon went to Ohio State to moderate a Veritas Forum on evidence for the historical resurrection. Afterward, a grad student named Matt Fields introduced himself. He was finishing a combined program in law and business. Matt loved the Veritas Forum and offered to help me run the national organization. Together with Howard, Don Lee and other friends,[2] we embarked on many road trips, wore many hats and slept on dorm futons. God kept Veritas Forums going around the country on a shoestring budget, two wings, some wheels and many prayers.

I invited more students to the cabin for weekends. We called our gatherings "Low Tide." I'd watch their faces change with the intake of oxygen while they paddled sea kayaks under the full moon, hearing the dripping and rippling of water off paddles. We had beach hikes and clam bakes. Sing-alongs, lobster and pies. The cabin's owners, Kim and Tudy, would show students the farm, the organic garden, the woodshop and art studio. The students thought Kim and Tudy were geniuses. Kim would laugh and say, pipe in mouth, "Nope, it's common sense—used to come with an eighth grade education."

I'd go into the henhouse with my lacrosse stick to liberate eggs from beneath the B.A.H. (Brooding Attack Hen). The smelly pigs would get the compost. Harry the dog chewed on rocks. He also had a knack for bounding into the bathtub and dropping muddy boots into the clean bubbly water.

Students and friends would arrive uptight and exhausted and leave in peace, with new energy. We were returning to our senses. We were beginning to see, to find an adequate basis of knowledge for hopeful action in the world. The healing required hope. As Harvard psychiatrist Armand Nicholi says, "I can't help but observe the limited resources available to one with no faith and no hope. . . . But what is hope? If hope is defined as belief, trust, and reliance, one cannot help but ask, 'Belief in what or whom?' One must have some basis, some reason for one's hope. It must be rooted in reality. . . . When we turn to the New Testament we read, 'In his great mercy, we have been born . . . into a life full of hope, through Christ Jesus rising again from the dead.'"[3]

This sustainable hope, strength and joy from Christ within us is not an intangible proposition. A person voluntarily plumbed the depths of what we have suffered, and more. To follow him is to draw his life into ours, to even become like him in his sufferings, to do and feel things for others. Our comfort zones expand as we live the full spectrum of life from suffering to joy and power. We enter the largest story.

The Secret of the Vine

A student I met once said of Christians, "Whatever drug you guys are on, I want it." Another said, "It's like you guys are plugged in, with huge bandwidth but wireless. What software are you running?"

Like the rest of us, students want healthy community, restored bodies and minds, love, a calling in life that is significant and good, a quality of life so rich that dependencies on externals like alcohol, drugs, money, status and sex pale in comparison. To both of these students I explained Jesus as the vine, the wine he offers being himself within us. He quenches our thirst.

Along with the students, I was learning that real faith isn't intellectual assent to the doctrine and data points of "belief in God," though that's a useful starting point since it's hard to entrust our lives to what we doubt as real. But faith is believing God's Word about all things and being grafted into God as our life. Biblical faith is an opening and receiving into oneself the gift of God—Jesus Christ and his Spirit. Inviting his life into our lives.

Just as the Creator heals our skin after puncture by various thorns, he desires to be the healer of our hearts, minds and relationships. He helps those who say, "Daddy, Abba, please help me." But many of us run *from* him rather than *to* him. We do not see his open-hearted, open-armed nature, as in Jesus' story (and Rembrandt's painting) of the return of the prodigal son. Instead we silently blame God for the thorns of betrayal or sorrow lodged deep within us. Bitterness takes root in our hearts and we lose faith, hope and love. We are disappointed with God. We compare our interior turmoil to other people's exterior calm, and we come up short. "God is for others," we say, "but not for me."

So, then, how do we thrive in a fullness of life while living in a skeptical and harsh world? Jesus, it turns out, is not only true north for wisdom, he is the True Vine for healing and for life. "I am the vine; you are the branches. If a man remains in me and I in him, he will bear much fruit. . . . I have told you this so that my joy may be in you and that your joy may be complete" (John 15:5-7).

When grafted into Christ by faith, the fruit of his Spirit is love, joy, peace, patience, kindness, goodness, gentleness, faithfulness, self-control (Galatians 5:22-23). It's a basic principle of ecology—drawing greater life into the lesser. In him we have the power and beauty of sustainable life. We reconnect with people as fellow branches in the Vine. When rerooted, obeying and drawing from the source of life himself, new things begin to happen.

Brenda visited the cabin during one of my exhausting bouts with Lyme disease. I was planning to catch a flight soon for California to meet with Veritas planners. But on a hike out to the tide, I had trouble making it back home, much less to the airport and across the country. It had been three years since I'd contracted Lyme disease and antibiotics hadn't cured me. When symptoms of paralysis, arthritis, lethargy and serious stupidity kept returning, specialists considered me a chronic Lyme patient. Though I was maintaining my Veritas Forum involvement by autopilot, my energy, mind and hope were nearly depleted.

When we did make it home, Brenda prayed for my healing. I fell asleep. When I woke up a few hours later, I knew the disease was gone from my body. I saw a Lyme specialist later who analyzed my blood, and he asked me to take the test again—he thought the lab had confused my blood with someone else's. After the second test came back negative, completely clear of disease, the doctors called it a miracle. So do I.

I don't know why God chose to heal me when others still suffer from various results of the Fall. I don't know why my heart and spirit took longer to heal than my body. I suppose injury to the soul is deeper. And the healing is more glorious. In the Greek, "salvation" also means "healing." I don't know when, or how, God will heal all our diseases and wounded hearts, but we've been instructed to err on the side of asking, risking and believing.

The New Wine of Christian Community

Believers together become a culture of life in which the gospel is plausible and the kingdom is more and more real. The first few questions at Veritas Forums are often intellectual ones. But as time goes on, the questions come from the heart. One common question is, "How does love last?" and beneath that question is often a broken heart. Nearly 40 percent of college students are from broken homes. Many feel ambiguity in a relationship with someone they love. They want intimacy but fear the pain of potential loss. Again.

In a Cambridge living room, friends were hanging out, talking about community and intimacy. A few in the group were single and content. Others wished they were married. One was raw with the pain of divorce. Some were newly married and in love, or in shock, or exhausted with work and small children.

"What does a Christian life look like?" we wondered. I thought of my lifelong friend Susan, who homeschools her nine kids, and how I often envied her. *Now that's the good life,* I often thought. But I later discovered that she desired aspects of my life—solitude, adult conversation, mission work and vacations.

After grappling with questions, we concluded that we would each be sane to the extent that we were connected to a life of community, worship, receiving and giving to others. Life in God's household, though sometimes a messy wonder, welcomes people whether married or single, poor or rich. Believing fellowships struggle like anyone, but we learn to press through and to help one another. The kingdom is a new kind of family. In it we grow in love with our spiritual brothers and sisters. The church is like a home, as G. K. Chesterton said, "that is bigger on the inside."[4]

The Shelter of One Another

It's often considered a little insulting to call someone "a sheltered child." But many people long to live in one another's shelter. Whether it's a biological family or friends, we long for intimacy and that rare balance of adventure and security, of wings and roots. We want the sanity of life with moral and relational fiber. Put simply, we need one another. The kingdom of God grows as we invite others, one person at a time, into the family of God and Christian community.

Once on the Guatemala-Belize border, nine of us grad students ascended the ruins of the Mayan pyramids in Tikal, which were formerly used for sacrificial atonement rituals. At dusk, looking down on the tropical canopy, we watched the lush rainforest come to life, full of color and the sounds of parrots and monkeys.

Later we said goodnight and went to separate bungalows in the jungle. I was alone in a grass hut without electricity or light. In the darkness I began to hear all around me a strange sound of breathing—in and out, in and out, louder and softer and then louder. I thought, *Something Scary Is Out There.* We were in the ruins of ancient sacrificial altars, after all. It sounded like I was inside a giant lung. I bolted the door.

When the breathing seemed almost deafening, I grabbed my flashlight and dashed outside through the ruins, feeling my way through the dark jungle looking for the nearest bungalow. I pounded on the door. "It's Kelly, let me in!" Nathan and Jeff quickly pulled me inside and bolted the door shut again.

"What's that sound?" they asked—as if I knew.

Another knock on the door. Two by two the others found us and we ended up all crammed together in one bungalow, singing to drown out the noise, talking the night away, finally falling asleep in the comfort of one another's shelter.

In the morning we stumbled to the "restaurant," which was a thatched hut with a generator, a toaster and a small refrigerator stocked with beer and asparagus soup. In walked the cook, who took one look at us and broke into laughter.

"How did you sleep last night?" he asked.

We just stared at him, and he laughed again. "They're howler monkeys,'" he informed us. "Very many, very cute, but loud at night."

"Thanks for telling us now," someone said. The cook joked about us being our own band of pale monkeys huddled together all night. We finally laughed too, after sunrise, once things were quiet.

On another trip, a bit sore from pouring cement for a Haitian medical clinic, we designated a Sunday as a "day of rest," so Bryan and

Heather Ruhm and I organized tackle football on the beach. The ball was a coconut. The fact that a poorly thrown pass could give you a mild concussion added a level of excitement to the game. Even more exciting, the ball was alive if it was floating on the surface of the water, and with twelve of us, this led to some impressive aqua-scrambles and pile-ons. At one point Jeff and John pulled a few of us out after we were stung by jellyfish. We had to count players after each play in case someone was stuck on the bottom or washed out to sea or laughing too hard to breathe. Shelter and joy.

Biblical Community Building

The Bible's exhortations toward wisdom, grace and love are like oil for the engine of community. God tells us to speak the truth. To worship him alone rather than dead cultural idols. He teaches us to love our neighbors as ourselves. To beware of pride and the love of money. He warns us not to covet our neighbor's spouse or oxen (or car) or home. He tells us to keep the Sabbath and the life-giving habits of ceasing, worship, feasting and celebrating life's goodness.[5] God counsels the wealthy to care for the poor who glean in the fields, who are always in God's thoughts. He teaches us to welcome the stranger, to love our enemy and to advocate for those without power or voice.

God teaches us to be true in heart. He changes us from the inside out. Those who follow him come clean, ask for forgiveness and forgive. We qualify for inclusion in the church simply by knowing that we've sinned and fallen short of the glory of God and by asking for mercy and a new life. We know we're saved by grace alone, not any good thing we've done. This refreshing and honest truth lifts a burden of pretense from our shoulders. We begin to connect to God and to other people in a new way. We gather for meals, for conversation, for retreats and hikes and prayer. We join churches that stand under the words of God. We enjoy creation and the world's largest family, and we give to others out of gratitude for what we've received from God. In such communities, the world looks new and full of potential goodness and beauty.

Philosophy professor Nicholas Wolterstorff wrote in *Finding God at Harvard*, "To be human is also this: to be that point in the cosmos where the yield of God's love is suffering. And sometimes when the cry is intense, there emerges a radiance which seldom appears: a glow of courage, of love, of insight, of selflessness, of faith. In that radiance we see best what humanity was meant to be."[6]

What emerged for me in the wake of my struggle with pain was a growing awareness of the love of Jesus as veritas. Suffering is a severe mercy—a gift revealing our utter dependency on God. Suffering breaks our self-reliance and throws us onto the mercy of God. I also was given a deeper gratitude for the privilege of friendship with people who know his love as well. They are salt and light. They are living proof of the gospel, for he lives in his people.

Like the first friends of Jesus, I'm a self-preserving coward on my own. But in countless moments I've thought, *This thing that I'm doing right now, I would not be doing except that I'm with my friends.* Climbing in the high Alps with skis. Working in the San Salvador garbage dump. Living with rodents and reptiles in the Dominican Republic. Speaking to hundreds at Harvard, Brown and Berkeley. It just wouldn't have happened without one of us being goofy enough to talk others into trying. The point is to listen to God's voice and to follow where he leads.

Though friends move in and out of Cambridge, we're still bound together by our shared adventures and by love deepening over time. Healing and community are both personal gifts and tools for building the kingdom. Grafted like branches into the tree of life, we are set into a larger and better story—one with depth of time, present meaning and future hope. His Spirit in us is for comfort, wholeness, grace with ourselves and one another, and engaging and blessing the world God loves.

13

Engaging the World
The Rise of Veritas

*What matters at this stage is the construction of local forms of
community within which civility and the intellectual and moral life
can be sustained through the new dark ages which are already upon
us. And if the tradition of the virtues was able to survive the horrors
of the last dark ages, we are not entirely without grounds of hope.
This time however the barbarians are not waiting beyond the
frontiers; they have already been governing us for quite some time.*

ALASDAIR MACINTYRE, *AFTER VIRTUE*

Had friends like Brenda not prayed and God not healed me, I
couldn't have caught the next plane for Los Angeles and driven up
the coast to visit Veritas planners at UCLA, UC Santa Barbara, Cal
Poly, Berkeley and Stanford. I began to care deeply again about students and universities. At the UCLA Veritas Forum Erwin McManus,
the pastor of a fellowship called Mosaic, spoke on the transition from
image to character.

"People who are depressed are living in the past," he said. "Forgiveness moves us from selfishness to wholeness to giving. Humility opens
up a new world of possibilities. Of love. Of hope."

Overwhelmed—if not already numbed lifeless—by images of violence and injustice, by sex apart from fidelity, and by the cynicism
and confusion of their own professors, many students are asking
about wisdom and even truth again. They want to know what lasts,
what matters and why. Discontent, many in our culture are rebelling
against the desacralized world with its appetite for abomination.
They are looking once again for meaning and for beauty in the ashes.

They want to change the world for good.

As individuals are revived, so can cultures be revived—by abiding in the Vine and then being and doing what he tells us. I am stubborn enough to believe that God hasn't given up on these universities that were founded in faith. Maybe those seeds beneath the surface aren't dead, only dormant—and potentially full of life. Perhaps the true king will indwell Gondor and "the race of men" once again.

A New Beginning for Veritas

Friends from Ohio had filled in sacrificially to support planners in many universities, which is like hosting twenty weddings a year in terms of planning and expenses. But eventually, with barely enough money to pay for fast food and a rental car to get from LA to San Francisco, I wondered how God would sustain Veritas with speakers, consulting and program expenses at an increasing number of schools.

My trip to California in 2000 catalyzed a new beginning for Veritas. Not only did planners host amazing forums at UCLA, UC Santa Barbara, Cal Poly and Stanford, but I met the person who would help lead Veritas into the new century.

A friend near the cabin had suggested that I visit Kurt Keilhacker, an unassuming grad student, brilliant business consultant and wise encourager behind the Veritas Forum at Stanford. I did. He asked how things had gone at UCLA.

"Well, here's what UCLA's impression is," I said and pulled out the student paper from the day before with a positive front-page story of Veritas and a photo of keynote speaker Os Guinness.

Howard, Matt and I soon asked Kurt to become our chairman, and he agreed. Kurt immediately recruited Ashley and Ted Callahan as bright and creative staff workers. In 2001 the Callahans and Kurt moved to Cambridge. Kurt opened his home for fellowship meals, parties, Bible studies and the Veritas office. As a team we began to strengthen Veritas as a movement with renewed vision.

We started by defining our mission: "We create forums for the exploration of true life. We seek to inspire the shapers of tomorrow's culture to connect their hardest questions with the person and story of Jesus Christ."

Ashley and Ted were soon visiting planners in New York, Minneapolis, Nashville and Los Angeles, encouraging the unity and creativity of vibrant Christian communities.

Within a year we were growing in quality and quantity with more and better forums, with planning resources, better consulting, and outreach beyond the ivory towers. People were able to watch forums on C-SPAN and through a powerful Veritas website offering iPod downloads and podcasts. Art Battson at UC Santa Barbara produced a weekly Veritas television series called *Let There Be Light* for the University of California cable system and for the DISH Network.

With the partnership of many fellowships, churches and foundations, Veritas planners included more than two hundred thousand participants in over sixty universities in the United States, Canada and England.

Kurt enrolled in a graduate program at Harvard while working and serving as chairman of the Veritas Forum. When Ted and Ashley went to business school at Dartmouth, we hired Harvard alumnus Daniel Cho as the new executive director.

Why Veritas?

Given the world's need, believers are neither fragmented nor idle. Collectively, Veritas is for students and others who are seeking true life. Though seminars had covered science, art and philosophy, the dominant theme of the Harvard Veritas Forum became love, community and intimacy. Consider this e-mail from Harvard undergrad Chiduzie Carl Madubata.

> Hey guys, if you haven't already read the cover story in today's *Crimson*, there is an article discussing how depression is prevalent on this campus. Eighty percent of students have felt depressed at least once, forty-seven percent have felt so depressed that it was difficult for them to function, and ten percent have seriously considered committing suicide.
>
> I think these are tragic statistics. I have a burden on my heart to ask you to pray for the campus in general, that God could carry

those who are feeling depressed and that he could assure them of his presence, and that we would be a friend to others who need a friend. I think this begins with prayer.

God bless,
Chiduzie

JOURNAL ENTRY

Twilight Zone. The administration just decided to fund a Harvard sex magazine but gave nothing to help Veritas—even though we have fourteen hundred students attending and are talking about love, truth and meaning. Do we keep trying despite the confusion, banality and addictions?

Yes. Because of these, press on. They are rich but poor. God will provide what we need through his people.

At about the same time, two Harvard students began a soft-porn magazine called *The H-Bomb*. Was it any wonder students continually expressed feelings of intense loneliness?

"Lord, why do you care about this place?" I sometimes asked. "They are defaming your glory." All I got was an image of Sam and Frodo against way too many orcs.

I sensed God saying, "Trust in the good end, and do the next thing. The humble will be saved, and I will be glorified."

The next forum centered on the question "Where is the love?"[1] It received the attention of various Harvard newspapers as well as national press. It was beautiful to see how deeply and constructively Veritas planners cared about students and welcomed them into Christian community.

The Courage of Students

An impressive undergrad on the UCLA soccer team named Andrew Dragos wrote to me at the cabin, wanting to catalyze a Veritas Forum on his campus. A portion of his letter read, "Please be in prayer. Trust me when I say that UCLA *needs* a Veritas Forum. Even if we're fighting an uphill battle, there is still hope."

The first of many UCLA Veritas Forums was led by Andrew and in future years by extraordinary undergrads and community friends.[2] In 2004, C-SPAN Books covered the forum's discussions of science and the emergence of biological complexity.

Vision for Veritas spread among students in Los Angeles to the University of Southern California. A 2005 article in the USC *Daily Trojan* titled "Enter the Depths of the Soul" read:

> Who are we? Do we have a soul? Are we a product of chance or purpose? While these are not easy questions, they will be tackled by the Veritas Forum at USC starting Feb. 22. The three-day event promises to be both thought-provoking and maybe a bit controversial, forum organizers said.
>
> "It's controversial but not confrontational," said Stefan Alexandroni, a staffer for USC's Veritas Forum and a senior majoring in biomedical engineering. "The objective is to ultimately get people talking about important issues that are not discussed in classrooms today . . . to get them to start asking questions about what they believe and why they believe those things."[3]

In 2002 Veritas at Northwestern University in Chicago welcomed more than three thousand people and unified over twenty fellowships as hosts. One of the student planners, Kathy Sievers, later wrote:

> I was invited to a reception for a student committee in the Northwestern Club and found myself talking to a recent president of Northwestern. He was wearing an elaborate robe and headpiece and around his neck was a gold medallion of our school seal.
>
> There was talk that our seal would be changed. It was considered archaic and unsuited for the university's modern image.

Northwestern's seal contains the words "Whatsoever things are true" in Latin taken from Philippians, and on an open book in Greek is the phrase, "The Word, full of grace and truth" from John chapter one.

When asked by a student what the Greek and Latin meant, our president replied, "It means 'Whatever is good is true' or something like that." I was surprised by the irony of his very postmodern answer. I felt shy to say anything but I also couldn't keep quiet. I explained the seal as well as I could and that "the Word, full of grace and truth" referred to Jesus Christ, as seen in the first chapter of the gospel of John.

Another student asked how I knew this, and I said we had explored the meaning of the seal in the Veritas Forum. Then I realized why God had placed me on that student committee—to share the name of Jesus and the truth of his Word with the president of my university.

This story reflects what has become a normal disregard of the giants on whose shoulders we sit, or, as C. S. Lewis called it, a "chronological snobbery" toward the past.

To Northwestern's credit, after the Veritas Forum the university decided to keep the original seal and motto and cancel the new design. I felt that this was a sign of hope and progress, not regress. Only rootedness in a living truth makes sustainable growth and new life possible in the midst of the challenges our world faces. Timeless truth is our hope, not modern trends that fade.

Welcoming All People and All Questions

Likewise, at the University of Wisconsin, Veritas planners asked a humanist student group whom they should invite to debate Bill Craig on the existence of God. The group requested the famous British atheist and philosopher Anthony Flew. Dr. Flew accepted. Bill Craig was gracious and gentle, but the evening was a landslide in favor of theism and the biblical worldview, even though Dr. Flew had influenced millions toward disbelief in his lifetime.

Dr. Flew has recently rejected his lifelong commitment to atheism and secular humanism. According to a 2005 essay, "Dr. Flew has turned his back on atheism, saying it is impossible for evolution to account for the fact that one single cell can carry more data than all the volumes of the Encyclopaedia Britannica."[4]

Veritas speakers are often invited into labs, faculty clubs and academic departments as well as auditoriums. Recently at Ohio State, the theater department asked Jody Sjogren, a Veritas speaker and medical illustrator, to speak to their cast of *Inherit the Wind,* the play based on the infamous 1925 Scopes Monkey Trial in Dayton, Tennessee. Jody's presentation of the emergence of biological complexity in science surprised the cast—they had not realized how strong the "creationist" data was. They talked with Jody for three hours. *Inherit the Wind* is primarily about free speech, Jody said, and in our universities we're still struggling for free speech when it comes to various views on the nature of the universe. She encouraged students to stand for that free speech, including the case for a Creator.

Changed Lives

Veritas Forums at UC Santa Barbara and Cal Poly included presentations by Darrell Scott, the father of Rachel Scott, who confessed faith in Christ before being murdered in the Columbine High School tragedy of 1999. Afterward a planner e-mailed:

> As I type to you I am emotionally weak and filled with an amazing feeling of God's presence. Never in my life have I been to an outreach event at UCSB where it filled up our largest lecture hall (which seats over 900 people). Instead of me going into all the details, please read through the quotes that students wrote down on the comment cards. We have 60 new brothers and sisters in Christ and 75 people made recommitments to Christ. Many more are now asking questions.

Likewise, I once sat in a philosophy class at UCSB. At 9 a.m., most of us were still groggy when the professor introduced guest lecturer Bill Craig. Dr. Craig began his lecture by saying that in the next forty minutes he was going to try to persuade us through logic and scientific evidence that the universe had a Creator who knew and loved each of us personally.

Judging by the students' body language, initial responses ranged from "weird" to "whatever." Bill began to speak about the likelihood of the big bang. By 9:15 most students were sitting upright. He then unpacked the anthropic principle of a habitable earth. By 9:30 they were leaning forward in their seats. Bill then spoke on the person of Jesus. At 9:45 a dynamic Q-and-A session was underway. At 10, a dozen students were surrounding Dr. Craig for further conversation. The host professor looked stunned, perhaps thinking, *This is what college should be for students.*

■ ■ ■

At Harvard, Archie Epps, the dean of students, had been part of the woodwork for three decades. Just before he retired in 2000 we ran into each other in the Yard. "Kelly," he said, "come to see me soon."

I did. Dean Epps wanted to say thank you for the Veritas Forum. He also talked about his own life, losing his childhood faith while a student at Harvard; however, later in the sixties, while watching an Ingmar Bergman film, he decided that he didn't want to live in a story of God's death anymore.

"I no longer believed it. And I wouldn't raise my children to believe it. I got up in the middle of the film and walked out. I went back to faith in God. And now, as I grow older, faith in Christ."

He continued, "I'm the one who sent the *Crimson* reporter to Veritas these past few years. And after reading your history of Christian Harvard, I want Veritas to have an office in Phillips Brooks House. I know the whole house is supposed to be used for fellowships, but at least one office is a start."

I thanked him. Within two months Dean Epps suffered a stroke, and two years later he passed away. I imagine that Veritas is all the more wonderful to him now. I miss him.

■ ■ ■

The drama department at the University of Kentucky partnered with us in 2004 by performing a stage adaptation of *The Great Divorce* by C. S. Lewis. Most of the actors had never read Lewis, and they asked the director what he meant when he spoke of glory, of heaven and hell, and of our choices toward either of these. The play was so popular with the community that they scheduled additional performances.

Several weeks after the Kentucky Veritas Forum, coordinator Brian Marshall told us that a student cast member named Hayden had died tragically in a plane crash. Brian said that Hayden had told another cast member that the play had forced him to rethink his beliefs. He later told the director that he was a Christian.

"Our hope," said Brian, "is that the play and his involvement in Veritas helped to move him toward deeper intimacy with God."

The entire campus was talking about the themes in Lewis's work, including the significance of small choices that move us closer to God, which we saw in Hayden's life and which seemed all the more poignant in his death.

■ ■ ■

Several years after the terrorist attacks on the World Trade Center, we learned about the public suicides at New York University. Several students had jumped from the crosswalks inside the library, crashing to the marble floor below. Our staff spent time with InterVarsity leader Kevin Oro-Hahn at both NYU and Columbia to help local volunteers plan Veritas Forums that included artists, *New York Times* journalist and Pulizter Prize-winner Nicholas Kristof, economist Jeffrey Sachs, scientist and theologian Vinoth Ramachandra, and two thousand students. Marketing guru and filmmaker Gordon Pennington volunteered for Veritas and spoke about the spiritual challenges of an image-based culture, and national media picked up on the phenomenon of academics talking about Jesus in New York.

Ironically, given the signs of despair, Columbia had recently removed references to Jesus from the seal and diminished the meaning of its three crowns, which once represented the Trinity. Richard John Neuhaus—Catholic priest, editor of the journal *First Things* and one of

Time's twenty-five most influential evangelicals—discussed another irony: the removal of the cross as a symbol by a university that claimed to value diversity.

The 2006 New York Veritas Forums explored the question "Suffering—Who Cares?" More than two thousand students heard of a God, according to Sri Lankan nuclear scientist and theologian Vinoth Ramachandra, "who is not distant but entangled in our world, who enters our suffering, who stoops to serve and to bless." Vinoth continued:

> Evil is a parasite. It is not reasonable or ordered, but irrational and inexcusable. Every attempt to explain evil trivializes it. It is not to be understood but fought. This is precisely what God himself does for us. On the cross God takes evil and turns it on itself.

On the cross, God defeats the devil at his own game by becoming the sacrifice for the sins of the world. And then rising from the dead to inaugurate God's new reign of love.

And so it was that many students at Columbia and New York University committed themselves to come alongside a Ugandan village of children orphaned by AIDS, war and famine.

InterVarsity's Ashley Byrd, one of a hundred volunteer planners, said, "The Veritas Forum has been catalytic in transforming our students' understanding of witness" at Columbia and New York University. While in Manhattan, we were encouraged by visits to Times Square Church, All Souls Episcopal and Redeemer Presbyterian. We benefited from teachings by Redeemer's pastor, and Veritas speaker, Tim Keller. And we attended classes by longtime Veritas advisor, speaker, jazz pianist and friend Bill Edgar.

International Work

In 2000, Matt Fields and I had been invited to New York City by a ministry involving people within the United Nations. These new friends explained that they had been given *Finding God at Harvard* as a gift, which went to several hundred U.N. ambassadors and heads of state. I said, "We're so pleased. Next you'll tell us that the moon is made of blue cheese." But they weren't kidding.

Over the next two years we met with various ambassadors who were reading *Finding God* and considering the gospel and God's desire to bless the nations. We also discussed issues of suffering and reconciliation, and several times we met to encourage and pray with people battling cancer or otherwise hurting.

■ ■ ■

It's not news to say that the European academy is on a prodigal path away from its Christian heritage, and believing students and professors there often feel marginalized and alone. Nishan de Mel, Ard Louis and Aaron Romanowsky, friends from the first Harvard Veritas Forum, eventually found their way to England to continue their studies. In partnership with Veritas they, and friends like Maithri White, initiated a spring conference for European scholars in an old mansion in Derbyshire, near the Peak District. Though participants teach or study at Cambridge, Nottingham, Oxford, Aberdeen and St. Andrews, these scholars are from France, South Africa, China and Sri Lanka. The following is a letter I wrote to Veritas staff:

> Though an England conference is across an ocean, I see our support as a consistent next step of encouraging and nurturing the seed of the first Veritas Forum in 1992. This is how I've seen every forum since the first one. The mode has been one of organic, relational growth, and I think it's an effective one.
>
> It's a story with a protagonist community of believing scholars influencing culture for God's kingdom here and now and exploring the brilliant lordship of Jesus in every sphere of life.

These Veritas friends in England are kingdom-oriented scholars. Nishan de Mel is finishing a doctorate in economics at Oxford while teaching undergrads. Ard Louis is teaching chemistry at Cambridge. Aaron Romanowsky (of the observatory dance fame) is doing a postdoc fellowship in astronomy at Nottingham. Together, in their own words, they wrote:

> We are called to allow God's perspective to direct our choices, our premises and our manner of inquiry and learning, and to strive after God's standards of excellence in our pursuit of truth. We are

called to take seriously our responsibilities as students, academics and/or future leaders in society. Our calling is to seek God's kingdom and make a difference both now and in the future, wherever God places us. We are called to fulfill and accomplish God's purposes in the world.

Their gatherings have been titled "Transforming the Mind: Christian Stewardship in Academia" and "Turning the World Upside Down." Seminars are punctuated by lively hikes, Ultimate Frisbee (my American contribution), worship, meals and laughter.

■ ■ ■

In 2005 Ted and Ashley Callahan left our staff for Ted to enroll in business school at Dartmouth, but not before hiring Harvard alumnus Daniel Cho as the new executive director. Dan attended the first Veritas Forum in 1992. He was a discontented freshman who considered transferring but changed his plans when he discovered a larger Christian community wrestling with the same questions he was.

Thirteen years later, Dan's first trip as Veritas director was to Asia, where *Finding God at Harvard* had been translated into Chinese and Korean. Through the Veritas community built over the past thirteen years, Dan made contact with officials, scholars and pastors in many Asian cities.

"Hunger for a university-caliber engagement with the truth of the gospel was palpable," he wrote. "The response was unanimous: Veritas is needed. Students want to explore pressing questions and to relate their education to the reality of troubled hearts and souls in rapidly changing cultures. Sound familiar?"

The previous year I'd received an e-mail from China:

Hi Kelly. We purchased fifty Chinese translations of *Finding God at Harvard* in a bookstore in Hong Kong. (It is a good translation, btw.) It is one of the most powerful books for removing barriers to faith for Chinese intellectuals who are meeting to discuss, perhaps the first meetings of their kind since 1949!

Emerging Excellence and Younger Scholars

Of all people, Christians are open to mystery and led by a sense of wonder. Nothing sustains a sense of wonder like treasures and discoveries along the way, so Veritas works with partnering ministries to see believers in every academic department. Bright young Christian scholars are emerging. Many have been student participants at Veritas Forums, some are now speakers and will soon be mentors. Theirs are the stories that will inspire us in the years to come.

They are friends like Ard Louis, a chemist/physicist at Cambridge University, who helps direct a Templeton grant on the emergence of biological complexity. Ard, the son of Dutch missionaries to Gabon, is fascinated by the immensity of creation, as well as by the precision of quantum mechanics. He and Fritz Schaefer are on the forefront of discovering what has yet to be seen in the world of the very small. Kirstin Johnson is finishing a doctorate on the theology and poetics of Scottish author and pastor George McDonald. Nishan de Mel at Oxford is refining assumptions about economics and policy that influence developing countries and the poor. Jennifer Wiseman, now the lead scientist for the Hubble Space Telescope Program, is advancing our ways of seeing and understanding the universe and our privileged place in it. Finny Kuruvilla just finished his M.D. at Harvard and Ph.D. at MIT in biotechnical engineering. He pastors a church in his home and writes books while he's a medical resident. Finny is advancing ways of seeing the interior of the body as well as ethics and the sanctity of human life at every age.

While Jeff Barneson's Cambridge home and loving family is a hub of student life, other friends have built Christian study centers at Cal Berkeley, Wisconsin, Virginia, Yale, Cornell and Florida. Societies of Christian scholars are developing and mentoring younger scholars and professionals. The Christian Union, led by Matt Bennett, supports programs in the "ivy league." The list of encouragers continues to grow, longing to see our culture move from information to wisdom.[5]

Vision for the Future

Ideas have consequences. College graduates change the world for worse or for better.[6] Universities are incubators of ideas and leaders who define the horizon of a culture and of a world.

Jesus and his followers care about universities. But impressive campuses too often become nervous and conformist fortresses, in some cases monasteries of secularism. Living off the legacy of the Christian past, many universities survive less on fresh passion and more on accruing fiscal endowments. Though Christian scholars have taken many blows, the church has and will weather many storms. Renewal will take time.

In the past century, the academy and the then-popular worldview were influenced by men, reductionists and materialists and relativists, like Nietzsche, Freud, Marx, Darwin, Kinsey and Derrida. Today their influence is eroding against the inevitable consequences of their ideas. Their ideas bore within themselves the seeds of their own destruction, but not without cost to countless millions.

But who and what will take their place of influence? Universities will be granted cultural authority, and they will be inhabited. The question becomes "by whom?"

Conversely, what ideas bear within themselves seeds of hope and a culture of life?

This is the challenge that Veritas enters. Ours is a season of opportunity. Dare we dream ahead to the year 2015 or 2025? We know that God could replace our work with something else, and we'd still be thankful for each story, for every student. But as long as he allows us to continue, we'll dream, plan and keep our hands to the plow.

We hope to grow in our partnerships with local fellowships and churches hosting Veritas forums, and to grow through ongoing conversations in the United States, Asia and Europe by adding spiritual, intellectual and cultural vitality to more than a hundred of the world's leading universities.

Ours is simply a model of encouraging unified witnessing communities, hospitable, bright and creative (embodying both grace and truth), emerging within leading universities around the world. Together with them, we'll encourage cynics to question, seekers to believe and believers to grow in Christlike brilliance and love.

In forums and, when possible, in mentoring relationships, we hope to continue to introduce thousands of younger students to mature Christian professors and professionals. We want to help students see through their lenses and to stand on the shoulders of giants. Though our preference is actual in-person community—and everyone is invited to Veritas at no cost—Veritas conversations and research will also be increasingly accessible remotely via the Web and Veritas Forum books.

Biblical truth is for the art of life. We'll work to excite students with the relevance and coherence of the gospel in the arts and sciences, from anthropology to zoology. We want to inspire those entering "secular" vocations with the biblical dignity of good work in the story of restoring a broken world to order, beauty and wholeness.

Veritas alumni are already scattered throughout the world, beginning to shape academic departments and research labs, the arts, corporations, relief and development projects, media networks, and governments. They are restoring conversation of "first things," such as right knowledge, responsibility, discovery and action in the world.

We'll continue to explore true life. To rejoice in the gift of life. To create a culture of life.

If I may borrow a sentiment from Professor J. R. R. Tolkien, a hopeful realist: there may come a day when believers will be called to abandon the university to itself, to its idols and self-deceptions, to its self-worship.

But it is not this day.

14

Seeing All Things

The Questions of Our Times

Many things are wrongly created because the artist does not rightly see.

DOROTHY SAYERS, *THE MIND OF THE MAKER*

I am learning that the Veritas Forum is about real life . . . making sense of our lives as whole pictures.

MARIAN HALLS,
STUDENT VERITAS PLANNER AT UCLA

I believe in Christianity as I believe in the sun. Not only do I see the sun, but by its light I begin to see all things.

C. S. LEWIS, *A MIND AWAKE*

Veritas isn't about religion; it's about life. It's about the art of life and a new way of seeing.

Veritas is truth whose nature is love and hospitality. Our approach is generally not debate but exploration. We find that Christians have as many questions as seekers and skeptics. A surplus of mystery is waiting to be revealed. We are learning to enjoy life's journey together. If Jesus is untrue and irrelevant, we want to know and to act accordingly. But if he is truth and life, we imagine that every sane person wants to know.

Veritas tries to avoid secular political categories and divisiveness. Forums welcome all questions and ideas and those who present them. We focus on the principles beneath the hot issues and trivializing slogans popular with the media and politicians.

We believe that in the perfect coherence of the three verifiable words of God (creation, Scripture, Jesus) we've been given a basis of knowledge and authority out of which right action is possible. Further, we've been given a source of power, the True Vine of Christ. And we've been given the fellowship of friends on the journey. Though we face many odds in this life, the gospel is the most world-changing possibility the human race has ever known.

The gospel is the corrective lens for our impaired vision. It challenges us to see life in relation to the mind and privileged insight of Jesus. We begin to see not only our own stories of pain and healing but all things in relation to the biblical epic of a good creation, a bad Fall and a promised redemption for those who believe.

What do we begin to see anew through the gospel's lens? To begin with, people become more precious. Our families and neighbors, even strangers and self-proclaimed "enemies" are valued and loved by God. Our minds and hearts are enlarged. Love naturally makes us more generous, creative and inclusive. Our sense of family expands to include people of various ethnicities, abilities, and socioeconomic classes. The world is mystery to explore, adventure to be attempted, and his kingdom of love and justice to be extended.

Those who are suspicious of the word *truth* needn't be. Consider this—the nature of the truth of the gospel is self-sacrifice. That gives us reason to trust rather than to fear. Yes, we make mistakes, but overall we taste good fruit from this tree of life.

Veritas is the mind of Christ, full not only of truth but also of grace in lovely fusion. Therefore, to grow in Christlikeness is to grow in grace. To listen before speaking. To seek God's mind and heart on all things. To allow one another mistakes and misjudgments, laughing at ourselves but taking wisdom seriously because it's the path of life in a hurting world.

As we grow, our instincts change from self-preservation to faith.

Our assumptions change from scarcity to abundance. Put plainly, life gets more fun. (When our home contains more people than chairs we thank God for such a wonderful problem. Fun is sometimes messy, and messy implies life.) Our growing sense of justice leads us from joining the privileged few to seeking liberty for all.

Jesus created the good germ of radical love that would spread through the entire world, turning this world upside down (or rather, right side up) wherever he is obeyed in faith. "Behold," he said, "I make all things new" (Revelation 21:5 KJV). And while being betrayed, just before choosing the cross, he said, "A new command I give you: Love one another. As I have loved you, so you must love one another" (John 13:34).

By sacrificing his body, Jesus created a new form of community— the body of Christ around the world. There are people like my friends, stories like our stories, everywhere he is believed and obeyed. His sacrifice reconnects us to reality, to truth, to who God is, to a clear vision of who we are without him and who we are with him.

Jesus is changing the way we see and treat one another. Individuals, free and personally responsible, governed by the Spirit and the Word written on our hearts, are able to live in community to the benefit of one another. We are being freed of external dependencies. We no longer reduce one another to bodies. We no longer steal but learn to give. We learn to live in the greater truth unveiled by the Word become flesh. Christian communities are created by his life, empowered by his Spirit, sanctioned by his authority, sustained by his presence. By his grace we forgive, live and learn. We learn to look freshly at the seemingly overwhelming questions of our day. Questions that are explored more deeply at Veritas Forums, but that I'll at least mention here.

We approach the question "What story are we living in?" by asking if an Author has told us of our human epic and our own subplot within it. Those who believe that the story involves the conquest of evil take courage in this life.

We are challenged in our heart's core, where seeing happens. The mind of Jesus is beyond right or left. He defines the center. He is deeply radical, which means "at the root of" the questions and issues.

Living in Skin

In a skin-tight tank top above her pierced navel and blue jeans below her hips she spoke. Her question at the Veritas Forum at Harvard was earnest. "Why can't we just do whatever we want with our bodies, with whomever we want—gay sex, group sex—whatever? Why is this still an issue?"

I hurt for her, but I understood her question. Present on every college campus are questions of sexuality, the body, intimacy and love. While sex is everywhere, intimacy based in faithful commitment is hard to find. A world starving for genuine intimacy seeks sex like salvation. But sex alone is a false hope, only skin deep.

A student at the Veritas Forum at Rice said that her parents divorced when she came to college, and then she and her boyfriend broke up after a year together. "How does love last?" she asked.

At Duke, Veritas addressed the compulsion of female students to strive for the appearance of "effortless perfection" with respect to their bodies, minds and achievements.

A recent Veritas Forum at Harvard explored true love. Several thousand students participated. We discussed the nature of the curse, but more importantly the goodness of life beyond the curse.

Veritas enters the realm of these primal questions. We see our desires in the context of being human in God's image—relational, loving, giving and receiving beings with conscience, will, discernment, emotion, reason, moral agency, spirit and creativity. We dive into questions of pain and healing.

We also dive into our potential as artists and lovers of beauty. Art is critically important because the artist translates ideas into cultural influence, and ideas have consequences. Whether false or true, abstract ideas become tangible through story, image and sound, through emotion and impression.[1] Musicians, dancers, designers, actors and filmmakers join Veritas Forums and share their art and ideas with us. With many believers at the forefront,[2] there is a movement of art to reclaim truth and beauty. Visually sophisticated, with intellectual depth, we are seeing a renewal of art that espouses hope, healing, redemption and homecoming.

These artists are reenchanting (singing into) our cultural void. For artists who embody truth and grace, our culture and our future is within reach. Inspired by the Spirit of the Artist, all is possible.

Questions of culture include conversations about race, multiculturalism and community. Jesus offers us privileged information. Our fundamental identity, he says, is neither gender nor ethnicity nor skin color. It is neither economic class nor cultural orientation. Our true identity, he says, is simply "child of God" (John 1:12). We now belong to one another—brother and sister, adopted into the same family by the same Father by faith. Biblical Christianity is the most inclusive family on earth. Each person is created in the image of God and endowed with intrinsic value. God empowers us to love and to rightly value every human being as beloved of God.

Jesus turns the world right side up by challenging every social and cultural identification. Once he has deconstructed our constructs, he rebuilds us by uniting us at the core of our human identity.

How do we see the poor in relation to our own resources? Poverty presents an opportunity for the wealthy, Christian or not, to bless countless individuals and nations. The Christian story is life-giving for the poor and for women as we share food and water and education, as we honor those without honor.

In Acts 2 when the Holy Spirit was given to believers, one result was that they shared what they had as any one had need. They distinguished needs from wants, and whether giving out of poverty or abundance, they gave to the world out of joy.

We are coming to understand a biblical view of wealth: that truly wealthy people don't accumulate so much as they scatter wealth, they invest in the needs of people and in the portfolio of the growing kingdom. They seed that which lasts forever.

Are beauty, truth and moral goodness universal and essentially human? The reality of beauty has been diminished in recent decades within the academy, the arts and pop culture. But why then do most of us find certain real things beautiful? Aqua water, wave upon wave, beating into white sand. Clouds ignited indigo and crimson by a setting sun. The innocent and shining eyes of a baby. The humble homecoming of a runaway teenager. A friend healed from the ravages of cancer.

We're discovering a family resemblance—we humans are made in the same image with the same Father—and our hearts were designed to see the most valuable things as beautiful.

And why, perhaps universally, do cultures value humility, honesty, courage, kindness, self-control, fidelity and love? Put conversely, what culture celebrates rape, child abuse, or addiction to pornography? Who is proud of exploiting the labor of poor women in sweatshops? Cultures everywhere produce laws to reinforce and reward universal values—not in exact similarity, and with varying degrees of punishment for violators, but on the whole a universal moral law is at work, much like physical laws.[3]

What originates in pride takes the form of lust, greed, sloth, rage or jealousy. But the fruits of humility are radiant with beauty: godly sorrow and honest confession, forgiveness, tears and then laughter and reconciliation. We see in the gospel a secret to peace among all people and all cultures.

Veritas conversations often include world religions. We see moral wisdom in many religious teachings. And we often see shadow myths of the gospel. But we find real differences as well. A student at the Harvard Veritas Forum told Indian-born philosopher Ravi Zacharias, "All religions are the same."

In front of seven hundred students Dr. Zacharias answered by paraphrasing poet Steve Turner, "The same except for their understanding of the character of God, of the cosmology and meaning of the universe, of human nature, of human value, of the nature of reality, of ethics, the good life, charity and kindness, sexuality, suffering, joy, hope, salvation and our eternal destination of either heaven or hell."

He got our attention.

"There are many paths up the mountain," the saying goes. But that assumes our ability to climb. Given our imperfections and the inevitability of death, we find that only one person made a path down the mountain, from the top, to love us.

Students ask, "What about the earth?" We begin to see the earth as we see our bodies—as entrusted gifts and ourselves as stewards of these gifts. Our choices about stewardship are related to our love of God, human beings and the rest of creation—leaning neither toward a worship of nature at the expense of human needs, nor toward greedy exploitation of nature for human indulgence. With wisdom and the ethic of stewardship, we learn that to care for the earth is also to care for our neighbor, the poor, children and generations to come.

What of new science, biotechnology and health care? Veritas has explored some recent wonders of science as a tool of discovering what God has created. Human achievements in science and engineering have helped alleviate some consequences of the Fall, such as disease and malnutrition. But we are now at a tipping point regarding our choices about things such as cloning, the use of embryos for research and nanotechnology, which may precipitate a category shift for human beings, something akin to a morphing of man and machine into techno sapiens.[4]

Veritas often emerges within medical and scientific communities. We see that the gospel is about health, life and wise progress. Healers and researchers are finding new ways to heal, to advance the quality of life without diminishing humanness or killing living beings in the process.[5] Researchers are learning to thwart the behavior of cancer cells and infectious diseases by turning other viruses against them. We look at the health-giving conditions of the first two chapters of Genesis, and botanists are finding healing properties within newly discovered plants. Biblical living in general corresponds strongly to health care, healing and quality of life.[6]

Francis Collins, head of the Human Genome Project and a believing Christian, models both wise restraint and cutting-edge research. He and others lead us into an exciting future of biotechnology and healing. Christians are also expanding the definition of "quality of life" more holistically to include the mind, spirit and community.

Students at most Veritas Forums raise the question of the problem of evil. How could a holy, powerful and loving God allow evil to exist in his world? Isn't this evidence of God's absence, impotence or indifference? We live in a world of natural as well as moral disasters. Scripture tells us of humanity, and a particular blue planet, out of order. Paul tells us in Romans 1 that even the earth groans for the redemption of the children of God. The God of the gospel doesn't just talk about evil, he doesn't just hate it, he enters into evil and takes it on. Evil is a greedy invader and colonizer, but it will eventually flee the power of those who abide in Christ. Darkness hates light.

We don't fully know why God allows evil in his world, but for the Christian the more relevant question becomes, What are we going to do about it? I think of my friend and Cambridge housemate Poh Lian Yap. When SARS hit Malaysia, she stayed in the hospitals in spite of natural fear, out of a sense of God's calling. Gary Haugen and the International Justice Mission follow Jesus into the dark realities of evil— into brothels to liberate little girls taken captive, into brick kilns and mines to free slaves.

Jeff Barneson and Harvard students ask, "Where is Jesus least felt in this world?" They spend weeks encouraging Bolivian prisoners and working for health care and human rights. Many relief, development and mission agencies rescue the oppressed, feed the hungry, are light in darkness. To follow Christ is to march into hell for a heavenly cause, knowing that you're playing on the winning team even if you lose your life in this world. Knowing the Real Story helps us live in the middle of it with clarity and courage.

For years I thought that evil, and even stupid mistakes and accidents, thwarted the plans of God. But Scripture reveals a deeper magic. God, who hates evil, allows it only because he trumps it—he redeems what evil intends. He uses it in some mysterious way to his good purpose. As Paul says in Romans, "In all things God works for the good of those who love him" (Romans 8:28). We can have joy in all things. This is evidenced by the genius of Jesus on the cross, reversing the curse right under the nose of the devil himself. This genius is known as the sovereignty of God. And so it was that the worst day in human history, when man killed the son of God, is now the day we call Good Friday.

Students ask, "What of the clash of civilizations?" Like the shifting and colliding of tectonic plates, the shocks and waves of our cultural clashes keep coming.[7] The academic world found Samuel Huntington's 1993 insight, that the "clash of civilizations" between Islam and the West is of a primal religious and cultural rather than political or economic nature, to be quite new, even prophetic. With all respect, such insights are ancient and familiar to students of Scripture.

After September 11, 2001, when the media looked for answers from the past few decades, believers explored the ancient origins of this conflict. (The Garden of Eden was near the confluence of the Tigris and Euphrates rivers not far from present-day Baghdad.) Muslims trace their lineage to Abraham through Ishmael, the son of Abraham and Sarah's surrogate, Hagar (see Genesis 15—21). Judeo-Christianity traces its lineage to Abraham through Isaac, the son of Abraham and Sarah. Islam, Judaism and Christianity each believe they are heirs to God's promise to Abraham that he would be the father of many nations. Christianity believes that inclusion in this promise is by faith, not biology.

A primal conflict between law and grace originated more than three millennia ago, as far back as Abraham. Islam asserts Allah's indivisible oneness, his holiness and law, but the Qur'an intentionally precludes God's act of divine sacrifice through Jesus "on the cross."[8] Christianity encompasses not only God's holiness but also his mercy toward us: he sent Jesus to break the cycle of evil and vengeance by taking our violence and brokenness into himself.

The Christian understanding is that no one needs to be sacrificed for human injustice and sin because Jesus satisfied our debt once and for all. Christians are now to become living sacrifices to bless the nations. Given this, and given other modern worldviews such as secular fundamentalism, what is the response of Jesus' followers? Prayer. Self-giving. Grace and truth. Wise restraint and conversation. For example, if the Christian instinct to protect the vulnerable might involve restraint of an oppressor, we must wisely discern the nature of justice and the right uses of power.[9] We consider the mind of Christ on the relationship between mercy and justice, and on diplomacy, trust-building and peace-making.

Waging Peace on the World

How do we wage peace, or what God calls *shalom?* Shalom is not merely the lack of conflict but also the presence of God's wholeness, prosperity, healing and salvation. This peace includes in its nature those whom Jesus called "the least of these." Shalom is about the complete reign of God over creation. Jesus is the Prince of Peace because he alone is the one who can bring such fullness as he rules the world from the right hand of the Father. We spread shalom as we embody and teach the love of Jesus.

The poet William Blake said, "The glory of Christianity is to conquer by forgiveness." Jesus-followers take many hits while waging peace. Christians fed the Roman Empire's poor while the Roman Emperor fed Christians to the lions in the Coliseum. When the Roman Empire fell by its internal demoralization and disorientation, not unlike our own, those same persecuted Christians harbored countless Roman citizens in their hidden churches as Rome burned to the ground.[10]

Paul taught believers how to live in all things. Though he wrote from prison, Paul gave us a new way of seeing in light of who Jesus is. In the second chapter of Philippians, his letter to the believers at Philippi whom he loved and addressed with a deep affection, Paul asked them to "do nothing out of selfish ambition or vain conceit, but in humility consider others better than yourselves. Each of you should look not only to your own interests, but also to the interests of others" (Philippians 2:3-4).

He continues, speaking a powerful truth beautifully:

Your attitude should be the same as that of Christ Jesus:
Who, being in very nature God,
    did not consider equality with God something to be grasped,
but made himself nothing,
    taking the very nature of a servant,
    being made in human likeness.
And being found in appearance as a man,
    he humbled himself
    and became obedient to death—
        even death on a cross!

Therefore God exalted him to the highest place
    and gave him the name that is above every name,
that at the name of Jesus every knee should bow,
    in heaven and on earth and under the earth,
and every tongue confess that Jesus Christ is Lord,
    to the glory of God the Father. . . .

Do everything without complaining or arguing, so that you may become blameless and pure, children of God without fault in a depraved and crooked generation, in which you shine like stars in the universe as you hold out the word of life. (Philippians 2:5-16)

We too can take the hits of a hurting culture and live in such a way that our culture will rise again. Jesus-followers don't sacrifice others, they give of themselves on behalf of others. Peace is waged. The kingdom is advanced on earth as it is in heaven. The kingdom's Prince of Peace is glorified.

Veritas is a new way of seeing and living. It begins with the humility to say that we know little on our own, and that we're open to the Author's words, his light, his presence. When we abide in him as a True Vine, branches bud and bear fruit. The world is "freshly storied" and the future is full of possibility.

This chapter is merely a sampling of how in Veritas Forums we consider questions as friends seeking wisdom together. Future Forums and books will be shaped by such conversations about the gospel's relevance in a hurting world. We explore the mind of Christ beneath issues that are divisive along the fault lines of calcified politics and public opinion. We listen beyond the noise in our heads to a still, small voice. We listen for the words of life. Like oxygen, the gospel opens up new possibilities. I am still learning and often personally mistaken, but together we are finding a new way of seeing and of living.

We not only see the sun, but by the light of that sun we are learning to see all things. This vision helps us build a lasting kingdom, and honor the lasting king.

15

The Lord of the Rings
and a Kingdom Among Us

So turn on the light and reveal all the glory
I am not afraid
To bare all my weakness, knowing in meekness
I have a kingdom to gain.

JENNIFER KNAPP, "MARTYRS AND THIEVES"

And I heard a loud voice from the throne saying, "Now the dwelling
of God is with men, and he will live with them. They will be his
people, and God himself will be with them and be their God. He will
wipe every tear from their eyes."

REVELATION 21:3-4

And he [God] made known to us the mystery of his will . . .
to bring all things in heaven and on earth together under one head,
even Christ.

EPHESIANS 1:9-10

We live in a time of intriguing existential irony. Postmodernism is often characterized as the rejection of the metanarrative, the big story, and yet millions gravitate toward grand epics and myths that help them make sense of their lives. The most popular of these epics include a shared meaning of history, the conquest of evil, the value of purposeful and adventurous friendship, the power of simple virtue and the eternal value of human beings—epics such as *The Lord of the Rings*, *The Passion of the Christ* and The Chronicles of Narnia.

Perhaps there really is a great story, a hero and a band of brothers and sisters, and perhaps we have heroic notions because there are battles to be won. Truth changes us as it changed the cowardly friends of Jesus who deserted him at the cross but were transformed by the resurrection. They were no longer afraid of death, nor life, nor the world and its idols.

Truth is not abstract and unembodied, but alive. Wanting relationship with us, in us, the Author risked entering his own play and became the sublime hero. He revealed that our lives are subplots in the epic that began before, and will continue after, our short time on earth—and that our lives are unending.

I've tried to share the supblot of the Veritas Forum, how it emerged through friendships, shared vision and organic growth from the grassroots up at each university. Protagonists are believing students, scholars, administrators and friends. The fellowship is found in cultural incubators such as Cambridge, New York, Los Angeles, Chicago and many kindred universities. Those in this fellowship are in the world but not of it. They are dedicated to the story of the brilliance and lordship of Jesus in every sphere of life and of God bringing all things together under his love and wisdom (Ephesians 1).

How are protagonist communities revolutionary, or potentially so? Think of the influence of a few friends who called their group "The Inklings"—C. S. Lewis, G. K. Chesterton, J. R. R. Tolkien, Dorothy Sayers, Charles Williams, Owen Barfield—they were a creative cluster who needed one another in order to change the world. Imagine now if there were hundreds of such clusters, perhaps thousands, with a commitment to mentoring others over the course of lifetimes.

I once asked poet Luci Shaw at her kitchen table if she had a creative cluster of writing friends. She said, "I've had two writing groups. The first met to critique one another's work. We lasted three months. The second group began for friendship, vision and encouragement. We're going strong after thirty years. Perhaps you've heard of some of them."

She mentioned some names: Philip Yancey, Eugene Peterson, Madeleine L'Engle, Walter Wangerin, Richard Foster, and her husband, John Hoyt. Yes, I'd heard of them.

Luci smiled and said, "If not for one another, no one would have heard of any of us. Our lives are bound together."

In Hebrews 11, sometimes called the "Hall of Faith" of the Bible, we read of the heroics of believers who by faith conquered kingdoms and injustice, sacrificed themselves and were "sawn in two," believed against all odds. I think of my own human heroes. They include believers in other countries who face persecution and those who serve the poor, adopt children, open their homes to strangers and pray for our world. Other heroes are Veritas planners who challenge the images and powers of Los Angeles and New York, Boston and Singapore, with the mind of Christ. They are professors, ministers and friends who give sacrificially in the world. They are Veritas presenters who graciously reason with any scholar who will step up to a microphone and voice their questions of knowledge, authority, philosophy, science, art, history and life, death and resurrection. They are Christians in the arts and sciences who create despite persecution by others who are bothered by the implications of their work.

And that's just the beginning of my list.

The Return of the King

Lovers of Tolkien are familiar with the chilling rhyme that echoes as a motif throughout *The Lord of the Rings.*

One ring to rule them all.
One ring to find them.
One ring to bring them all,
and in the darkness bind them.

I believe that there is a real Lord of the rings—not a dark lord, but one of light and brightness. A servant-king who will reconcile the race of men and the whole cosmos to himself, for God loves the cosmos, including us. And the gates of hell shall not prevail against him.

I have a vivid memory of the advent of the third millennium. It was

New Year's Eve 1999. I was at a party with grad students and young professionals dressed in East Coast black with chic haircuts, hip glasses and sophisticated accents. All eyes were on the large-screen television. Networks positioned cameras on the frontiers of time zones around the world, transmitting images by satellite. The first celebration: the island of Tonga.

The Tongan villagers in native dress danced on a beach around a large bonfire. What a contrast to my urbane gathering. We expected the Tongans to break into traditional, perhaps animistic, ritual or song. But instead the Tongan people began a beautiful tribal dance and started singing with uplifted hands, from Handel's *Messiah:*

The kingdoms of this world have become
The kingdom of our Lord
And of his Christ, and of his Christ.
And he shall reign for ever and ever!

The room was in quiet shock.

What those European and American grad students didn't realize was that the Christian movement is exploding almost everywhere in the world but North America, Europe and Muslim countries. Thousands of Chinese come to faith every day. The same is true in Africa, South America and even India.

The gospel is not a small story, but the great story that our hearts have desired and known since we were children, before we were taught to stop listening to our hearts and to good reason.

Though the music is often discordant and our instruments damaged, I have come to believe that all of life is becoming a symphonic and coherent whole in relation to this One. All cultures and nations and arts and sciences.

His kingdom is both now and not yet. And for now, the work of the kingdom is always with us. It begins right where we are planted, best in fellowship with others. Bringing water to the thirsty. Good news to the poor. Binding up the broken-hearted. Announcing freedom to captives. Dancing where there was mourning. Revealing dignity where there was shame and praise where there was despair.

This is our great adventure, even though lived an hour at a time. Culture-making, world-changing, kingdom-advancing is about the faithful commitment to build in the ruins. Not to coerce but to shine forth a light so lovely that all will be drawn to his presence.

And So We Sing

There is a lot of sound in universities, and some students make sound that is, well, full of hope and even joy. It is a strange sound in those places, always beautiful, often harmonic, and I have heard it many times.

I hear it in Sanders Theater in Harvard's majestic Memorial Hall, with eleven hundred students singing to consummate the Veritas Forum:

Amazing grace, how sweet the sound
That saved a wretch like me.
I once was lost but now am found.
'Twas blind but now I see.

I hear it at InterVarsity's Urbana mission convention with twenty thousand students singing:

O the deep, deep, love of Jesus.
Vast, unmeasured, boundless, free.

I hear the African American spirituals at Duke and many Veritas Forums:

Ride on, King Jesus,
No man's gonna hinder thee.

I hear the singing at a Princeton Christmas party:

Mild he lays his glories by,
Born that man no more must die.
Born to raise the sons of earth,
Born to give them second birth.

I hear the singing at Cal San Diego at Easter:

Jesus Christ is risen today, alleluia!

I hear them at USC in Los Angeles:

I will build my church, and the gates of hell shall not prevail against it.

I hear Brenda's voice calming me at the cabin:

I am not ashamed of the name of all names.
It has the power to heal and to save.
Strength for the weary, peace for the troubled soul.
It's the name of Jesus. It's the name of Jesus.
Mightier than mountains, he lives among the weak.
Ruler eternal, and lover to me.

During a lightning storm, heard and seen through massive arching windows of Harvard's Paine Hall, singer-songwriter Pierce Pettis closed a Veritas Forum with his guitar and lyrics adapted from Paul's first letter to the Corinthians, chapter 13:

Knowledge and prophecy will fade and tongues will all fall silent.
Love that lives is here to stay solid and defiant.
I know it's hard to see these things like through a dark glass straining,
But when we're standing face to face the truth won't need explaining.

I have only about three notes to contribute, but I join in. We sing while hanging drywall with Habitat for Humanity in Boston and while ski-hiking Tuckerman Ravine. We sing while quilting in Cambridge and while building a school for kids with polio in the rainforest of Peru. We sing while riding low in the back of a dusty pickup across war-torn El Salvador. We sing at the weddings and funerals of friends. The Lord is our song, and so we sing.

Our beloved Vera Shaw passed on in 2004. She, along with her husband, Jim, had been faculty encouragers and spiritual parents to the Harvard-Radcliffe Christian Fellowship for fifty-five years. Kay Hall and I visited Vera in the hospice a few days before she went to be with the Lord. Vera let go of the morphine pump in order to hold our hands. Jim looked adoringly at her, as he had for sixty-some years. Vera's blue eyes still sparkled though her body was failing. She asked us to pray with her, but during that time she only prayed for us, for our circle of friends now in many countries, and for Veritas and the gospel in universities. (As she'd prayed each day for decades.)

After her "Amen," I asked through tears, "But Vera, how might we best pray for you?"

She looked at me with knowing, shining eyes. She smiled and said, "Just give thanks, dear. Just give thanks."

At Vera's memorial service I saw Rob's wife for the first time in four years. We embraced. "Vera brought us back together," she said.

All believers live in the reasonable hope, grounded in the resurrection of Jesus, that our fellowship and our love for one another is unending. As Vera used to say, "Honey, the future is as bright as the promises of God."

I expected in Cambridge to find something new, something beyond Jesus, but instead I found more of him. I saw how the pure light of God's truth refracts and falls in every direction with color and grace. I found him in the color of crimson, in the iron and stone of the gates of Harvard Yard and in the symbols on the college seal. I could see his truth in the work and eyes of fellow students, in rare books, in a friend's chemistry lab, the observatory, and in the legacies of founders and alumni who, whether living or beyond this life, would befriend and teach us.

After I eventually moved home to Ohio, students who planned a Harvard Veritas Forum invited me to return to Sanders Theater to speak on themes of true love and the person of Jesus. Once again I climbed onto that stage with its massive woodwork and the *Veritas: Christo et Ecclessiae* shields highlighted before us. I suggested that the question wasn't really what we thought of Jesus, but rather, how did he understand himself and our need of him?

And so I simply read from Luke 4, where Jesus read to announce who he was, thus fulfilling prophecy:

> The scroll of the prophet Isaiah was handed to him. Unrolling it, he found the place where it was written:

"The Spirit of the Lord is on me,
  because he has anointed me
  to preach good news to the poor.
He has sent me to proclaim freedom for the prisoners
  and recovery of the sight for the blind,
to release the oppressed,
  to proclaim the year of the Lord's favor." (Luke 4:17-19)

I read the longer passage from which Jesus was reading: Isaiah 61 about the coming of the Messiah:

He has sent me to bind up the brokenhearted . . .
to bestow on them a crown of beauty
  instead of ashes,
the oil of gladness
  instead of mourning,
and a garment of praise
  instead of a spirit of despair.
They will be called oaks of righteousness,
  a planting of the Lord
  for the display of his splendor.

They will rebuild the ancient ruins
  and restore the places long devastated;
they will renew the ruined cities
  that have been devastated for generations. . . .

Instead of their shame
  my people will receive a double portion,
and instead of disgrace
  they will rejoice in their inheritance; . . .
  everlasting joy will be theirs.

"For I, the LORD, love justice;
  I hate robbery and iniquity.
In my faithfulness I will reward them
  and make an everlasting covenant with them . . ."

For as the soil makes the sprout come up
  and a garden causes seeds to grow,
so the Sovereign LORD will make righteousness and praise
  spring up before all nations. (Isaiah 61:1-11)

Then Jesus "rolled up the scroll, gave it back to the attendant and sat down. The eyes of everyone in the synagogue were fastened on him," and he said to them, "Today this scripture is fulfilled in your hearing" (Luke 4:20-21).

Jesus understood himself to be the long-awaited fulfillment of the promises of God for those who believed. He understood himself to be God's Messiah who would rescue not only Israel but the entire human race from death to life. He understood himself to be the servant-king who, by way of sacrifice, would open wide the door to God's kingdom of love and justice on the earth.

Jesus is the avant-garde of God's new covenant. God's law will no longer be written on stone but on the hearts of those who love him. God's Holy Spirit will enliven the souls of those who receive him, making their lives abundant from the inside out.

I have found in Cambridge, and in many communities across the globe, a beginning of what could heal the world—the veritas of God's love embodied in beautiful fellowships of friends, set free from the self-seeking struggle with pride, greed and unreality. If Veritas can find us at Harvard or Berkeley, he can find us anywhere.

Smart people join these fellowships. Wise people become this wherever they are.

When our knees finally bend at each university, when we are made brighter and more curious by that humility, I believe that one Person will remain standing. On the far side of complexity, of our questions and angst, may his still, small voice, that lilting melody, be the one we hear.

Veritas does hold a secret. Its ancient truth is the golden key to our present and our future. "Christ in us," says Paul, "the hope of glory."

Through his eyes, the world is reenchanted and full of possibility.

With the eyes to see, we find a great story and kingdom to which we all belong. We sing with those who've gone before us and those at our side, warmed by the knowing that all things shall be well, one day.

We remember the prophet Jeremiah, to whom the Lord said, "Do not say 'I am only a youth. . . . Be not afraid. Stand and speak what I tell you. Today I appoint you over kingdoms to uproot, to build and to plant. . . . They will oppose you but will not overcome you, for I am with you and will deliver you" (Jeremiah 1:7-10, 19, paraphrased).

And so we find courage in ages past, the age to come, and this age which, by grace alone, is ours.

May our first light be our lasting light. The one from whom all beauty flows.

Veritas, in Christi gloriam.

Epilogue
Coming Home

Praise the Lord, O my soul,
*   and forget not his benefits—*
who forgives all your sins
*   and heals all your diseases,*
who redeems your life from the pit
*   and crowns you with love and compassion,*
who satisfies your desires with good things
*   so that your youth is renewed like the eagle's.*

PSALM 103:2-5

It's hard to know one's own story, of course. And I am a slow learner, overanalyzing before laying hold of things for myself. As a twenty-something I was in perpetual motion, often confusing activity with significance. I volunteered to work with the 1980 Lake Placid Olympic organization. Then, after my last college exam in Ohio, I drove to Colorado to intern for the U.S. Olympic Committee. I later returned to Lake Placid to try out for the U.S. luge team, unsuccessfully, but volunteered at the 1984 Sarajevo Winter Games. After that I worked in media production, had a near miss at love, went to grad school part-time and led Young Life in a local high school (I get dizzy just thinking back to it all).

My thirties were purposeful according to my passions—Veritas, friends, mission work, sports, creation. Cambridge was full of life, and

I thrived on its dynamics. I was known as the person who almost always wanted to get a group together. According to others I was famous for saying, "Hey guys, what if we . . . ?" There were days, in fact years, when I was in the zone. Like Indiana Jones looking for the holy grail, when I stepped out, the path appeared before me.

But there were other days and even years—rather dark ones—when I wondered if I'd made a wrong turn in the road. I began to realize that I wasn't going to be able to do everything. I'd made choices and, as a consequence, excluded certain possibilities, dropped options and closed doors. I stayed busy, but often I felt at a deep level I had missed God's will for my life. That nothing would be right again.

The pain of heartache especially caused me to question my choices. I was in my mid- to late thirties, a chaplain and single woman, traveling between Cambridge and the cabin where I practiced both solitude during the weeks and hospitality on weekends. I was grateful for both the emotional and physical healing I'd experienced. And it felt good to be reuniting with my community of friends and my work with students.

And yet I wondered. Had the work and travel for Veritas and the book *Finding God at Harvard* been too costly personally? Was the benefit worth the cost? Had I gotten off track somewhere and missed God's calling? I'd reached a point in my life where I needed to know.

I asked God to tell me my story. Was I headed down the right road? He took me up on it, and still does, in his timing. I always knew that my work came out of love for my family and for our culture. At one level, I was hoping that God would redeem my own family, injured by the false ideas of the secular culture. It is a gift to now see family members considering, and some believing, the gospel. And I'm hoping that the mind of Jesus will shine again in the universities so that pride and its consequent disasters don't continue to devastate our culture, one child or one family at a time.

In my thirties, I found myself curious to know why my great-grandparents came to America. What would compel them to leave Ireland and Norway? I had it in my heart to visit each place over two consecutive summers. I visited Norwegian friends of friends and camped in my blue tent by stunning Hardanger Fjord with an earthy Christian environmental group called CrossWay. We played volleyball until 2 a.m. in the land of the midnight sun. I then went to the immigration library and found, well, nothing about my mother's family.

It wasn't until a Veritas Forum at Cal Poly that I met my mother's only living cousin, Heidi, who asked me, "Have you seen our family genealogy and history book?"

"No," I said. "When I was in Norway I didn't find much. I had no idea that there was a book."

She replied, "I have an entire book on the lives of several generations moving from Norway and Sweden to Wisconsin."

Amazed, I took out my camera and shot photographs of photographs—of my grandmother dancing as the jitterbug champion of Wisconsin. Of her father, a state senator, who was no doubt embarrassed by his jitterbugging, banjo-playing, baton-twirling daughter whom I would one day call "Aunie." I didn't have time to read the whole book, so Heidi said she'd copy it and send it to me.

A short time later, I was packing for a trip to Ireland to bike with girlfriends and then to golf with family and learn a bit about our paternal history. I found myself still wondering if my life had taken a random or mistaken turn. If God was really there upholding me. On the day I was to leave, I received a phone call from someone I was to talk to that day and never again.

"Hello," a stranger said, politely introducing himself. "I'm in your office in Harvard Yard. I'm sorry to bother you, but I'm in Boston only for the afternoon. I'm reading *Finding God at Harvard* and I caught a cab to the Yard and looked for your office, hoping I might talk with you. The secretary gave me your home number. You see, the book has changed my life. Do you have time to meet?"

"I'd love to," I said, "but I'm a bit rushed, packing for two weeks abroad and I leave tonight with too much to do."

"Are you flying out of Logan?"

"Yes."

"May I meet you at the airport? Which terminal?"

Deciding whether I should feel stalked I said, "The international terminal."

"Me too," he replied. "Do you mind if I ask where you are going?"

"Ireland."

"Forgive me, but is there any chance you are on World Air flight 4202?"

I looked at my itinerary and, feeling a bit nervous, said, "Why do you ask?"

"If you are," he said, "I am, too."

There was a silent pause of disbelief. Now, I'd never been to Ireland before, and this man had never called me before. But somehow we were both going to Ireland, apparently together.

"Yes, I'm on that plane," I answered.

"I'll see you on board," he said. "I think I'll be able to find you."

My seat was in back pinned between the window and a sweet but very drunk Irish boyfriend and girlfriend who were both terrified of flying. The more fear they mustered, the more they drank. The more they drank, the more loudly they swore. Except for the lack of smoke and music it was like being in a crowded Irish pub. Soon the steward-ess came and notified me that I was in the wrong seat. I looked at my ticket and said, "38C."

She said, "It's been changed to 1-A."

Taking a hint, I crawled over the by-now snoring Irish lad and lass and went up to sit near the cockpit.

Once we were at cruising speed over the Atlantic, one of the pilots came into the main cabin and sat in the empty seat next to me. "Kelly?" he asked.

"Yes," I said.

"I'm Lawrence. We spoke on the phone today. I think that we were meant to meet."

Turns out Lawrence was a flight specialist who trained and certified new international pilots and normally flew through Dallas or New York. "I'm rarely in Boston, and that's why I called today."

"Nice timing," I said, also smiling, "because I've never been on a plane to Ireland. Good to meet you. Thanks for the ride."

Lawrence explained that he'd become an atheist in grad school studying philosophy in the seventies. Disillusioned, he dropped out and became a pilot.

He continued, "I saw your book and began reading it. I now see how a love of wisdom, what I thought philosophy would be in college, does point to God. I love fiction and I want to write books. I want to do mission work in South America and help people."

Though in times of heartbreak, illness and exhaustion life did at times seem mistaken, in times like this extraordinary coincidence I sensed God saying, "See, Kelly, I'm here. I've been here all along. Trust me, child, trust me. I'm in the pain and in the pleasure; I feel all of it with you. My grace is sufficient for you. I love you."

I also sensed him saying, "And I love this pilot, whom I will bless. I will restore the years that the locusts have eaten. I save up every tear. I lose nothing, and I lose no one who loves my truth."

I fell asleep, and though I looked the next morning, I did not see the pilot again. He had given me his business card, and after my two-week trip I called the number on it. He had left his airline. I don't know where or how he is, but I believe God is holding him in the palm of his hand.

Coming Home

These adventures, life in and out of Cambridge, were unforgettable and wonderful, but I began to feel that it was time to fall forward in a new way. I'd been thinking about settling down and becoming more of a tree and less of a bird. I also had been thinking of adopting children. Once on a winter mission trip to St. Petersburg, Russia, two orphans asked if I would take them home with me. I began to pray.

At the same time, Veritas advisors and staff in my hometown of Columbus wanted to work together more closely. And after a series of clear dreams, and also missing my parents, I decided to leave the cabin and go home to Ohio. I bought a house out of which I could help run Veritas around the country and possibly raise adopted children. The words of Thoreau resonated, who after months in a canoe on the Concord and Merrimac rivers, and after reading seafaring novels, longed for "the quiet beauty of one fair, particular shore." My one fair, particular shore became my hometown with parents, old friends, church, and Veritas board and staff. Finally I would be near my lifelong friend

Susan and her nine children back home. Though Ohio isn't everyone's vacation destination, it was home and full of good people: the salt of the earth.

So, after that spring's Grad School Christian Fellowship sendoff, I said goodbye to friends and students. Beneath the lighted candles and carved woodwork of Appleton Chapel, Harvard's original chapel in the Yard, friends prayed that I would be able to let go of Cambridge enough to lay hold of what is ahead—desires that seemed lost, desires that might again rise to the surface. Desires that I'd set aside while trying to fight the fight and change the world, however slightly. Steph and Cathy prayed that God would open my eyes to see his faithfulness and his path of abundance. I said goodbye to students, to friends and dogs and sheep near the cabin, to the red barn and to Jeff. Brenda and I took a last walk around Walden Pond, and she prayed that God would make all things new.

I loaded up a truck and drove to Ohio after thirteen years, and this time I didn't turn back except to visit.

Several weeks after arriving back home in Columbus, I learned that the two Russian children were not legally available for adoption, which was a disappointment.

Then a Veritas advisor, old friend and bright apologist named John Hansel suggested to a friend of his, David Kullberg, that he call me to discuss sharing the gospel with someone. David came over and I handed him a wooden spoon to stir the chili for the college fellowship that met in my house. He was a writer and a father raising five children on his own and writing in the wee hours between bedtime and car pool. We ended up discussing a draft of his novel, *The War Against God*. The title reminded me of the only surviving book in John Harvard's library, and the story itself revealed the beauty of faithful people who care less about being "left behind" and more about loving God's world back to life.

To my surprise he called the next day and then most days after that. Unwittingly, we became the world's smallest writers club, meeting at Caribou Coffee near Ohio State. I thought that we were "just friends" until someone asked if she could join our writers club, and David announced with a grin that "she was welcome to apply; however, as the chairman of the membership committee, he was obliged to mention that there was currently a two-year waiting period for new members."

"Why?" I later asked him.

"Because I always wanted a best friend," he said.

He became the world's biggest fan of Veritas, of *Finding God at Harvard*, saying, "I want my children to live in a story like yours, full of faith and meaningful adventure."

His enthusiasm for Veritas fueled my own. He drew out of me every story that became this book, and then some.

I was also challenged by his faith in God's sovereignty in the midst of suffering, having lost his wife to cancer at age forty-three, leaving him with five children at home to raise. I remembered my night in 1995 in a café, waiting out a monsoon, with Madeleine L'Engle. It was a wrinkle in time because now, a decade later as I write, I realize that my conversation with Madeleine about loss, grief and hope occurred during the same spring that the man I would eventually marry lost his first wife to cancer. The Word of God was falling into his heart, and he was sustained by grace to raise five children on his own for an irrational but truthful season.

Seeing the faith, hope and love that could emerge radiant in that suffering, I grew in my trust in God's power to make all things new. And I came to trust David. The rest, as they say, is history. I fell in love with David and then with the children: Michelle ("Tweetie Bird"), Joshua, John, April and Keya.

When Josh learned that I didn't know the difference between King Kong and Godzilla, he asked, "What have you been doing all this time?" Good question. The youngest, Michelle, full of life, is now fifteen, but that doesn't stop me from reading her *Winnie the Pooh* by the fire. Our barely germinated band, the Mildly Sensitive Tomboys, features April and Michelle as lead singers, yours truly and John on guitar, Josh on drums, and David who plays the triangle and drives the still-but-barely-living Lunch Box to our imaginary gigs.

We were married in the same sanctuary in which I hid as a hurting teenager while taking in the musical Passion play. The man who played the role of Jesus twenty-eight years before, Dave Fullen, led worship at our wedding. My youth pastor, now senior pastor Paul Ulring, led the ceremony. Brenda came from Boston and sang at the piano.

That night in the circle of one another, a few hundred of us danced under the stars to Celtic music—like the country dance that inspired the idea of Veritas more than a decade before. We danced within the dance of the Trinity. Jeff, Brenda, David, Kay, Katie, Andy, Jo, Jennifer, Martha, Dellynne, Rick, children, the Armbrusts and Hansels, the Lees and Watkins, parents, brothers, Father, Son, Holy Spirit. We danced.

Given the gift of our marriage, and ready-made family, life is forcing me to grow from child to adult, from receiver to giver, from guest to host. David has all the quiet virtues that I lack, and so our ship stays afloat while I slowly learn.

God has kindly given me the image of a garden plant in his parable of the mustard seed. It begins as a small seed. I imagine it's blown around a lot, but once it falls to the ground and takes root in good soil, it grows to become "the largest of the garden plants, and the birds of the air gather in its branches" (Luke 13:18).

Now, as a daughter and wife and mother and friend, I am becoming a bit less of a bird and a bit more of a tree in which the birds of the air can eat and rest and be blessed, protected and encouraged. College students, teenagers, neighbors, grandparents, the OSU Veritas planners—a healthy tree is wonderfully biodiverse. I'm learning by watching my husband that such trees are particularly good at drawing life from beneath the surface, from the roots up, for the fruit of love, patience and kindness.

For now, we're content to abide and to live with open arms under an open sky. We long for our children, and for ourselves, to live in an immediate reality—to break through virtual deception and into visceral truth. To play in the mud, to have adventures and skinned knees. We muck stalls, ride horses, hike and ski in the same little Ohio valley with the nine Armbrust kids. It's not the mountains of New England or South America, but it's only an hour away. We pick apples and collect honey from bees. David often reads to our family by the fire after Sunday dinners.

My life is becoming more about roots than wings, though I still have both. My idea of high art is Michelle's seventh-grade painting of us on the *Dawn Treader*, InterVarsity's sailboat on Lake Huron. My idea of theater is Josh's eighth-grade production of *Tom Sawyer*. I'd prefer dancing with David in the kitchen over a springtime waltz in Harvard Yard on, well, most nights.

We still marvel at God's world, even more so through the eyes and minds of children. At Cedar Campus, Michelle leapt and danced in the sand one night under the starry sky. "It's so beautiful!" she cried, and I knew then that I belonged in a family—this family in particular. Whether by biology or other kinship, connection to children is a gift from the Lord. I cry and laugh more. I am challenged to define family as Jesus seemed to: adopted not by blood but by faith. Shared by those who together call the Lord of heaven and earth Daddy.

When I came to believe in Jesus in high school, I saw a new way of living, a creative and joyful vitality that I did not see in the conformist university. In response to my own many questions, I was also struck by the reasonableness of the gospel. I felt a calling to restore an understanding of the person and brilliance of Jesus to the most secularized and influential sphere of our culture—the academy. I also did this in love and honor of my parents and their own journeys still unfolding.

My calling and passion is still Veritas. Veritas as True Vine. I can't presume to give to others without first receiving from him. I depend on his ecology. It is the only dependency I know that feels like freedom and life. I guess I believe in miracles mainly because my life is filled with them. I sense inklings of redemption. I've been healed physically. I'm given many of my heart's desires—though, with the unique sorrow of miscarriage, not all. But joy is possible without every desire fulfilled. I'm learning contentment, which in Latin means "to be held." I increasingly sense the miracle that we all share—of our small stories being grafted into the great story, with time, depth and future hope.

■ ■ ■

A wedding gift arrived from my second cousin Heidi. It was a family genealogy from Scandinavia to Wisconsin. My mother read aloud to us a section of the book, a letter from a Norwegian immigration museum.

"Dear Mrs. Johnson, I have found the ship [on which your ancestors departed] registered in our files. . . . Unfortunately, there seems to be no picture of the ship in the museum collection. But we can tell you that it was built in Sunderland, 1831, and in 1887 the ship was classified *Veritas*."

Acknowledgments

I would like to thank some, among many, wonderful friends and partners: To my wonderful **family** of Monroes, Kullbergs, Sengelmanns and Armbrusts.

To my **readers and editors:** David Kullberg, Al Hsu, Dan Cho, Martha Linder, Katie Milway, Carol Williams and Ted Callahan.

For our Veritas "trail map," thank you Jody Sjogren.

To **various fellowships** that unite as a communal witness and host; many independent local fellowships and churches, InterVarsity Christian Fellowship, Campus Crusade for Christ, Ivy Jungle, Navs, Alpha, Chi Alpha, ABSK, RUF, Campus Ambassadors, Reasons to Believe, Mosaic, Upper Arlington Lutheran Church in Columbus.

To Jeff Barneson and the Harvard Grad School Christian Fellowship, along with Harvard undergrads.

To **administrative support** from universities, such as offices of the provost, student government, various sponsoring deans and academic departments.

To the **Veritas board,** including my fellow present members: chairman Kurt Keilhacker, Daniel Cho, Katie and Michael Milway, John Kingston and Ted Callahan; and my fellow past board members: chairman Jerry Mercer, Nancy Donner, David Mann, John Hansel, Larry Johns, Bill Edgar, Morse Tan, Don Lee, Howard VanCleave, Eric Roy, Matt Fields, Charles Kwon and Jim Zangmeister.

To our small **Veritas staff** led by Daniel Cho, along with several regional coaches and interns, hundreds of volunteers, who serve hundreds of thousands of participants. In the 1990s: Ken Brown, Jeri Lynn Brooks and Matt Fields; in the 2000s: Ashley and Ted Callahan, Andy

Crouch, Daniel Cho, Ana Maria Schlecht, and interns Candace Shreve, Faith Sadar, Paul Choi, Ryan Lincoln, Theresa Brosnan-Johnson, Liz Hawkins and Louisa Thomason.

For **media and website** help: Don Lee, Buck McCallum, John Walsh, Grant Olsen, Art Battson, Eugene Adams, Justin Smith, Kyle Doerksen and Scott Cannon. See <www.veritas.org> to join our journey and to enjoy many presentations.

To **Veritas speakers,** most of whom are Christian scholars, professors and professionals, doctors and scientists, researchers, pastors, and artists responding to the hardest questions of the university, society, and the human heart. These presenters include: David Adeney, David Aikman, Ron Akers, Ray Aldred, Denis Alexander, Dave Anderson, Mary Ellen Ashcroft, Ric Ashley, Marc and Patty Baer, Dennis Bakke, Steve Ballinger, Randall Balmer, Jeff Barneson, S. Scott Bartchy, Wendy Bannister, Carey and Randy Bare, Lilian Calles-Barger, Jeff Barneson, Art Battson, Elisabeth (Overmann) Baumann, Michael Behe, Jeremy Begbie, E. Calvin Beisner, T. March Bell, Harold Berman, Brenda Birmann, Bradley Birzer, Diane Bisgeier, Alf Bishai, Roger Blackwell, Avis Blair, Craig Blomberg, Marcus Borg, Scott Bolinder, Steven Bouma-Prediger, Greg Boyd, Jane Boyer, Walter Bradley, David Bradshaw, Paul Brand, Alice Brown-Collins, Jay Budziszewski, Doug Bunnell, Rudy Caarrasco, Anthony Campolo, William Carlton, Corbin Carnell, Richard Carrier, Ben Carson, Stephen Carter, Vikram Chand, Gary Chapman, Honora Chapman, Peter Clark, Matthew Coburn, Sharon Cohn, Jack Collins, Charles Colson, Matthew Conolly, Brian Cox, William Lane Craig, Andy and Catherine Crouch, Daniel Curran, Robert D'Agostino, Austin Dacey, Darrell Darling, Marva Dawn, David Deamer, Matt DeJongh, Michael DeRobertis, Gary DeWeese, Calvin DeWitt, Nishan de Mel, Henry Delcore, William Dembski, Alan Dershowitz, Bob DiSilvestro, Larry Donnithorne, John and Todd Dorman, Mike Duggins, Jeronima Echeverria, William and Debbie Edgar, Bruce Edwards, Jean Bethke Elshtain, Susan and Charles Emmerich, Casely Essamuah, Dan Everett, Sabrina Fairchild, Peter Feaver, David Fitch, Alex Flather- Morgan, Daniel Flemming, Anthony Flew, Brian Foster (for Brent Foster), Serrin Foster, David French, Ron Fritts, Tim Fry, Charles

Futrell, Sharon Gallagher, Richard Ganz, Steven Garber, Ward Gasque, Saleem Ghubril, David Gill, Gale Gnade, Ari Goldman, Peter Gomes, Hon. James Graham, Frederica Matthewes-Green, David Grizzle, Greg Grooms, Peter Gomes, Greg Grooms, Douglas Groothius, Os Guinness, Judith Gundry-Volf, Terry Gustafson, Gary Habermas, Brian and Kay Hall, Molly Halvey, Ron Hansen, Garrett Hardin, Annalise Harding, Robert Harper, Dennis Hassell, Daniel Hastings, Gary Haugen, Wally Hawley, Walter Hearn, Ken Heffner, Philip Hefner, Bryan Hehir, Paul Hensleigh, Bruce Herman, Laura Hermann, Roberta Hestenes, Jon Hinkson, Eric Holter, Antonye Holyde, Thomas Howard, John Hoyt, Bruce Huber, William Hurlbut, Ian Hutchinson, Sabastian Huynh, Lee Irons, Mary Irwin, Kay Cole James, David Lyle Jeffries, Douglas Jesseph, Greg Jesson, Robert Jewett, Kirstin Jeffrey Johnson, Phillip E. Johnson, Jo Kadlecek, Lauris Kaldjean, Sudarshan Kapoor, Patrick Kavanaugh, Guy Kawasaki, Christine Keeling, James Keesling, Kurt Keilhacker, Timothy Keller, John Kennedy, Dean Kenyon, Tom Key, Dick and Ben and Mardi Keyes, Joseph Kickasola, Jim Kidder, John F. Kilner, Rebekah Kim, Diane King, John Kingston, Phillip Kitcher, David Koepsell, Liz and Pravin Kothapa, Robert Koons, Ken Krabbenhoft, Peter Kreeft, Nicholas Kristof, Catherine Kroeger, Bruce Kuhn, Finny Kuruvilla, Madeleine L'Engle, Mark Labberton, Joy Jordan Lake, Todd Lake, James Langley, David Larson, George Lebo, Mike Licona, Ard Louis, Jack Lunsford, Jay Lynch, Jed Macosko, Bill Malarkey, Robert Maldonado, Habib Malik, George Marsden, Paul Marshall, Eff Martin, J. Stanley Mattson, Roy McCloughry, Gene McConnell, Norma McCorvey ("Jane Roe"), Erwin McManus, Sam Meier, Eric Metaxas, David Miller, Don Miller, Scott Minnich, Katie Smith Milway, Michael Milway, John Monsma, John Warwick Montgomery, J. P. Moreland, Hyatt Mousa, Barbara Mouser, Richard Mouw, Karen Mulder, Thomas Mundle, Mary Naber, Ron Nash, Thomas Nechyba, Glen Needham, Paul Nelson, Richard John Neuhaus, Robert Newman, John Newsome, Armand Nicholi, Mark Noll, Marvin Olasky, Adeyemi Olufolabi, Gwendolyn O'Neal, Dean Overmann, Sam Overstreet, Billy Park, Richard Parker, John Patrick, Ryan Pazdur, Nancy Pearcey, Bill Pearson, Gordon Pennington, Derek

Perkins, Rodney Peterson, Charles (Tony) Pfaff, Susan Phillips, Daniel
Philpot, Rosalind (Roz) Picard, Kerry Pierce, Alvin Plantinga, Pablo
Polischuk, Sir John Polkinghorne, Bonnie Poon, Sanjay Poonen, Mary
Poplin, Becky and David Porteous, Paul Post, Richard Pratt, William
Provine, James Pyne, Vinoth Ramachandra, Fazale Rana, John Rankin,
Condoleezza Rice, Fazale Rana, Larry Reed, George Rekers, John
Mark Reynolds, John Richardson, Benjamin Rodriguez, Bill Ro-
manowski, Aaron Romanowsky, Richard Rorty, Hugh Ross, Heather
(Tallman) Ruhm, Jeffrey Russell, Leland Ryken, Jeffrey Sachs, Krister
Sairsingh, Lamin Sanneh, Henry "Fritz" Schaefer, Jeffrey Schloss,
Thomas Schmidt, David Schugart, Jeffrey Schwartz, Suzanne Rozell
Scorsone, Darrell Scott, Marlan Scully, Niall Shanks, Robert Shapiro,
Luci Shaw, Vera and James Shaw, Joe Sheldon, Michael Shermer, Rob-
ert Shapiro, Lawrence Shattuck, Ron Sider, Jennifer Siggers, David
Simms, Steve Simmons, Nancy Simpson, James Sire, Jody Sjogren,
Laura Smit, Estella Smith, L. Murphy Smith, Betsy Inskeep Smylie,
David Snoke, Scott Snook, Mark Somma, Tim Stafford, John Staple-
ford, Michael Strauss, John Stott, Rick Strawbridge, Lori Strehler, Ele-
onore Stump, William Stuntz, Wayne Talarzyk, Joel Tanis, Stanley Tay-
lor, Antonio Tendero, John Teter, Charles Thaxton, Terry Thomas,
Chuck Thorpe, Robert Thurman, James Tour, Drew Trotter, Bob Trube,
James Tumlin, Carl Upchurch, Howard VanCleave, Kyle Van Houtan,
Mary Stewart Van Leeuwen, Deb Veth, Gene Edward Veith, Paul Vitz,
Constance and William Walker, Jerry Wall, Alan Wallace, Stan Wallace,
Jim Wallis, Raleigh Washington, B. J. Weber, William "Chip" Weiant,
Kathy Donovan Weigand, Richard Weikart, Jonathan Wells, James
Westgate, Clif Wilcox, Dallas Willard, Lauren Winner, Arthur Wint,
Jennifer Wiseman, Ben Witherington, Larry Woiwode, Nicholas
Wolterstorff, Edson Wood, Dudley Woodberry, Dana Wrensch, N. T.
Wright, Paul Wylie, Edwin Yamauchi, Philip Yancey, Michael Yang, Poh
Lian Lim (Lim) Yap, Kris Young, Frank Young, R. V. Young, Mark Young,
Scott Young, Ravi Zacharias, David and Micky Zartman.

To those who participated in **Veritas outings,** including: mission
and eco-adventures in South America, with Food for Hungry, Wycliffe,
Prison Fellowship; wetlands hikes with Cal DeWitt at the University of

Wisconsin and University of West Ontario; surfing at UCLA, UCSD and UCSB; salmon runs at the Columbia River Gorge at Oregon State University; ski trips and hiking in Rockies, White and Green Mountains, Sierra-Nevadas and the Andes; tours through museums, rare books libraries and research labs; two-steppin' at Anne and Walter Bradley's in College Station, Texas; star gazing "cosmos tours," at Ohio State, Harvard and MIT; and "treasure hunts" through art museums at Harvard and Carnegie-Mellon.

To **Veritas musicians, artists and performers,** including: Jars of Clay at the University of New Hampshire and Hope College; Michael Card at Harvard University; the UCLA grafitti performance and art exhibit; Over the Rhine in concert at Hope College; *An Evening with Champions,* hosted at Harvard by Olympic skater Paul Wylie; "C. S. Lewis on Stage" and a scene from Revelation by actor Tom Key at Harvard University; *The Great Divorce* by C. S. Lewis, performed by University of Kentucky drama department; *The Screwtape Letters* actor Tom Key at the University of Pennsylvania; "C. S. Lewis on Stage" by David Payne; *The Gospel of Luke, Tales of Tolstoy* and *Acts* by Broadway actor Bruce Kuhn; gospel choirs in many universities, such as Harvard's Kuumba; Haydn's *Creation* by Virginia Tech orchestra; Handel's *Messiah* in Harvard's Dunster House; "One Artist's Spiritual Journey" by Bruce Herman at Harvard; Keith and Kristyn Getty singing new Irish hymns at Ohio State University; Joel Tannis in concert; "The Sense of an Ending" by Jeremy Begbie; Pierce Pettis in concert; J. S. Bach, *St. Matthew Passion;* "Heaven in a Nightclub: The Christian Roots of Jazz" by Bill Edgar and Ruth Naomi Floyd, at Rice, Duke, Brown, Harvard and LSU; and "The Spiritual Lives of the Great Composers" talk by Patrick Kavanaugh, and violin performance by Mary Irwin at Ohio State.

To those who participated in the **film and documentary discussions** of *Hamlet; A Man For All Seasons; Chariots of Fire; A Walk to Remember; The Fellowship of the Ring; The Return of the King; The Lion, the Witch and the Wardrobe; Luther; The Passion of the Christ; Glory; Jesus of Nazareth* (Zefferreli)*; Life Is Beautiful; The Spitfire Grill; The Truman Show; Babette's Feast; Brother Sun, Sister Moon; The Matrix; The Mission; Dead Man Walking; Quiz Show; The Privileged Planet; Unlocking the Mys-*

teries of Life; Bonhoeffer; Icons of Evolution; Teresa; Weapons of the Spirit; How Shall We Then Live? with Francis Schaeffer; and *Fatal Addiction* (Ted Bundy's final interview) with James Dobson.

To the thousands of **Veritas planners and volunteers**—they are the human heroes of Veritas—though impossible to name them all, some include those at the following universities.

The East. Brown University—Matt Coburn, Gordon Sigler, Peter Han, Joseph Hong, Sue-Lin Nurse, James Langley, Jason Loscuito, Irene Eng, Mark Hidenbrand, Alex and Debbi Thomas, Alfred Ricci, Kari Klassen and Ross Meuller;

Carnegie-Mellon University and the University of Pittsburgh—Tom Grosh, Mike Milano, David Baynes, BJ Woodworth, Karen Stevenson, Sandie Starr, Gary Myers, Eugene Tibbs, Leland Albright, Randy Bryant, Richard Cox, Dan Everett, Robert Griffiths, Christian Hallstein, Barry Luokkala, Katherine Lynch, Gary Patterson, Ed Sell, Ann Smiley-Oyen, David Snoke, Chuck Thorpe, Richard Zimmerman;

Columbia University—Ashley Byrd, Kevin Oro-Hahn, Ben and Heather Grizzle, Ken J. Lee, Tien Lun Chuang, Jesica Lee, Emily Lo, Norman Yung, Carol Chuang, Kai Chang, David Cho, Albert Wu, Ben Lyons, Fr. Jacek Buda, Susan Field, Gordon Pennington, Scott Strickman, Reyn Cabinte, Terri Thompson, Katie Roland and Sharon Park;

New York University—Jeff Jacob, Elizabeth Kallop, Jackie Ling, Ian Lau, Paige Hinkle, Trevor Agatsuma, Matthew Schultz, Benjamin Roberts, Daria Ng, Christopher Goodenough, Terri Tsai, Andrea Woodward, Susan Field, Ann Hrivnak, Peter Trautmann, Johnny Pyon, Father John McGuire, Seth Freeman, Ben and Heather Grizzle, and Matt Rose;

Duke University—Luke Condra, Jason Dean, Cindy Wang, Peter and Karen Feaver, Kyle and Kelly Van Houtan, Ken Elzinga, Steve Hinkle, Cindy Wang, IV Grad and Faculty, FCA student leaders, Joseph Ho;

Harvard University—DJ Snell, Jeff Barneson, Mark Gauthier, Jim and Vera Shaw, Kay and Brian Hall, Dean Truog, David Cist, Debbie Edgar, Elisabeth Overmann Bauman, Tricia Lyons, Nishan de Mel, Glenn Lucke, David McGaw, Laura Singleton, Laura Johnson, John Kingston, Kristin Brunner Thurlby, Kirk Reickhoff, Phil Coburn,

Dave Brunton, Rebekah Kim, Daniel Cho, Kevin Offner, Jim Shaw, John Ratichek, Rich Lamb, Andy Crouch, Heather (Woodruff) Grizzle, Ben Grizzle, Ben Littauer, Rich Halverson, Heather Tallman, Poh Lian Lim, Bonnie Poon, Angela Um, Kurt Keilhacker, Ashley and Ted Callahan, Jay Minga, Grace Hou, Jeff Dean, Deborah Morton, Caitlin Stork, Katherine McEnaney, Aaron Barth, Garrett Grolemund, Emily High, Rich Halvorson, Matt Salvatierra, Mark Hill, Joel Mitchell, Anne Haig, Molly Lin, Victor Li-Ban, Brad Smith, Yannis Paulus, ABSK (Asian Baptist Student Koinonia's fantastic dramatic production), Jordan Hylden, Jacob Luke Bryant, Jennifer Whiteside, Rick Buhrman, Dave Toniatti, Kathy Goodson, Jeanette Park, Shang Chen, CT Chin, Chiduzie Matubata, Tina Teng, Stephen George, Jon Scruggs, Marcus Moreno, Adam Benitez, Teddy Styles, Ellie Campisano, Saul de La Guardia, Jason Scoggins and Faith Sadar;

Penn State University—led by Keith Maurer;

Princeton University—Scott Luley, Keith Brewer, David H. Kim, Clay Porr, Bill Boyce, David Buschman, Matt Bennett, Ryan Bonfiglio, Thomas Mullelly, Ryan Anderson, Laura Bennett, Robert Kaita, Robert Prudhomme, Gary Deddo, Jim McCullough, Undergraduate Student Government (USG), Joe Williamson, Tom Breidenthal, Bob and LaDonna Lally, Jon and Patty Sweemer, and Kirk and Brenda Lowery;

University of Pennsylvania—Dave de Huff, Michael Atchison, Richard Landis, Rob Roy MacGregor, John P. Dormans, Donald Ewert, Steve Dunning, Horace DeLisser, Michael Moore, Kevin Bauder, Steve Baker, J. D. Atkins, Michael Pollack, Ashok Kurian, Margaret Jankowsky, Cindy Groff, Jessica Benash, Tim Fryett, Steven Mitchell, Michael Hu, Elizabeth Lovett and Noel Greenberger;

United States Military Academy, West Point—chaplain Ron Fritts;

Yale University—Donald Dacey, Greg Ganssle, John Hinkson, Eric Gregory, Dave Mahen, Stewart Davenport and Chris Green;

Bryn Mawr and Haverford College—Sharon Bain, Jonathan Malone, Michelle Kim, Phil Zhang, Joel Kwabi, Joe Chai, Anita Lai, Nicole Wood, Astrid Rodrigues, Amanda Fegley, Jes Chung, Leah Blankenship, Kimberly Beaton, Lilly Yoon, Alice Oh, Jenny Lom, Susie Matter,

Kelsey Smith and Mary Kim;

University of New Hampshire, Durham—Sue Foster;

University of Western Ontario, Canada—Michael Venema, Clive Waugh, Christian Naus, Jim Neufeld, Pat Taylor, Michael Wagenman, Kenji Saito and Jason Perry;

York University, Canada—Eva Sham, Yury Baik, Shiao Chong, Kathy Cook, Phil Cummings, Rob Fish, Jimmy Kim.

The Midwest. Ohio State University—Howard and Debbie Van-Cleave, Micky and David Zartman, Bob and Marilyn Trube, Peggy and Gary Nielson, James and Kyle Pyne, Paul Post, Glenn Needham, Julie DeLavergne, Larry Schirm, Jody and Jack Sjogren, Jack Chapin, Debbie and Mark Splaingard, Andrew Moon, Stephanie Rummel, Allison Brooks, Michael Mattes, Don Lee, David, Kelly, April and John Kullberg, Mimi and Craig Taylor, Chip Weiant, Jim Wyland, Nancy Donner, Terry Gustafson, Matt DeJongh, Bill Mowry, Jim Lett, Joe Zickafoose, Tim Montgomery, Wayne Talarzyk, Matt Fields and Bryce Kurfees;

University of Minnesota—Bob Osburn, Luke Brekke, Ben Stevens, Tylor Wagner, Nicole Anderson, Steve Spaulding, Sarah Decker, Chris Cook, Cole Reis, Matt Kahl, Julie Moch, Bruce Harpel, Leon Longard, Doug Schulz, William Monsma and Joe Mulvihill;

Hope College—Marc and Patty Baer, Meg Gustafson and Joel Tannis;

Northwestern University and the University of Chicago—Rick Ashley, Morse Tan, Ethan Schrumm and Jay Sivitts;

Indiana University—Jim Tomasik and the Hon. David Welch;

Ball State University—Jim Tomasik, Bruce Geelhoed, Larry Roberts and Norman Van Cott;

University of Iowa—led by Keith Bateman;

University of Kansas—Jason Brown;

University of Michigan—Charles Roeper, Daniel Balbach, Robert Adgate, Abe Radmanesh, Kevin Richardson and Bruce Robinson;

University of Nebraska—led by Ray Boeche;

University of Wisconsin, Madison—Jim Tanner, Vern Visick, Cam Anderson, Terry Morrison and Jon Dahl.

The South. University of Tennessee—Mike Maxey, Susan and Doug

Messer, Jim Kidder, Terry Weber and Julian Reese;

University of Kentucky—Maureen and Mark Jacus, David Bradshaw, McKinley Neal and Brian Marshall;

University of Louisville—led by Doug Borchman;

Rice University—led by James Tour;

Louisiana State University—led by Sung Joon Jang, Ann Ledet, Howard Tull and Robyn Verbois;

University of Florida—Michael Sorgius, Eddie Gilley, Matt Gordon, Aaron Read, James Keesling, George Lebo, James Keesling, Jay Lynch, Corbin Carnell and Clif Wilcox;

University of Georgia—led by Bill Hager;

Emory University—led by James Tumlin;

Oglethorpe University—led by Michelle Harrington;

University of North Carolina, Asheville—Marty Johnson and Dean Miller;

University of Texas, Austin—Greg Grooms and John Cogdell;

University of Virginia—Drew Trotter, Tony Giles, Russell, Skip Burzumato and Tripp Sanders;

Texas A & M University—Ann and Walter Bradley, and Michael Neely;

Virginia Tech—led by Dean Bork, Kristin Ammons, Steve Brown, Elizabeth Grotz, Hank Tarlton, J. R. Woodward, Tabatha Crostic, Loren Rees, Wayne Leininger, Kwa-Sur Tam, Bill Robinson, Mark Newell, Don Ohanehi, Cliff Ragsdale, Dave Broadwell and Matthew Vahlberg.

The West. Cal Poly, San Luis Obispo—Jamey Pappas, Avery Blackwell, Josh Jeter, Dan Fogal, Mike Swanson, Trevor Aclinard, Scott Fults and Christiana Williams;

Oregon State University—led by Gary Hough and Steve Mayer;

University of Oregon—Richard Beswick, Mike Alverts, Kathryn Voyak, Mike Edsall, Mia Kubu, Ryan Moore, David Rapp, Corey Rose and Dan Smith;

Stanford University—Libby Vincent, David Dettoni, Bruce Huber, Phillip Brennan, Tom Sheehan, Jonathon Smith, Kurt Keilhacker, Bianca Dorman, Josh Ralston, Ron Sanders, Pete Sommer, Scott Scruggs, Steve Stenstrom;

University of California, Berkeley—Susan Phillips, Sharon Gallagher, Doug Bunnell, Carrie Bare, Randy Bare, Daniel Curran, Jason Jensen, Bruce McCluggage, Dave Fang, Mark Labberton, Paul Ruud, Tom Bryce, Clay Radke, Al Tizon, Phillip E. Johnson, Vivian Lau, Nancy Muff, Erina Kim, Felix Theonugraha, Josh Ong and Elliot Au;

University of California, Los Angeles (UCLA)—Andrew Dragos, Soon Chung, Kyle Gladden, Marian Halls, Ashley Starkweather, Marc Janoff, Tim Shulz, Faith St Jean, Craig Nishimoto , Andrew Mcdonnell, Ryan Richards, John Book, Matthew and Lucy Pearl Conolly, John Griffin, Clarice Law, Alfred Wong, Heather, Heather, Peter;

University of Southern California (USC)—Courtney Churukian, Anya Thomas, Brooke Fullmer, Lydia Lee, Natasha Huang, Stephen Cathers, Brandon Dion, Ian Dale, Jonathan Whitmore, Greg Triplett, Neil Walker and Stefan Aledroni;

University of California at Santa Cruz (UCSC)—Pam Urfer, Susan Bentley, Jason Reikewald-Schmidt and Karen Keen;

Fresno State—Henry Delcore, Gary Lentell and Steve Cates;

Arizona State University—Ben Johnson, Mike;

University of California at San Diego—Elliot Hui, George Varghese, Bill Howden, Liam Palmer, Rick Lieber, J. Bracht, James Choung, Sharon Narita, Jeremy Kua, J. Norris, G. Huber, S. Dexter, K. Beardsley, M. Choi, N. Gallaher, L. Rice and P. Neukom;

University of California, Santa Barbara—Art Battson, John and Vicky Kennedy, Daniel Philpot, Chris Comstock, Scott Wilson, Ed Birch, Christy Whiddon and Eric Agol;

University of Colorado, Boulder—Jim Cook, Steven Jolly, George Morgenthaler, Jack Twombly, Gordon Brown, Paul Todd, Ed Miller.

United Kingdom. Maithrie White, Nishan de Mel, Ard Louis, Mike Clifford, Debbie Dickson, Ian Tarrant, Aaron Romanowsky, Chye Foong Yong and Mike Jeggo.

And with gratitude for special **friendships and partnerships** over the years, including: Cam Anderson, Patty and Marc Baer, Carol and Dick Baer, Carie and Randy Bare, the Barnesons, Kim and Tudy Bartlett, Art Battson, Elisabeth Baumann, Matt and Monty Bennett, Brenda Birmann, Gary Bollinger, Marcia and Pete Bosscher, Sandy and Rick Bowen, Anne and Walter Bradley, Bob Brindell, the Brunners, the Bunnells, Ashley, Ted and Sam Callahan, Colleen and Craig Caruso, Daniel Cho, Eric Convey, Sandy Corbitt, Marva Dawn, Julie DeLavergne, Carolyn and Bob Durfy, Barb, Debbie and Bill Edgar, Nathan Estruth, Matt Fields, the Fieldstead Foundation, David French, Bob Fryling, Mark Gauthier, Krystyn and Keith Getty, Cynthia Gonzalez, Eric Gregory, Douglas Gresham, Os and Jenny Guinness, Kay and Brian Hall, Eric Halvorsen, Anne and Bryan Hamlin, Craig Hammon, the Hansels, Darlene and Walter Hansen, Susan and Charles Harper, Bruce and Meg Herman, Kirstin and Greg Johnson, Laura and Jeff Jones, John and Vicky Kennedy, Dick and Mardi Keyes, Frank and Judy Kifer, Jung Joo Kim, Diane E. King, John and Jean Kingston, Drew Ladner, Todd and Joy Jordan Lake, Susan and Louis Lataif, Martha Linder, Ard Louis, Glenn Lucke, Hugh Maclellan, Stan Mattson, Tom McCallie, Doug McCallum, Elisabeth, Furmann and Denise McDonald, Carole McMillen, Jerry Mercer, Gayle Miller, Katie and Mike Milway, David and Pam Mann, Nishan de Mel, the Nagy family, Kevin and Amy Offner, Ruth and Jim Olsen, Cary Paine, Gordon Pennington, Roz Picard, Elaine and Gene Pierce, Mary Poplin, Becky and David Porteous, Steph Powers, John Reichart, Nancy and Diego Ruiz, Heather and Bryan Ruhm, the Rules, John Sage, James Shaw, Steve and Mary Jane Simmons Laura Singleton, Mallory and Mary Ann Smith, DJ Snell, Lou Soiles, Grady Spires, Dellynne and Rick Strawbridge, the Stull family, John Stott, Kristin and Trace Thurlby, Kathy Tuan-McLean, Paul Ulring, Howard and Debbie Van-Cleave, Abraham Vema, Nina and Meirwyn Walters, Tammy Watkins, Andy Webb, Richard West, Woody White, Dallas Willard, Ron Williams, Jennifer Wiseman, Poh and Vong Yap, Susie and David Young, Micky and David Zartman, Leslie and Steve Ziesler.

Thanks for the **inspirational music** of: Eva Cassady, Joni Mitchell, James Taylor, Dan Fogelberg, J. S. Bach, F. Handel, Kenny G, Loreena McKennit, Chris Rice, David Wilcox, Michael Card, Fernando Ortega, Amy Grant, Jill Phillips, Nickel Creek, Bebo Norman and, oh well, too many to mention here.

And with thanks for the **Bible teaching** of Beth Moore, N. T.

Wright, Joel Nagy, Kay Arthur, Tommy Nelson and John Stott.

And in the vivid memory of Vera Shaw.

With deepest thanks to each of you. This story would be my gift to you if it weren't first your gift to me and to many.

A moment of silence for nearly two hundred pages of stories and ideas on the editing floor. See many photos, stories and talks to accompany this book on our web site—<www.veritas.org>.

Purposes and profits from this book are dedicated to the mission of the Veritas Forum, helping students Explore True Life.

Join us for more photos, friends and stories at <www.veritas.org>.

Harvard's shield translates, "truth, for Christ and the church." It's first motto was "for Christ's glory."

The Harvard Grad School Christian Fellowship (GSCF).

Jeff Barneson in front, with colleagues (Kathy Tuan-MacLean and Lou Soiles) and GSCF student leaders.

Kelly journaling above Machu Picchu, Peru, en route with friends to build a school in the Amazon with Food for the Hungry.

War orphans caring for one another, and even befriending us, in El Salvador.

Students build a medical clinic with Haitian workers in the Dominican Republic.

Rebuilding houses after a civil war in (Mayan) Ixil villages of Guatemala. L to R, Nathan Estruth, Kelly, Heather Ruhm, Will Schroer and Brian Ruhm.

One of many ski trips with friends in the Rockies, Sierras and New England.

Mother Teresa's letter from Calcutta, about the *Finding God at Harvard* book.

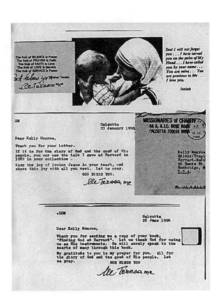

In Cambridge, absorbing the light and love of Vera Shaw, our spiritual grandmother, whose very name (Vera) means "truth."

Kelly reading student questions at the first Veritas Forum at Harvard Law School in 1992. Far right edge: DJ Snell. (Photo by Jeff Barneson.)

Keynote speaker Ravi Zacharias on "Is Atheism Dead? Is God Alive?" Twenty presenters explored questions of more than 700 participants.

Soon after, many forums become a symphony of disciplines and cultures. (Photo by David Herwaldt.)

Kuumba Gospel Choir on stage of Sanders Theatre, Harvard. (Photo by Debbie Edgar.)

Christina Folch listens to talks on wholeness and community. (Photo by David Herwaldt.)

The posters welcoming Kelly to her talk, "The Bible and Feminism," at SUNY, Albany.

Second Veritas Forum at Ohio State University; Jerry Mercer in middle front with light jacket.

Students ask about origins, authority, science, meaning and purpose, evil, morality, and hope. (Photo by Julie DeLavergne.)

The Lux et Veritas Forum, at Yale University.

Yale: Kay Cole James,
Lamin Sanneh,
R. J. Neuhaus,
N. T. Wright and
Nicholas Wolterstorff.

What Does It Mean to Be
Human? Veritas explores
essential questions.

Kelly moves to a cabin forty miles northeast of Cambridge on Cape Ann.

Near the ocean and islands—pain, forgiveness and the red barn run.

At the cabin: Harvard students Ben Grizzle and Ben Littauer, Jen Whiteside, with Eric Convey, the Hermans and the Milways.

Brenda Birmann and Kelly at the cabin.

England, with Veritas speakers and friends: Becky Porteous (and Benjamin in stroller), Ard Louis, Kelly, Nishan de Mel at Cambridge University.

Stanford: USC philosopher Dallas Willard with students in a midnight fireside chat after his Veritas talk, exploring humanness, authority and truth.

Texas A & M: Physicist Hugh Ross after a talk, late into the evening.

Ted and Ashley Callahan (in cool shades) with Kurt Keilhacker (at right) and other friends in Harvard Yard.

New Veritas Board (L to R): Kurt Keilhacker, Daniel Cho, Michael Milway, Kelly, Katie Milway, John Kingston.

Ohio State Veritas volunteers with historian Ben Witherington (middle). Far right: OSU leader Howard VanCleave.

Ivy League Christian Fellowship leaders gather for unity, hosted by Christian Union.

Veritas planner Susan Phillips welcomes Condoleezza Rice to Cal Berkeley.

Philosopher William Lane Craig with students.

Los Angeles: UCLA students led by senior Marian Halls (3rd from left).

Princeton and Penn: Veritas focuses on bioethics, physics and ethics.

New York City: Veritas Forums at Columbia and NYU on truth, pluralism and suffering. One result: students befriend a village of Ugandan war and AIDS orphans.

New York City: *Finding God at Harvard* read within the United Nations.

New York Times journalist and Pulitzer Prize-winner Nicholas Kristof and human rights journalist Benedict Rogers speak on "Publishing the Cries of the Oppressed" at the Veritas Forum at Columbia in 2006.

Jeff and Tara Barneson with Zach and Ezra in Cambridge.

A big party: Kelly and David's wedding.

Like a New England country dance long ago, once again, we danced.

L to R: Veritas at Ohio State, friends Steve and Taryn Gehlert with Kelly's new family—April, Michelle, Josh, John, Kelly and David (more volunteers!). Not pictured: Keya.

The Kullbergs aboard *The Dawn Treader*.

A Parable

True North on a Dark Sea

While sea-kayaking off the coast and between the islands near the cabin, my questions about knowing converged in a metaphor. I occasionally got carried off course by strong currents or got disoriented in the fog. I learned the benefit of having a friend with me, like Eric or Tudy or Bruce in my boat, who knew the coves and the ocean, who knew how to navigate in relation to True North. Next time you're lost, just ask a sailor or a pilot about navigation.

Our postmodern loss of bearing, it seems to me, is as though we're adrift in a boat on a dark sea. Imagine a situation where, say, our machines fail and we need to live immediately (without technological mediation). Our boat's engine stops. Then we find that our GPS, radar and radio are down. Our wallets are of no use. And our luggage is mostly dead weight. Our experience, for the moment, is honest, immediate, real.

For us to act with confidence and competence as a community, against all odds, we need a fixed point of reference outside of ourselves by which we might find our way (or else we are only winging it). Someone asks for a compass or map by which we might triangulate and find ourselves. Another says she no longer trusts maps because we can't know the mapmaker's motives. Someone asks about the North Star, Polaris. Perhaps True North is out there somewhere, but our vision is clouded. Without it, and without light inside our boat, we can't even read our map. Without True North we are quite simply—lost.

We're left to our own interior and subjective sense of things alone. This begins with civility. Has anyone been in these waters before? Will the boat hold? Which way do we feel we should row? Each has his own opinion, her own idea. Apart from a lucky guess, there is little hope for finding land before food and water are gone or before the cold sets in too deeply. Thirsty and lost, we are tossed more by waves than we are led by purpose.

Time is running out. A direction must be chosen. Various conversations quickly devolve into arguments, power struggles, and the most vocal "alliance" wins. The most forceful ones decide to row with the current and hope for the best. "This gets us somewhere faster," says the self-appointed captain. Several agree. Intense rowing goes on for several hours into the darkness, with no knowledge of either progress or regress. Only blind faith. Several begin to think of discarding those who aren't pulling their weight.

The sun rises but no land is in sight. Exhausted, hypothermic and hungry, even the strongest ones begin to weep. One will miss his wife and children, whom he has never fully loved or been faithful to. One woman wishes she had married her hometown sweetheart before going off to college. Perhaps, she thinks, we would have had children and been a family together. One wonders why he ever left the family farm, which, after his father's death, fell into disrepair and had to be sold after seven generations in the family. Another wishes for a chance to follow his dream of becoming a surgeon. Everyone has unfinished business of apologies, and forgiving, and thanking. Most begin to think of God.

Apart from occasional sobbing, it becomes quiet—quiet enough to hear a calmer voice.

"I sail," a man says from the stern. There is a long pause.

"What?" says the once-strong rower and self-appointed captain.

"I sail," he repeats as a matter of fact.

"So what?" says a man with an oar.

"Your strength won't get us there. We need the stars for direction, the wind for power and wisdom for right decisions. I know where we are and where we need to go."

Silence stills the boat. People begin to murmur, how do we trust him, his truthfulness and competence? We put him to the test.

"Why didn't you say something before?"

"I did. You weren't listening. But then some began to talk to me, silently."

"So you've been in this situation before?"

"Yes, worse than we are in it now. I've sailed through hurricanes like Francis and Ivan and delivered people to safety."

"You know the sea?"

"Yes (I made the sea), we're almost two hundred miles off the coast to the northeast."

"Do you have a map and compass?"

"Yes (my Word is the map and compass. I separated the land from oceans and know them). I'll triangulate to get us home using the North Star as the fixed point of reference."

"You've seen the North Star?"

"Yes (in creation, God has made himself known . . . all are without excuse, according to Romans 1), the North Star, Polaris, was carefully set in place (by my Father) and is constant (like my Father) among all that changes." He points to it, still visible in the early dawn.

"That distant light can help us in this boat?"

"Yes, because I am (the light of the World) along with you in this boat. (The light shines in the darkness but the darkness has not understood it according to John 1.)"

"But you want to sail against the waves and current? What if it's not the way we want to go?"

"The place I have in mind is better," he says.

"And if you're wrong, we die?"

"Correct," says the sailor. "But you'll die anyway. You've come to the end of your strength, and you don't know how to sail. My intent is not only that you would live but that you would be thankful for this night because we will become friends forever."

What a strange fellow. We ask a few more questions and with each response we begin to sense that he is neither a poser, nor a lunatic. In fact he is strangely brilliant, humble and confident, without fear. In a moment of humility we give him a chance with the boat and with our lives. After all, we have nothing left to lose and everything to gain.

He takes the helm. He tells us to unfurl the main sail and, soon after, the jib. He acts in utter confidence. He seems to know the sea, the dark, and he seems to desire life—not his so much as ours. He also seems to know us intimately, for he not only sails, but he sings to cheer our hearts. Before long we find ourselves singing along. He teaches us how to sail as we go, as if this disaster-adventure was meant to happen and could happen again. He speaks of fixing our eyes on what is constant. He teaches us how to read the invisible wind. By speaking of the water, of his experiences and of the island for which we're headed, he assures us of the reality of things hoped for though not yet seen.

He asks us to huddle low together for warmth and for ballast. Those with food and water and clothing are asked to share it as needed. We are to throw overboard any unnecessary baggage that slows us down. Some allow themselves moments of hope and of rest.

Before the sun sets, we see land. Not our intended vacation destination, it is unfamiliar terrain, but he said it would be. Some weep, but this time for joy. After bringing the boat ashore, he builds a fire for heat and light around which we dry and thaw. Some help him find food for our meal. We talk and begin to see our lives differently. Everything and everyone seem rescued from a shipwreck, less like drab continuum and more like miracle. After sleep there are hugs of farewell. Most, but not all, thank the sailor—for his words, deeds, and presence were truth and life. They entered what Veritas speaker N. T. Wright calls "a freshly storied world."

How do we know truth? For anything like confidence, we need both True North and the Sailor in our boat—we need both objective and subjective knowledge of God. God himself is most aware of this, for he made us people of mind and heart. The Creator of the cosmos is not distant. He is not silent. He is "God with us," transcendent yet present. He has spoken and shown his face.

Notes

Chapter 1: Through the Darkness
[1]The passion play and musical is called *Tetelestai*. Written by Joel and Russ Nagy, 1972, Upper Arlington Lutheran Church, Columbus, Ohio.

Chapter 2: Bewildered in the City
[1]My thesis was titled "The Gospel in the Information Age" (Ohio State University, 1989). The "Religion and Media" course was taught by the very helpful Hugh Jessup.
[2]To see more on this and the historical Jesus, read Todd Lake's story in *Finding God at Harvard* (Grand Rapids, Mich.: Zondervan, 1996).
[3]See Jacques Ellul, *The Technological Society* (New York: Alfred Knopf, 1964), Wendell Berry's essays and Marva Dawn's *The Hilarity of Community* (Grand Rapids: Eerdmans, 1992).
[4]Associated Press, "Web Porn Results in Harvard Dean's Forced Resignation," *The State News*, April 27, 1999 <www.statenews.com/tech/990427/harvardporn.html>.

Chapter 3: Rumors of Another World
[1]Jeff taught us to work both at the grassroots level with the poor and from the "top down." Later in the week we visited a former president of Peru who was once a fellow at Harvard's Kennedy School of Government. He welcomed us as kindred spirits but couldn't relate to our work as missionaries. He was comfortable talking to us about his political vision for Latin America but was surprised that we would come so far to help women and dying children in a shantytown a few miles down the road. He took us on a tour of his home and then, in a small motorcade of armored cars, to lunch at his rowing club. He kindly listened to us about the conditions and people of La Boca.

Chapter 4: Veritas Envisioned
[1]I soon moved in with the ninety-five-year-old and still brilliant poet Amos Wilder. And after his death I lived with grad fellowship friend Heather Tallman and then Bryan and Anne Hamlin.

[2]Wonderful staff colleagues over the years included Kathy Tuan McLean, Kevin Offner, Mark Gauthier, Glenn Lucke, Dave McGaw, Andy Crouch, Rich Lamb, Dave Fountain, Eric Schenkel, Val Nordby, Serema Syme, Bill Pearson, Lou Soiles, John Ratichek and others.

[3]Dallas Willard, "Spiritual Disciplines in a Postmodern World" <www.dwillard.org/articles/artview.asp?artid=56>.

[4]Physicist Hugh Ross has calculated the probability of a random evolution of the universe far smaller than 10^{-38} (see <www.reasons.org>).

[5]Methods of seeing are mainly mathematical given the extreme smallness at the sub-atomic level. The reference to paradox here includes the wave-particle duality.

[6]The universe is accelerating, according to Hubble's constant and Einstein's theory of special relativity. All things are relative to a constant: the speed of light. Note Jesus' claim to be "the light of the world" (John 8:12).

[7]The Cambrian explosion was not gradual as Darwin speculated but a burst of life during which perhaps as many as seventy animal phyla appeared in the fossil record. Arguably, no new phyla appeared after this date. The Cambrian explosion may be referred to in Genesis 1:20-21. See www.reasons.org.

[8]Including Kay and Brian Hall, Anne and Bryan Hamlin, Becky Baer, Jim and Vera Shaw, Poh Lian Lim, Kate Grozier, Susan and Louis Lataif, and Ed Wu.

[9]John Downame, *Christian Warfare,* 1634. This book is kept in the Houghton Library, but the text can be accessed via Early English Books Online <eebo.chadwyck.com/home>.

[10]The Shaws also discovered that many endowments and funds for Christian purposes had disappeared or been neglected. After decades of questioning the administration about this, they have received few answers.

[11]The passage the administrator was referring to is Acts 5:27-42.

Chapter 5: The Veritas Forum Begins at Harvard

[1]Becky Baer, an American graduate student in ethics; Ruth Gana, a Nigerian law student; Nishan de Mel, a Sri Lankan undergrad in economics; and Tim Shaw, an Indian American undergrad in political theory.

[2]Mark Gauthier and Glenn Lucke with Campus Crusade for Christ, Rebekah Kim with the Asian Baptist Student Koinania, and Jeff Barneson each brought over a hundred students and were great encouragers.

Chapter 6: Road Trip

[1]The idea of Julie Loesch Wiley, Feminists for Life, Washington, D.C.

Chapter 7: Veritas Beyond Harvard

[1]Harvard College Laws, 1642. The earliest known account of Harvard College. Also appears in *New England's First Fruits* (London, 1643), quoted from "Rules and Precepts

That Are to Be Observed in the College."

[2]John C. McCullough. Quoted by Robert Bellah in his Nobel lectures.

[3]New Creations Foundation helped with matching funds and a wise board, including Jerry and Adele Mercer, Don Lee, Dave Mann, John Hansel, Eric Roy, Larry Johns, Susan Armbrust, Ken Brown, Nancy Donner and Jeri Lynn Brooks.

[4]Planners included Art Battson, Daniel Philpott, Christie Whitten and many others. Sixteen campus fellowships cosponsored Veritas; eighteen community churches joined them. Twenty-six donors exceeded a national Veritas matching grant. Since 1998, annual UCSB Veritas Forums have been smaller in scale, attracting more faculty and community members in addition to undergraduates.

[5]Wendell Berry, "Standing Sabbath of the Woods," in *A Timbered Choir* (Washington, D.C.: Counterpoint, 1998).

Chapter 8: Searching for Clues

[1]David Brooks's excellent essay in *The New Atlantic*, "The New Elite: Meet the Organization Kid," explored the nature of the new elite by describing Princeton students.

[2]Speakers included Michael Behe, John Patrick, Matthew Conolly, Fritz Schaefer, Bill Edgar and Walter Bradley.

[3]The Wests, Parkers, Dahlbergs and others are salt and light at Dartmouth. In the meantime, several Dartmouth families began a deep fellowship that grew and flourished over the years. Craig Parker took students skiing and winter camping and spent summers in Africa, Latin America and inner cities in the U.S. He invited several writers of *Finding God at Harvard* to speak to students.

[4]Others who played key roles included Trish Lyons, Debbie Edgar, Elisabeth Overman, David McGaw, Todd Lake, Joy Jordan Lake, Drew Trotter, Bruce Herman, George Windgate, Vikram Chand, Nishan de Mel, Kirk Reickhoff, Katie Smith Milway, Susan Drake, Dave Brunton, Vito Nicastro, Eric Nelson, Vera and Jim Shaw, Ginny Viola, the Maclellan Foundation and the Mustard Seed Foundation.

[5]Here is an update on a few of the *Finding God at Harvard* authors: Yale professor Lamin Sanneh's story, "Jesus More Than a Prophet," is used as a catalyst to explain the mercy of God through Jesus to Muslims and to begin explaining Islamic faith and culture to Christians. Krister and Nancy Sairsingh are now teaching in Moscow. Psychiatrist Robert Coles explores with students the literature of social reflection and the spiritual wisdom of children. Students are challenged by Armand Nicholi's course on the conflicting ideas of Sigmund Freud and C. S. Lewis, the topic of a recent PBS special. Peter Feaver is teaching government at Duke. Michael Yang, an atheist before attending Harvard Medical School, and now an ophthalmologic surgeon, wrote the fascinating book *Reconsidering Ayn Rand*. Aleksandr Solzhenitsyn returned to his Russian homeland. Peter Clark is initiating programs to help Afghans, Iraqis and Rwandans rebuild communities. Bill Edgar at Westminster Seminary and Dick Keyes at the Boston L'Abri

community remain extraordinary cultural apologists and musicians. Todd and Joy Jordan Lake energized student life at Baylor and now Belmont.

[6]Johannes Wellebius's *The Abridgement of Christian Divinitie* was obligatory reading for Yale students in the early years of the eighteenth century. In it students learned that *Urim v'Thummim* "did signify Christ the Word and Interpreter of the father, our light and perfection." Also see "Divining the Meaning of Yale's Insignia," *Biblical Archeological Review,* March-April 2005.

[7]The Yale forum was to discuss the light and truth of the gospel. In his opening remarks, Donald spoke of truth as oxygen, by which we live and breathe and act with confidence in the world. We heard a panel that included quantum chemist Fritz Schaefer, Kay Coles James, Richard John Neuhaus and Yale professors Nicholas Wolterstorff and Lamin Sanneh, a former Muslim.

Chapter 9: East to West

[1]A catalyst was Doug Bunnell, college pastor at First Presbyterian Berkeley. He and other leaders began a Berkeley "Veritas Fellowship" of ministries committed to partnership in subsequent years. This committed group included Susan Phillips and Sharon Gallagher of New College, Carrie and Randy Bare of InterVarsity Christian Fellowship and Westminster House, Daniel Curran of Campus Crusade for Christ, and Mark Labberton, senior pastor of First Presbyterian Berkeley.

[2]The 2001 Stanford Veritas Forum, with several thousand participants, was orchestrated by Dr. Dorman's daughter Bianca. (Bianca's great-grandfather helped to found the American University of Beirut, with the motto from John 10: "I came that they may have life, and have it to the full.")

[3]He wrote this story from the 1999 Veritas Forum in his book *Ruthless Trust* (San Francisco: HarperSanFrancisco, 2000), pp. 17-19.

Chapter 10: Forgiving

[1]Ben Grizzle and Ben Littauer.

Chapter 11: Knowing and Believing

[1]Two closely related Greek words are *logos* and *rhema. Logos* is usually translated as "word" but also as "reason" or "meaning" and is used in Greek philosophy to describe the principle of coherence undergirding the universe. In the Septuagint, *logos* translates the Hebrew *dabar,* the creative "word" of God, which is parallel to *sophia* ("wisdom") as a mediator who acted for God in relation to his creation. In John 1:14 and Revelation 19:13, Jesus is called "the Word of God." This is an important development for Christology: it is an assertion that the Word who was God's agent in creation was to be identified with the human figure of Jesus of Nazareth (John 1:46). W. R. F. Browning, *Oxford Dictionary of the Bible* (New York: Oxford University Press, 1996).

[2]Please see Guillermo Gonzalez's *The Privileged Planet* (Washington, D.C.: Regnery, 2004) to explore earth's design and location for discovery. It has been this hitchhiker's guide to the galaxy. See also the writings of Karl Barth.

[3]David Wilcox, "Big Mistake,"*Big Horizon* (A&M, 1994).

[4]George Gilder, sidebar to "The Crusade Against Evolution," *Wired*, October 2004.

[5]A beautiful camp in the Upper Peninsula of Michigan owned by InterVarsity Christian Fellowship. Organized by Howard VanCleave and made possible by Jerry Mercer, three hundred Veritas speakers, planners, friends, families and ministry leaders joined together as an extended family.

[6]She and many others were assisted by the wonderful work of Bob Lupton and his ministry in Atlanta.

[7]In Matthew 27 we read that at the moment Jesus "gave up his spirit," the curtain in the temple was torn in two. That curtain, like a wall, symbolically confined the Holy Spirit to the most sacred core of the temple. When Jesus died on our behalf, I believe the Holy Spirit was free to burst forth and enter God's better temples: flesh-and-blood human beings.

Chapter 12: Healing and Friendship

[1]Eric Convey, a.k.a. "Christopher Robin," artists and dear friends Carole McMillen, Meg and Bruce Herman, Bonnie Loring, Craig Hammon, Kay Hall and family, Jo Kadlecek and Chris Gilbert, Lil Copan, Katie and Mike Milways and kids, Martha Linder, Dellynne and Rick Strawbridge, Linda and John Howell, Pravin and Liz Kothapa, Kyle Dugdale, Li-Lan Tan and others.

[2]Such as Don Lee, Nancy Donner and several charitable foundations.

[3]Kelly Monroe, ed., *Finding God at Harvard* (Grand Rapids: Zondervan, 1996).

[4]G. K. Chesterton, *Brave New Family* (San Francisco: Ignatius Press, 1990).

[5]See Marva Dawn's book *Keeping the Sabbath Wholly* (Grand Rapids: Eerdmans, 1989).

[6]Monroe, *Finding God at Harvard*.

Chapter 13: Engaging the World

[1]Led by Ben Grizzle, Ben Littauer, Rich Halvorsen, Bonnie Poon, Jordan Hylden, Jacob Luke Bryant, who have led Veritas at Harvard in recent years. Speakers included Gary Chapman, Don Miller, Os Guinness and Bill Edgar.

[2]Such as Kyle Gladden, Marian Halls, Heather Ashley Starkweather. Speakers have included Dallas Willard, Os Guinness, Stan Mattson, Matthew Conolly, Jed Macosko, Erwin McManus and local artists, scientists and students. Erwin's church, Mosaic, meets in an artist loft of sorts. When Matt Fields and I visited we watched sculptors and painters at work during the service, worshiping with hands as well as voices.

[3]Tony Chiorazzi, February 18, 2005, p. 1.

[4]Uwe Siemon-Netto,"Science, 'Frauds'Trigger a Decline in Atheism,"United Press International, 2005.

[5]Just a few: Randy and Carrie Bare in Berkeley; the Andersons, Morrisons, Gartlands and Dahls in Madison; the Zartmans, Trubes, Splaingards, VanCleaves, Weiants, Manns, Rules, Carusos and Pynes along with Allison Brooks and Julie DeLavergne in Columbus; Jack Gilbert, Act One, Campus Crusade and InterVarsity in Hollywood; Tim Keller, Redeemer Presbyterian and other great churches in New York; and the Edgars in Philadelphia.

[6]We think of the influence of men and women such as Margaret Sanger, Alfred Kinsey, Betty Friedan, Timothy Leary, Allen Dershowitz, Jacques Derrida and Stephen Jay Gould. But we also think of the contributions of professors and professionals, men and women, such as Isaac Newton, Galileo, Blaise Pascal, Johannes Bach, Rembrandt, Hildegard Von Bingen, Christopher Wren, Martin Luther, John Calvin, Jonathan Edwards, John Wesley, Abraham Lincoln, Hellen Keller, C. S. Lewis, George Washington Carver, Marie Curie, Václav Havel, Francis Schaeffer, Pope John Paul II, Ken Elzinga, Fritz Schaefer, Phillip Johnson, Michael Behe, William Edgar, Walter Bradley, Michael Strauss, Elanore Stump and many others.

Chapter 14: Seeing All Things

[1]With thanks to David Kullberg for helping me appreciate the power and role of art.

[2]This movement finds artists like Makoto Fujimura, Jeremy Begbie and Bruce Herman among the vanguard, along with journals such as *Image*, writing workshops such as The Glen, the C. S. Lewis Foundation and Summer Institute in Oxbridge, excellent fine art and music and drama departments in Christian colleges, Act One and others in Hollywood, Redeemer Presbyterian in New York City, Christians in the Visual Arts (CIVA), MasterWorks music institutes, theater groups like the Lamb's Players in San Diego, Mosaic and many churches, and Matthew House Project.

[3]The important question of moral law is addressed by C. S. Lewis in *Mere Christianity*, by Glenn Tinder, by Augustine, by Thomas Aquinas, and more recently by Veritas presenters.

[4]See Jacques Ellul, *The Technological Society* (New York: Alfred Knopf, 1964); Rosalind Picard's MIT website http://affect.media.mit.edu; Neil Postman, *Technopoly* (New York: Alfred Knopf, 1992), and *Amusing Ourselves to Death* (New York: Viking, 1985).

[5]I commend the work of Leon Kass, John Patrick and the Christian Medical Society, Dave DeHuff, Lauris Kaldjean and Matthew Conolly.

[6]See the research of the late David Larson, the founder of the National Institute for Healthcare Research.

[7]See the writings of Lamin Sanneh, Edward Said, Meic Pearse (*Why the Rest Hates the West* [Downers Grove, Ill.: InterVarsity Press, 2004]) and Christine Mallouhi (*Waging Peace on Islam* [Downers Grove, Ill.: InterVarsity Press, 2002]; *Miniskirts, Mothers and Muslims* [Oxford: Lion, 2004]).

[8]The fourth sura of the Qur'an denies the sacrificial death of Jesus on the cross, and it prescribes punishment for any "infidels" who believe in it. For Muslims, there is law and holiness but no atoning act of divine mercy for unholiness; therefore, there is no bottomless well of mercy from which to draw. The cycles of vengeance cannot otherwise be broken.

[9]See the Stanford Veritas Forum talk by Gary Haugen on <www.veritas.org>.

[10]See Augustine's *City of God.*

 *The* ·VERITAS·FORUM

Mission Statement

We create forums for the exploration of true life.
We seek to inspire the shapers of tomorrow's culture
to connect their hardest questions
with the person and story of Jesus Christ.

About The Veritas Forum

The Veritas Forum helps create university events that engage students and faculty in discussions about life's hardest questions and the relevance of Jesus Christ to all of life. We seek to restore an understanding of the Gospel to promote intellectual, spiritual and communal vitality for tomorrow's leaders. The forums are created by local university students, professors and ministers while guided by the national Veritas Forum team.

The Veritas Forum believes that the search for truth, which is the search for reality, is our human responsibility and privilege and the principle endeavor of the university. Each Veritas Forum is an opportunity for the entire university community to explore the possibility of truth, beauty and goodness in every aspect of our academic and personal lives. By asking the pressing questions on campus and seeking answers with respected university voices, we hope to engage the entire university in fruitful discussion and restore to culture a sense of wonder, meaning and true life.

Our story began at Harvard University in 1992 when a group of students and ministers, challenged by the emptiness around them, decided to face their hardest questions about life and truth. At the first Veritas Forum writers of the book *Finding God at Harvard* gathered to share of their own sufferings, journeys and discoveries with the Harvard community. Students, faculty and friends came together to discuss how the pursuit of knowledge in the university related to the truth claims of Jesus Christ.

Veritas Forums have now emerged on more than sixty campuses across the country, involving almost a quarter-million student and faculty participants and hundreds of speakers. Veritas Forums have been featured on ABC's *World News Tonight,* C-SPAN Book TV and National Public Radio, and in books and many campus newspapers. *Finding God at Harvard: Spiritual Journeys of Thinking Christians* won a Christian Booksellers Association Book of the Year award and appeared on the bestseller list of the *Boston Globe.*

You are invited to join the Veritas journey in three ways: in person at campus forums, on the web with recordings of hundreds of Veritas talks, and in this book and others that are forthcoming from InterVarsity Press. To find out more about The Veritas Forum, visit our website at www.veritas.org.

VERITAS FORUM BOOKS
FROM INTERVARSITY PRESS

As a partnership between The Veritas Forum and InterVarsity Press, Veritas Forum Books connect the pursuit of knowledge with the deepest questions of life and truth. Established and emerging Christian thinkers grapple with challenging issues, offering academically rigorous and responsible scholarship that contributes to current and ongoing discussions in the university world. Veritas Forum Books are written in the spirit of genuine dialogue, addressing particular academic disciplines as well as topics of broad interest for the intellectually curious and inquiring. In embodying the values, purposes and mission of The Veritas Forum, Veritas Forum Books provide thoughtful, confessional Christian engagement with world-shaping ideas, making the case for an integrated Christian worldview and moving readers toward a clearer understanding of ultimate truth.